BEYOND THE RTI PYRAMID

Solutions for the First Years of Implementation

WILLIAM N. BENDER

Solution Tree | Press

a division of

Solution Tree

555 North Morton Street
Bloomington, IN 47404
800.733.6786 (toll free) / 812.336.7700
FAX: 812.336.7790

email: info@solution-tree.com
solution-tree.com

Visit **go.solution-tree.com/rti** to download the reproducibles in this book.

Printed in the United States of America

13 12 11 10 09   1 2 3 4 5

Library of Congress Cataloging-in-Publication Data

Bender, William N.
    Beyond the RTI pyramid : solutions for the first years of implementation / William N. Bender.
        p. cm.
    Includes bibliographical references and index.
    ISBN 978-1-934009-12-3 (perfect bound) -- ISBN 978-1-935249-21-4 (lib. bdg.) 1. Remedial teaching. 2. Learning disabled children--Education. 3. Learning disabilities--Diagnosis. I. Title. II. Title: Beyond the response to intervention pyramid.
    LB1029.R4B458 2009
    371.9'043--dc22

2009014353

President: Douglas Rife

Publisher: Robert D. Clouse

Director of Production: Gretchen Knapp

Managing Editor of Production: Caroline Wise

Copy Editor: R. C. Gokulakrishnan

Indexer: Appingo

Proofreader: Elisabeth Abrams

Cover and Text Designer: Orlando Angel

Acknowledgments

Solution Tree Press would like to thank the following reviewers:

Cherry Boyles
Assistant Director of Curriculum
Kentucky Department of Education
Frankfort, Kentucky

HsuanFang Hung
Doctoral Student in Department of Specialized Education Services
University of North Carolina at Greensboro
Greensboro, North Carolina

Kristin Sinclair
Doctoral Student in Department of Specialized Education Services
University of North Carolina at Greensboro
Greensboro, North Carolina

Richard Skinner
Principal
Bel Air Elementary School
New Brighton, Minnesota

Gretchen Smallwood
Doctoral Student in Department of Specialized Education Services
University of North Carolina at Greensboro
Greensboro, North Carolina

Cheryl Tremble Smith
Adjunct Instructor
North Carolina A & T State University
Greensboro, North Carolina

Summer Stanley
Doctoral Student in Department of Specialized Education Services
University of North Carolina at Greensboro
Greensboro, North Carolina

Kendra Williamson
Doctoral Student in Department of Specialized Education Services
University of North Carolina at Greensboro
Greensboro, North Carolina

Visit **go.solution-tree.com/rti** to download the reproducibles in this book.

Table of Contents

About the Author

William Bender, PhD, is an international leader in instructional tactics with an emphasis on differentiated instruction, response to intervention, brain compatible instruction, and classroom discipline. He is an accomplished author and presenter who consistently receives accolades for his workshops from educators at every level.

Dr. Bender began his education career teaching in a junior high school resource classroom, working with adolescents with behavioral disorders and learning disabilities. He earned his doctorate in special education from the University of North Carolina and worked in teacher preparation in various higher education institutions. He has written nineteen books in education, and has published over sixty research articles. Today, he consults full time, writes professional development books, and is in demand providing workshops for educators throughout North America. His numerous bestselling titles include *Response to Intervention: A Practical Guide for Every Teacher*; *Differentiating Instruction for Students With Learning Disabilities* (second edition); *Introduction to Learning Disabilities* (sixth edition); *Relational Discipline: Strategies for In-Your-Face Kids* (second edition); *Differentiating Math Instruction* (second edition), and *Reading Strategies for Elementary Students With Learning Difficulties: Strategies for RTI* (second edition).

Introduction

School districts across the nation are gearing up their educational efforts to implement the recent emphasis on *response to intervention* (RTI). The RTI process involves targeting specific areas on which students are struggling and applying increasingly intensive research-proven interventions until the threat to learning is alleviated. The process is, thus, aimed at assisting all students in their educational and social development (Kame'enui, 2007; East, 2006; Torgesen, 2007). RTI also involves documentation of how students respond to scientifically proven interventions when those interventions are delivered in a multitiered format (Bender & Shores, 2007; Kame'enui, 2007).

> The RTI process involves targeting specific areas on which students are struggling and applying increasingly intensive research-proven interventions until the threat to learning is alleviated.

The impact of RTI in education is hard to overestimate. Recently, RTI was described as a "dramatic redesign of general and special education" to assist all students in meeting their individual educational goals (East, 2006). RTI has resulted in impressive academic gains by many struggling students as well as a general reduction in the number of students requiring special education services (Torgesen, 2007). As a result, educators nationwide are gearing up for this emerging instructional model (Buffum, Mattos, & Weber, 2009; Kavale & Spaulding, 2008; Kemp & Eaton, 2007).

The multitiered set of interventions is typically presented as a "pyramid of interventions," beginning with high-quality instruction and frequent performance monitoring for all students and incorporating progressively more intensive tiers of interventions intended for smaller numbers of students who demonstrate increasing difficulty in an academic or behavioral area (Buffum et al., 2009; Kemp & Eaton, 2007; Torgesen, 2007). Thus, the primary focus of RTI is provision of effective instruction for all students as well as targeted interventions for all students who need further assistance (East, 2006).

Since December of 2004, it has been possible to use an RTI process to document the possibility of a learning disability because of changes in the federal legislation, namely the Individuals with Disabilities Education Act of 2004 (IDEA) (Bradley, Danielson, & Doolittle, 2007; Cummings, Atkins, Allison, & Cole, 2008; Kame'enui, 2007; East, 2006). However, while the federal government did allow for the use of such a procedure, the government did not specify extensive guidelines as to how to conduct an RTI process, leaving many questions unanswered (Kavale & Spaulding, 2008; East, 2006). For this reason, many educators turned to some of the early books that were published on that topic for initial implementation suggestions (for example, Bender & Shores, 2007; Kemp & Eaton, 2007).

Of course, the first collection of books on the market had a body of research on RTI on which to draw, and those books provided guidance and suggestions that were available from the existing literature, literature dating from the 1990s through approximately 2005. However, in the brief time since the early books were published, some educators have moved significantly beyond the need for introductory-level information, and need more practical guidelines for actual implementation of RTI during the first, second, or even the third implementation year. In fact, because many districts were undertaking educational initiatives similar to RTI even before the legislation was completed in 2004, educators in various workshops that I have conducted across the nation have indicated they are struggling to plan for implementation of RTI during year two, three, or four of implementation. For this reason, there is a need for information on implementation of RTI beyond the introductory level.

> Educators have moved significantly beyond the need for introductory-level information on RTI, and need more practical guidelines for actual implementation of RTI during the first, second, or even the third implementation year.

Several efforts have been made recently to document how states and school districts across the nation are implementing RTI (Berkeley, Bender, Peaster, & Saunders, 2009; Spectrum K12/CASE, 2008). For example, in March of 2008, a commercial software company teamed with the Council of Administrators of Special Education to conduct a nationwide survey of special education administrators to investigate how school districts were implementing RTI. More than four hundred respondents completed the survey, and while many indicated their district's RTI implementation efforts were preliminary, data indicated that 60 percent of districts are either piloting or implementing RTI; those districts now need concrete implementation suggestions (Spectrum K12/CASE, 2008).

Berkeley, this author, and our colleagues (2009) surveyed the states relative to the RTI procedures they recommended or required, as described by various state departments of education. We sought to develop a "snapshot" of how RTI was being implemented only one year after the final federal regulations were completed in August of 2006. Each state department of education website was searched for information on that state's plan for RTI, and subsequently, a telephone interview was conducted with one knowledgeable person at each state department of education to verify that the website information had not changed and to ask additional questions on RTI implementation. While this book will refer throughout to the results shared in that article, here it will suffice to say merely that a fairly wide range of RTI procedures was being implemented across the United States by the fall of 2007.

In many instances, even the state governments did not produce detailed instructions on how to actually do RTI, preferring to merely publish some general guidelines and then see what the different school districts themselves developed (Berkeley et al., 2009)—again leaving school personnel with little practical information on how RTI should look in years one, two, three, or four of implementation.

This early survey did reveal one interesting piece of good news (Berkeley et al., 2009). Many states have presented RTI to teachers not as merely "a new way to identify students with learning disabilities" but rather as a new way to assist all struggling learners in various areas of the curriculum and/or behavior. While the literature on RTI had emphasized reading and literacy and investigated in depth how RTI in those areas may be used to document eligibility for learning disabilities (this was the only substantive RTI emphasis in the learning disabilities literature from 2000 until approximately 2005), states planning their own implementation of RTI have frequently gone further to include a wider variety of areas such as RTI procedures aimed at curbing difficulties in mathematics, behavior, and other areas for all struggling students. Thus, even without firm guidelines from the federal government, many states and school districts have decided to move forward with an expanded version of RTI that presents RTI as a general educational instructional procedure designed to assist all students with academic difficulties in all subject areas and behavioral problems as well (Spectrum K12/CASE, 2008). RTI today is seen first and foremost as an intervention process that is a function of general education and that seeks to identify and alleviate all threats to a child's learning and behavioral development. Eligibility issues are secondary to this larger educational goal of helping all students succeed in general education (East, 2006).

> RTI today is, first and foremost, an intervention process that is a function of general education, and seeks to identify and alleviate all threats to a child's learning and behavioral development. Eligibility issues are secondary to this larger educational goal of helping all students succeed in general education.

Clearly, many educators today have moved "beyond" the RTI pyramid in the sense that they need more than merely introductory information on how to proceed with RTI in reading (Kame'enui, 2007) as well as other areas. Rather, these educators need practical planning and implementation suggestions that can assist with the difficulties that arise during the actual implementation of RTI. Furthermore, these educators need some insights into how other educators in other areas dealt with the same problems and issues, since ideas from one school district or state are frequently very applicable in another. The transitioning roles of educators—special education teachers, general education teachers, or even nonteaching personnel such as speech language pathologists (SLPs) or school psychologists—are now being discussed in the literature (Cummings et al., 2008), and educators need information on how these individuals may be used to support and enhance the RTI efforts. Furthermore, RTI may impact specific groups of students such as students with math disabilities or students with English as a second language (Baskette, Ulmer, & Bender, 2006; Haager, Calhoon, & Linan-Thompson, 2007; Rinaldi & Samson, 2008), and information is needed in those areas. Finally, districts that have been implementing this procedure for two or three years need suggestions for how to improve RTI efforts.

The purpose of this book is to address those needs and to help educators move beyond the introductory RTI pyramid and the level of information that was available on RTI two to three years ago. This is not to suggest that the RTI pyramid is not useful or is no longer applicable, rather, that much more detailed suggestions, ideas, and strategies for RTI implementation are now necessary. Given the wide variation that states have allowed in how RTI is implemented (Berkeley et al., 2009; Kame'enui, 2007; Spectrum K12/CASE, 2008), this book provides substantive discussion of how RTI is implemented, how it functions with diverse groups, and how it seems to impact the roles of a broad spectrum of educators.

Moreover, I intend to highlight problems with RTI procedures and provide some solutions for those problems. Practitioners in the field have developed many of the suggested solutions herein, and I will draw on hundreds of individual conversations with teachers I have had, while conducting scores of workshops on RTI during the last several years, in various states around the country. Of course, I will also draw heavily from the published work on RTI. These suggestions and recommendations will be highlighted in feature boxes throughout.

Chapter 1 presents the most commonly used national model for RTI—the three-tier model (Kame'enui, 2007; Spectrum K12/CASE, 2008)—and provides some suggestions on what an RTI process may actually look like in the typical general education classroom and the actual experiences of those implementing this model. It highlights substantive differences between the intended model and the implemented model. In addition, chapter 1 briefly reviews the research supportive of RTI and how RTI relates to meeting adequate yearly progress (AYP) and high educational standards; educators nationwide should understand this research to be effective proponents for RTI.

Chapter 2 presents recommendations for forming a school-based RTI task force and implementing a faculty-planning tool for RTI implementation. In my workshops on RTI, I have recommended a school-based RTI task force as one mechanism to get the educational leaders and master teachers involved in the RTI process. To get started, they can use a planning grid that aligns the tiers of intervention with critical implementation questions and issues; chapter 2 discusses this planning grid and suggests possible solutions for the questions and issues. Completion of the planning grid on a school-by-school basis will highlight the resources that the school currently is using for various tasks (for example, how does the general education faculty in Tier 1 monitor progress of struggling readers?). The completed school-level grid also highlights areas of deficit where school faculty will have to apply resources to achieve full implementation. An RTI case study serves as the basis for discussion of several points within the grid.

Chapter 3 addresses the single most challenging issue in RTI implementation—making time for RTI—by presenting a discussion of resources for RTI. General education teachers, once introduced to RTI, often lament, "How can I get this done?" This chapter will directly address providing or reallocating resources to support general education teachers in RTI. In addressing that issue with school faculty who are successfully implementing RTI, I have discovered a wide variety of practices that can be revenue neutral, including the following, among others: (1) using paraprofessionals, under the guidance of teachers, to implement structured curriculum interventions at Tier 1 and Tier 2; (2) using technology for time savings; (3) class sharing or teaming to provide small numbers of students with tiered interventions; (4) creative scheduling; (5) finding creative new roles for special education teachers, reading coaches, literacy specialists, and so on. Each will be presented along with extended examples.

Chapter 4 will present suggestions for how to implement an RTI procedure in mathematics. To date, the vast majority of the work on RTI has taken place in reading, though virtually every educator realizes that RTI interventions in math will likewise be necessary for some students. Perhaps 10 to 15 percent of students with learning disabilities, or those suspected of having learning disabilities, have disabilities in the area of math only. Furthermore, approximately 80 percent of students with a learning disability in reading likewise present lower achievement and perhaps a related disability in math. This chapter presents several practical suggestions for implementing RTI procedures in mathematics as well as a case study including a response to intervention procedure in mathematics.

Chapter 5 presents some guidelines for how to complete an RTI procedure in the area of behavior. Many states or school districts have implemented RTI in the form of a split pyramid that emphasizes academic RTI on one hand and behavioral RTI on the other (Berkeley et al., 2009; Spectrum K12/CASE, 2008). Of course, the multitier RTI framework has been implemented to provide positive behavioral supports for students for a number of years, now, with positive results. This chapter synthesizes these areas and also presents a case study to show what a behavioral RTI might entail.

Chapter 6 presents some suggestions on how to implement RTI in middle school and/or secondary classes. RTI is more frequently emphasized as a general education intervention model and as such, implementation of RTI in secondary content classes will be necessary. Of course, RTI also addresses eligibility issues, and most identification of students with learning disabilities has taken place historically in grades 3 or 4. Implementation of RTI is likely to move that time frame even earlier since universal screening—one component of RTI—will now begin in kindergarten. However, there is still likely to be some need to determine eligibility for learning disability services for students in late elementary, middle, or even high school. Furthermore, students struggling with reading, math, subject content, and behavioral issues in middle and secondary classes will always need assistance. This chapter presents a discussion of the issues of RTI implementation in middle and secondary schools and suggests a number of instructional procedures to facilitate that implementation.

Finally, chapter 7 examines the changing roles of various educators, including speech language pathologists (SLPs), school psychologists, special education teachers, lead teachers, and mentor teachers. Clearly, RTI will involve many educators who are not teachers, and these persons play an active intervention role in certain intervention tiers. For example, the role of many SLPs has changed recently toward more intensive service provision options involving multiple weekly sessions. This change presents the opportunity for these persons to become very involved in RTI interventions.

Again, this book is not intended as an introductory book on RTI. Today, many educators are beyond those initial introductory stages and need more practical information that has evolved from those who have done the process during a year or two. This book is intended to provide that information.

In closing, I should also state that I am a strong advocate of a comprehensive RTI initiative. I believe that RTI procedures should be used to enhance and enrich the total school experience for all students including struggling learners, and thus RTI should be applied in reading, math, behavioral areas, and perhaps writing. I concur with the position statement of the National Association of State Directors of Special Education that the RTI implementation effort around the nation may fundamentally restructure how teachers respond to the individual needs of students in their classes. Thus, RTI represents a paradigm shift in both general and special education (East, 2006).

> RTI implementation effort around the nation may fundamentally restructure how teachers respond to the individual needs of students in their classes.

After all, virtually every general education and special education teacher wants nothing more than to find a way to meet the needs of every student in his or her class, and to have access to the necessary support and resources to adequately address those needs. In my experience, every educator wants the time and resources that will allow him or her to seek out *all threats* to learning and development and provide constructive, intensive remediation to alleviate those problems. What teacher has not lamented, "If I just had a bit of time, I could help little Billy [or Sarah, or Noshawn] with his reading?"

RTI is the answer to that question, and in that sense, RTI represents teaching for the twenty-first century! It is a vehicle of empowerment for general and special education teachers and moves our education system into a fundamentally new mode of teaching—seeking all threats to learning and behavioral development and providing intensive remediation. For educators who are already heavily involved in implementing this RTI process, and for those who are just becoming involved, I sincerely hope these suggestions, ideas, and problem solutions are helpful.

1

Beyond the RTI Pyramid

Most educators have been introduced to the common conception of a three-tier RTI pyramid (Kavale & Spaulding, 2008; L. S. Fuchs & Fuchs, 2007), and that model has provided a mechanism by which educators across the nation could initiate RTI efforts. However, teachers who have been involved in the initial implementation of RTI have found that there were some incorrect assumptions resulting from the three-tier pyramid and how that pyramid was initially presented. In this chapter, after an initial discussion of the origin and implementation of the three-tier RTI pyramid, we will also investigate the fairly significant differences between the early implementation descriptions of the three-tier RTI pyramid and the actual experiences of teachers following that model.

The Three-Tier RTI Pyramid

In the commonly used three-tier RTI pyramid, Tier 1 is a general education tier that represents instruction that is presented to everyone in the class. Proponents of that three-tier model suggested that this "typical" instruction in general education classes should meet the needs of perhaps 80 percent of the students in the school population (Bradley et al., 2007; Boyer, 2008; L. S. Fuchs & Fuchs, 2007; D. Fuchs & Fuchs, 2005; Gersten & Dimino, 2006; Kavale & Spaulding, 2008; National Joint Committee on Learning Disabilities, 2005; Spectrum K12/CASE, 2008). Furthermore, the general education teacher is considered the primary facilitator of instruction for Tier 1 and is expected to deliver whole-group instruction, limited small-group instruction, and differentiated instruction based on the needs of the students in the general education class. These expectations are not new and are not related directly to the implementation of RTI, but rather represent effective instructional techniques used in general education classes as a grounding for later RTI interventions. In this model, that general education teacher is also expected to monitor student performance in a variety of ways, perhaps with some assistance from other educational personnel, as allowable by the instructional demands of the class and the time constraints on the teacher.

Tier 2 in this pyramid has been presented as a targeted supplemental intervention for a small group of students who are struggling in reading (Cummings et al., 2008;

Linan-Thompson, Vaughn, Prater, & Cirino, 2006; D. Fuchs & Fuchs, 2005, 2006). This tier is typically described as meeting the needs of perhaps 15 percent of the school population. In a typical class of perhaps twenty-two students, one might expect that between four and six will struggle in reading and thus require a level of supplementary instruction that is more intensive than the instruction offered to the entire class (that is, Tier 1 instruction). Again, in most state models, the general education teacher is expected to deliver this level of instruction for those struggling students (Kavale & Spaulding, 2008) since general educators often form small groups for targeted instruction. However, there are exceptions; New York, for example, uses other educators, perhaps reading coaches or math specialists, to deliver Tier 2 interventions, and other states have various educators deliver the Tier 2 instruction.

Tier 3 is most often described in the literature as an additional, more intensive educational intervention tier, and is occasionally presented as instruction that takes place after a child is identified as learning disabled and declared eligible for special education services; thus, this has been presented as a post–special education placement intervention tier (L. S. Fuchs & Fuchs, 2007; Kavale & Spaulding, 2008). Alternatively, others present Tier 3 as a highly intensive intervention that takes place in general education *before* a determination of eligibility for learning disabilities services (East, 2006). This level of intensive intervention is frequently described as one-to-one instruction designed to meet the needs of the remaining 5 percent of the school population (D. Fuchs & Fuchs, 2005). Figure 1.1 summarizes the tiers and their corresponding predicted percentages. Given a class of twenty-two students, we might expect that one or perhaps two students will require this level of intensive intervention, as predicted by the three-tier pyramid.

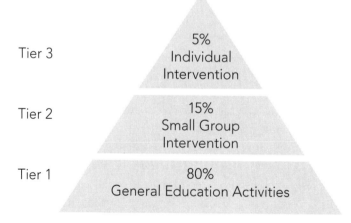

Figure 1.1 The three-tier RTI pyramid.

Embedded within this pyramid are a number of elements that seem common to most state models (Boyer, 2008; Kavale & Spaulding, 2008). First, almost all models are rooted in the concept of universal screening to identify students struggling in various subjects. Next, almost all models present some concept of increasingly intensive education interventions, typically called *tiers* of intervention (Boyer, 2008). Next, most models require the use of research-based curriculum, and in that sense, RTI is similar to other national initiatives such as No Child Left Behind (Kavale & Spaulding, 2008). Next, frequent monitoring of each individual child's progress is required, and finally, data-based decision making must be used to interpret the child's progress relative to curricular standards. These common elements (highlighted in table 1.1) can provide guidance for planning RTI efforts at the school level.

Table 1.1 Emphases of Most RTI Models

Universal screening to identify struggling students
Increasingly intensive education interventions presented in tiers
The use of research-based curricula in all tiers
Frequent performance monitoring of each child's progress in each tier
Data-based decision making when moving from tier to tier

Origins of the Three-Tier Pyramid

Because this three-tier pyramid is the most commonly used RTI model across the nation (Berkeley et al., 2009; Kavale & Spaulding, 2008), one may well ask where this concept came from. It often surprises teachers new to the concept, but before the recent legislation on response to intervention, there were a wide variety of different pyramids of instruction in the educational literature. Thus, both the concept of RTI and the three-tier pyramid model existed prior to the recent national discussions of RTI as an eligibility tool for determining the placement of students with learning disabilities. This three-tier pyramid was first used in public health (Kame'enui, 2007) as well as in several other contexts as both a model for reading intervention and a positive behavioral supports model for curbing inappropriate behavior (Fairbanks, Sugai, Guardino, & Lathrop, 2007; Horner & Sugai, 1999). In addition, Reading First programs around the nation used this three-tier model as the primary intervention model to assist students struggling in reading (Torgesen, 2007).

In fact, the early research on RTI in the literature on learning disabilities often referred to these Reading First programs as one model of how to implement RTI (Bender & Shores, 2007; Torgesen, 2007). For that reason, many states—Tennessee, Florida, West Virginia, and Texas are examples—built their RTI initiative as a three-tier model based on or in conjunction with their ongoing Reading First programs.

Of course, teachers in those Reading First schools were already applying a three-tier model of progressively intensive reading interventions for students struggling in reading, which gave them a certain advantage when it came time to consider how to implement RTI for eligibility purposes. For example, in West Virginia, forty-two schools were identified as Reading First schools, and the state department of education used data from those schools as one indicator of the early success of RTI implementation (Boyer, 2008). In that state, there were also thirty-six other schools that were designated as pilot schools specifically for early trial implementation of RTI (Boyer, 2008), and the data from those schools have been combined with the data from the Reading First schools to justify the value of RTI.

> Teachers in Reading First schools have been applying a three-tier model of progressively intensive reading interventions for students struggling in reading, which gave them a certain advantage when it came time to consider how to implement RTI for eligibility purposes.

In Texas, as a result of the national emphasis on reading, legislation was passed time-specific that required an extra thirty minutes of reading instruction daily for all students not meeting benchmarks in reading during the early grades. Based on that legislation, it is fair to say that before the RTI initiative, Texas had already implemented a second tier of reading intervention, involving a more intensive instructional experience for struggling learners and resulting in significant increases statewide in reading scores. Of course, this reading initiative also provided an excellent basis for RTI in Texas. Tennessee tapped its state coordinator of the Reading First program to lead the RTI initiative, specifically because the teachers in the Reading First schools were already using a three-tier intervention pyramid!

Clearly, it is not surprising that the three-tier model from Reading First programs became the most common for RTI implementation in the nation. In this text, we will use the three-tier model as the basis for our subsequent discussions because it is the most commonly used model. However, educators should realize that this is not a universally adopted model. Georgia and North Carolina adopted a four-tier RTI model, for example, and other states adopted five-tier RTI models. Educators from states that did not adopt the commonly used three-tier model should feel free to interpret the discussion in this text based on their state's RTI model. To facilitate such interpretation, in addition to talking about the three-tier model, I will describe the various intervention tiers at length as the *first supplemental intervention* or *the second supplemental reading intervention*.

Teachers' Initial Understanding of RTI

The premise of this book is that many educators have been introduced to the RTI concept, and that most schools have begun this process at this point. However, even in schools that have had preliminary RTI discussions, it may be advantageous to have teachers complete a self-assessment on RTI to provide a starting point for planning and implementation. A self-report needs-assessment survey for elementary teachers is provided in table 1.2 for this purpose (see page 192 for a reproducible form, or visit **go.solution-tree.com/rti** to download it). This self-assessment addresses four specific areas of RTI and should provide the lead teachers, administrators, and RTI facilitators with a snapshot of exactly where educators in their building are in relation to RTI implementation. A form for middle and secondary teachers is provided in chapter 6, along with a discussion of the challenges for RTI implementation at those levels.

Table 1.2 Response to Intervention Self-Report Needs-Assessment for Teachers of Elementary Grades

Circle one numeral for each descriptive indicator.					
1 = I have little knowledge and want additional in-service on this.					
2 = I have some knowledge, but some additional in-service will be helpful.					
3 = I have a good understanding of this, but need to put this into practice this year.					
4 = I have complete understanding and have reached proficiency at this practice.					
N/A = Not applicable for our state, school, or district.					
General Understanding of RTI					
1. The pyramid of interventions in our state and district	1	2	3	4	N/A
2. The problem-solving model for our state or district	1	2	3	4	N/A
3. The tiers of intervention in our school	1	2	3	4	N/A
4. The intervention timelines for each intervention tier	1	2	3	4	N/A
5. How RTI applies to all students	1	2	3	4	N/A
General Knowledge of Universal Screening and Progress-Monitoring Procedures					
1. The reading screening tests used in our school	1	2	3	4	N/A
2. The assessments of the five components of reading used in our school	1	2	3	4	N/A
3. The math assessments used in our school	1	2	3	4	N/A
4. Progress-monitoring procedures during interventions	1	2	3	4	N/A
5. Data-gathering procedures (weekly or daily) for RTI	1	2	3	4	N/A
6. Progress-monitoring procedures in content areas	1	2	3	4	N/A
7. The benchmark scores in reading and math	1	2	3	4	N/A
8. The data management system for RTI used in our school	1	2	3	4	N/A
Knowledge of Interventions to Facilitate Student Progress					
1. The reading instructional programs used in our school	1	2	3	4	N/A
2. The supplemental math programs for RTI used in our school	1	2	3	4	N/A
3. Behavioral programs to foster positive behavior	1	2	2	2	N/A
4. Frequency and intensity of interventions	1	2	3	4	N/A

continued on next page →

5. How to use flexible grouping for Tiers 1, 2, and 3	1	2	3	4	N/A
6. How to use creative staffing to make time for interventions	1	2	3	4	N/A
Knowledge of Literature on the Effectiveness of RTI					
1. Effectiveness of RTI in reading	1	2	3	4	N/A
2. Effectiveness of RTI in math	1	2	3	4	N/A
3. Effectiveness of RTI for struggling students	1	2	3	4	N/A
4. Effectiveness of RTI for English language learners	1	2	3	4	N/A
5. Impact of RTI on adequate yearly progress	1	2	3	4	N/A
My Contributions and Suggestions for RTI in Our School					
1. In what instructional intervention areas can you share suggestions for other teachers?					
2. In what RTI areas should we plan further staff development?					
3. What suggestions can you offer for making RTI work better for students in our school?					

A self-assessment survey will provide the lead teachers, administrators, and RTI facilitators with a snapshot of exactly where educators in their building are in relation to RTI implementation.

Does RTI Really Work?

Educational leaders must serve as proponents of and advocates for RTI, and thus, these leaders must prepare for the question, why are we doing this RTI business? General educators will surely ask this question when they realize that RTI responsibilities will necessitate some modifications in their teaching techniques such as increased performance monitoring, increased small-group supplemental instruction, and other changes in their use of instructional time. While this book cannot present a comprehensive review of the RTI literature, all proponents of RTI must be prepared to address this extremely relevant question, on the basis of the RTI research: Does RTI work?

As educational leaders advocate for RTI, they must be prepared for the questions, Why are we doing this RTI business? and Does RTI work?

RTI Works for Struggling Students

The answer to the questions is both simple and resounding: we do RTI because research has shown that it works for almost all struggling kids! Both research and the early practitioners of RTI have found several significant results from RTI implementation, and leaders should present these positive results boldly as school faculty move into the RTI process.

> We have undertaken the RTI initiative nationally because research has shown that RTI works for almost all struggling kids!

First, research has consistently shown that intensive supplemental instruction for relatively brief periods of time can alleviate the academic and behavioral problems when students are struggling academically and put kids back on track toward long-term success (Fairbanks et al., 2007; L. S. Fuchs et al., 2005; Torgesen, 2007; Vaughn et al., 2009; Vellutino, Scanlon, Small, & Fanuele, 2006). In particular, recent research in the area of reading has demonstrated convincingly that students struggling in reading will benefit from a supplemental, phonemically based, explicit reading instruction, and that the academic growth resulting from those interventions will be maintained over time (Denton, Fletcher, Anthony, & Francis, 2006; Simmons et al., 2008). In fact, a large number (if not the majority) of students at risk for reading failure in kindergarten do respond positively and early to a phonemically based, intensive, supplemental reading intervention (Simmons et al., 2008; Torgesen, 2007).

While some of these early studies tended to investigate efficacy of interventions directly, others documented the efficacy of multitiered interventions in a complete RTI process. Hughes and Dexter (2008) reviewed the research on the efficacy of the entire RTI process, and those studies indicated that this procedure assists struggling students in improving their academic performance. While results vary significantly, the broad body of available research suggests that between 40 and 60 percent of students who are struggling in either reading or math will have those academic problems alleviated or eliminated by a Tier 2 intensive supplemental intervention (Hughes & Dexter, 2008; O'Connor, Fulmer, Harty, & Bell, 2005; Simmons et al., 2008; Torgesen, 2007). Of course, that means that these students will not be classified with learning disabilities or other disabilities since they *have* responded to the instructional intervention, and that is an extremely positive outcome of RTI (Torgesen, 2007).

Furthermore, Vaughn and her colleagues (2009) have demonstrated that many students who do not respond positively to a Tier 2 intervention will respond positively to a more intensive Tier 3 intervention. Research has also demonstrated that only a small percentage of students who struggle in reading (between 5 and 7 percent) will continue to demonstrate problems after a third, more intensive intervention tier (Linan-Thompson et al., 2006). Thus, provision of multiple tiers of interventions in an RTI process seems to alleviate reading problems for something like 90 percent of the students who initially struggle in reading. In short, an RTI process works!

RTI Works for English Language Learners

One persistent concern among educators is provision of effective instruction for students with a primary language other than English, commonly referred to as English language learners (ELLs). As a group across the nation, these students all too frequently fail to meet AYP in moving toward high educational standards, and this has become a challenge for educators. Research has now demonstrated that RTI provides a very effective way to address that concern (Linan-Thompson, Cirino, & Vaughn, 2007; Lovett et al., 2008; Rinaldi & Samson, 2008).

In one study involving ELL students, Linan-Thompson et al. (2006) used a control-group design in a longitudinal study from the beginning of grade 1 through the end of grade 2 to investigate the impact of supplemental RTI reading interventions. The reading interventions were delivered over two years, in English for one experimental group and in Spanish for another. Almost all students in each experimental group responded positively to a daily, intensive, supplemental, phonemically based reading instructional program by the end of the first year. Among 103 students, only 3 (one in the Spanish intervention and two in the English intervention) failed to respond.

Other recent studies support this result, and while research on use of RTI with ELL students is still somewhat limited, there is a growing body of research indicating that RTI is highly effective for these students (Kamps et al., 2007; Linan-Thompson et al., 2007; Lovett et al., 2008). Again, this research is vitally important, since ELL students continue to present challenges in meeting AYP in many districts nationwide. Thus, an RTI process works for ELL students, and in most cases, eliminates their reading difficulty; this process also provides educators with a research-proven strategy to enhance learning and continue to meet AYP concerns. Given the critical and nearly universal nature of the worries about meeting AYP for ELL students, these results should be trumpeted to educators nationwide. RTI works for ELL students!

RTI May Reduce Disproportionality

In addition to these research findings, some interesting anecdotal evidence has emerged on the efficacy of RTI in addressing another persistent concern among educators—disproportionality. *Disproportionality* is best defined as the overrepresentation of minority students in special education, which suggests some inadvertent racial bias in eligibility procedures. Preliminary reports from the districts that have implemented RTI suggest that it might significantly reduce disproportionality. For example, in New Hanover County, North Carolina, during the 2004–2005 academic year, African American students were 1.7 times as likely to be placed in special education as were white students (Abernathy, 2008). This clearly suggests a disproportionately high percentage of placements for African Americans. However, after the county implemented RTI in 2006–2007, African American students were only 1.2 times as likely to be placed in special education (Abernathy, 2008), suggesting a significant reduction in disproportionality. While long-term research is not yet available on this question, early anecdotal reports are encouraging, and if subsequent research continues to document this type of decrease in disproportionality, then nationwide implementation of the RTI process will have addressed another ongoing concern among educators.

> Early anecdotal evidence suggests that implementation of RTI has reduced disproportionality in some school districts.

RTI Reduces Overidentification

Another long-term concern among educators has been the overidentification of students as needing special education services for learning disabilities (Abernathy, 2008; Spectrum K12/CASE, 2008). RTI should help address that problem. In one anecdotal report on pilot district implementation of RTI in North Carolina, the data indicated that 83 percent fewer students were documented as eligible for special education services after RTI was implemented (Abernathy, 2008). Torgesen (2007) summarized results of a Reading First multitier initiative in Florida and indicated that the percentage of the school population in kindergarten through grade 3 who were diagnosed as learning disabled was reduced from 10.4 to 6 percent during the three years of the reading initiative. Furthermore, the 318 schools in that study included schools with high levels of English language learners and students from impoverished homes. Even if these are extreme results, the research data do suggest the possibility of addressing educational needs before delivery of special education services.

RTI Empowers Teachers

As RTI has been implemented across the United States, this new instructional emphasis has resulted in enhanced instructional performance on the part of general education teachers. Of course, many teachers have long demonstrated the necessary skills for RTI, and elementary teachers, in particular, are specifically trained in various reading interventions. RTI basically involves provision of intensive small-group and differentiated instruction for struggling kids, and again, most teachers are qualified and experienced in that regard. What has changed is the availability of supports to allow teachers to provide this supplemental instruction and monitor students' performance more systematically.

In fact, under RTI, teachers are empowered to provide enhanced supplemental instruction, and this, again, is an extremely positive outcome for both struggling students and for general education teachers. Advocates of RTI should encourage teachers to see RTI as empowerment to alleviate educational problems.

RTI Facilitates Powerful School Improvement

RTI has been described as a dramatic redesign of general and special education (East, 2006), and as such, this initiative is perhaps best understood as a school improvement effort. As mentioned previously, schools across the nation have been challenged to provide high-quality effective instruction for several specific groups of students who exhibit significant learning challenges, including ELLs, students already diagnosed with disabilities, students from impoverished homes, and other groups. The mandate to meet and exceed AYP with these specific subgroups has proven highly challenging for schools and has left many educators ready to throw in the towel.

The good news from the initial research on RTI implementation should be shared with every educator and parent across the nation. RTI is a powerful instructional process that addresses each of the long-standing concerns, and results in extremely impressive academic gains for all of these groups of students! For this reason, many districts as well as several states (for example, Ohio) have emphasized their RTI efforts under the overall umbrella of *positive school reform*. In short, if schools wish to meet and exceed AYP for even the most challenged kids, those schools should implement RTI in an effective, forceful, and long-term manner.

> RTI has been described as a dramatic redesign of general and special education, and should be understood as a powerful research-proven opportunity for school improvement.

Unanswered Questions

There is one important caveat on the question of the efficacy of RTI. While research has shown that it is highly effective for assisting struggling students, research has not addressed all of the questions on its efficacy (Hughes & Dexter, 2008; Kavale & Spaulding, 2008). For example, it is not yet clear how RTI affects the determination of eligibility for services for learning disabilities (Baskette et al., 2006; Bender & Shores, 2007; Kavale & Spaulding, 2008). How many students will be identified for special education services using this new procedure? Will the overall number of students with learning disabilities ultimately increase or decrease? While evidence in some studies has suggested that the overall number of students diagnosed with learning disabilities may decrease (Torgesen, 2007), those studies are not definitive as yet. In fact, Kavale and Spaulding (2008) suggest that the overall number of newly identified students with learning disabilities may *decrease* in the lower grades, as it did in Torgesen's (2007) summary of the data from Florida schools in the primary grades, but *increase* in higher grades! Clearly, this is not the intended outcome. Educators serving as proponents of RTI should state its efficacy for struggling students, but they should also bear in mind these unanswered questions.

Advocacy for RTI

In the context of research-based advocacy for RTI, educators should have a general understanding of the research discussed in this chapter. While RTI work will involve much more than merely discussion, some knowledge of this body of research is critical for successful advocacy for RTI.

Furthermore, to more effectively promote RTI, I believe it is critical that educational leaders present RTI in terms of school reform efforts that positively impact all students, rather than as merely a new way to identify students with learning disabilities. In fact, that is the recommended approach among proponents of RTI (East, 2006), and is used in this text because teachers respond much more positively to that proactive approach for enhancing education for all students. While it is true that our recent RTI discussions have resulted from changes in special education eligibility guidelines, RTI is correctly understood as a *general education* response to delivering effective instruction for all students struggling in schools. Furthermore, this new RTI process represents the best instructional model available! In one recent survey of special education administrators, three out of every four participants indicated that RTI resulted in improvement in terms of meeting or exceeding AYP (Spectrum K12/CASE, 2008). Based on that evidence, I strongly recommend presenting RTI as effective teaching for the twenty-first century!

> RTI should be presented to educators as effective teaching for the twenty-first century: an instructional paradigm that works for all struggling students!

In summary, proponents of RTI must clearly state the fact that RTI provides the assistance that many struggling students need and alleviates—and in some cases, eliminates—their educational problems. Furthermore, it is effective for English language learners and students with various other educational challenges, and may result in more fair identification procedures with less racial bias. These results, when shared forcefully with educators, will provide a strong motivation to move into a comprehensive system of response to intervention.

Educators' Practical Experience With the Three-Tier Model

With this history and research basis on the three-tier RTI model noted, we can proceed to the actual experiences of those who have implemented RTI. Unfortunately, implementation of this model for RTI has created some degree of confusion on a number of questions.

What Do the Three Tiers Actually Mean?

In the original Reading First pyramid, all three of the initial intervention tiers were considered functions of general education, and most children participating in those three tiers of intervention in Reading First schools were not considered eligible for special education. Rather, all three of those initial intervention tiers were considered to be general education endeavors. In fact, many in special education view the three-tier model as three tiers of instruction that are the responsibility of general education (East, 2006). Of course, this is considerably different from what some educators understand as the three-tier model.

In several states, this traditional three-tier model provided the basis for an expanded four-tier model. Like states such as Texas, Tennessee, and California, educators in Georgia and North Carolina began with a three-tier model representing three general education intervention tiers (that is, instruction in the general education class, and two distinct supplemental intervention tiers). However, educators in Georgia then insisted on a fourth intervention tier, since educational interventions also took place *after* placement within special education. In short, they added a fourth tier to represent educational interventions that take place either as post-eligibility interventions or other specialized interventions (for example, interventions for ELLs or migrant program interventions). Therefore, the four-tier model in Georgia means essentially the same thing for general education teachers as does a three-tier model in Tennessee or Texas!

However, as noted previously, the three-tier model has likewise been described in quite different terms in the more recent literature on RTI and learning disabilities (Denton et al., 2006; D. Fuchs & Fuchs, 2005; L. S. Fuchs & Fuchs, 2007). L. S. Fuchs and Fuchs (2007), as one example, recommend use of the three-tier pyramid, but their recommendations describe Tier 3 in terms of a post–special education placement intervention and therefore not as a responsibility of general education. They suggest that only one supplemental intervention (in their proposed model, this would be considered a Tier 2 intervention) should separate general education from special education because of the difficulty in designing more than one supplemental tier of preventative intervention that is truly distinguishable from interventions that might be offered in the context of special education (L. S. Fuchs & Fuchs, 2007). As one example, while the New Jersey Department of Education does not provide extensive specifics on RTI implementation, some districts in that state (for example, Chatham, New Jersey) are considering this model as the basis for their RTI work. According to the initial RTI planning in that district, Tier 3 interventions will take place only after an eligibility decision has been made.

However, a recent study of implementation of RTI found that most states were considering the first three tiers of intervention as general education interventions (Berkeley et al., 2009). This is consistent with the view of the NASDSE (East, 2006) as published in a recent article, "Myths About Response to Intervention," which describes all three tiers as functions of general education. Most states seem to be following this model. In most states, Tier 1 seems to be considered a provision of the "typical" instruction in general education. That general education instruction seems to be followed by two distinct supplemental intervention tiers of instruction within general education, both of which would typically be completed before consideration of eligibility for special services. Thus, in those states, a child study team would consider possible placement in special education only after the child had not responded in *all three* of those general education intervention tiers.

While overall summations are difficult to draw, it does seem that not many states wanted to call together a child study team to make an eligibility decision based on only one supplemental tier of instruction (Berkeley et al., 2009). Most state RTI plans suggested conducting a minimum of two distinct supplemental interventions, beyond the educational program offered to everyone in general education, before considering a referral for special education or other specialized programming (for example, programs for ELLs or migrant programs). The use of at least two supplemental interventions may also protect the child suspected of having a learning disability, in the sense that the child has been presented with multiple opportunities to respond to instruction. If the child still does not respond positively after supplemental instruction, educators can then feel more confident that there is considerable evidence for some type of disability.

Finally, another point of confusion results from the fact that some states have adopted a very flexible model relative to this question. In some states, students reach an intensive Tier 3 intervention through *either* special education placement or more traditional reading remediation efforts such as Reading First programs. In both Tennessee and Texas, for example, some students receive a Tier 3 intervention once a child study team declares them eligible for learning disability services, whereas other students land in the same intervention as a result of moving through the levels of intervention used in the Reading First model—without a child study team declaring them eligible for services.

Clearly, this question of the exact timing of Tier 3—before or after special education referral and placement—holds the potential to be quite confusing for students, parents, and general education teachers. In particular, if a teacher should relocate from one state to another, that teacher may find that the three-tier pyramid holds different meanings in various locales, or that a three-tier model in one state means essentially the same thing as a four-tier model in another (that is, three intervention tiers in general education). At a minimum, this could clearly result in some communication problems over the long term, and school districts should carefully consider this question before implementation.

As a general recommendation, I tend to suggest the RTI process that seems to have been implemented by most states (Spectrum K12/CASE, 2008); that is, I recommend a three-tier model in which all three tiers are a function of general education, and only after a student fails to respond to intensive supplemental interventions in both Tier 2 and Tier 3 should a referral to special education or other specialized programming take place.

> I suggest a three-tier model in which all three tiers are a function of general education. In this model, only after a student fails to respond to intensive supplemental interventions in both Tier 2 and Tier 3 should a referral to special education take place.

I believe that this adequately protects the child from unnecessary referral, and further, that this encourages educators to actively seek creative ways to offer supplemental intensive interventions geared to the specific needs of the student. Of course, districts should follow the model adopted by their states, and in most instances, they determine protocol by accessing the state department of education website and searching for RTI.

How Many Interventions Can Be Done in General Education?

Another confusion resulting from the three-tier pyramid involves how many distinct interventions a general education teacher should expect to initiate. This issue represents a fundamental distinction between how RTI was initially presented across the nation and the actual experience of educators implementing RTI. In the descriptions of the three-tier model presented earlier, the literature suggests that the general education teacher might be expected to teach all the students in Tier 1 as well as implement a supplemental Tier 2 reading intervention for some students. It is often suggested that 20 to 25 percent of the students in a typical class will have reading difficulty, and thus, four to six students might require a supplemental Tier 2 intervention (National Joint Committee on Learning Disabilities, 2005).

Furthermore, many of the early descriptions of this model (for example, Reading First models), describe Tier 3 as a function of general education and thus involve the general education teacher in implementing those interventions. Of course, this placed a very heavy burden on them.

Unfortunately, the early proponents of the three-tier model never adequately explained how this was supposed to actually work in the classroom. Specifically, what was the general education teacher going to do with the sixteen to twenty students who did not require a Tier 2 intervention while he or she worked with the four to six students who did? And then how did that same teacher then make the time to work with the students who required a more intensive Tier 3 supplemental intervention?

Based on hard-won initial experience with RTI, many educators now question how this three-tier pyramid of interventions really works in the classroom. In fact, the experience of many teachers around the nation who are actually implementing this procedure suggests that the original three-tier model may have been something of an oversimplification. There are considerably more interventions for the general education teacher to complete than were originally discussed in the literature, and teachers quickly discover this as they initiate RTI procedures.

> There are considerably more interventions for the general education teacher to complete than were originally discussed in the early descriptions of the three-tier RTI model.

Here is a more realistic scenario, based on actual experiences of many teachers across the nation. If, in a typical grade 3 class of twenty-two students, one expects 20 to 25 percent of the students to experience some degree of difficulty in reading, perhaps five or six students will require a Tier 2 intervention. For most Tier 2 interventions, I suggest a time frame of thirty minutes per day, delivered for three days per week over a six- to nine-week grading period, since many intervention curricula are structured to allow for implementation in that type of time frame.

> For most Tier 2 interventions, I suggest a time frame of thirty minutes per day, delivered either every other day or for three days per week over a six- to nine-week grading period.

While many states have actually provided minimal time requirements (for example, thirty minutes per day, five days a week is a common recommendation), I tend to suggest a Tier 2 intervention that involves only three days per week because that level of additional instruction can easily meet some remediation needs, including a wide variety of early reading problems. Delivering Tier 2 interventions on three days per week gives the teacher some flexibility in instructional time.

In this scenario, we will follow my suggestion. Still, even if the teacher gives the Tier 2 intervention only three days per week, the obvious question is, what are the other seventeen students doing while the teacher works intensively with five students?

While that question presents some important concerns, experience has shown that even this question is not realistic. For example, of the five students struggling in reading at grade 3, three might need an intervention dealing with phonemically based decoding skills, whereas the other two might require an intervention dealing with reading fluency and/or comprehension. Thus, the general education teacher in this scenario would have to find or make time not to deliver *one* thirty-minute intensive intervention three days per week, but in fact to deliver *two* different Tier 2 interventions—one with three students on phonemic instruction and one with two students on fluency and/or comprehension. Clearly, educators should not make the assumption that given five students with reading difficulties, all five will require the same intervention! Unfortunately, this assumption was the basis of some of the early RTI discussions in the literature.

Of course, in some cases, that is an accurate assumption. For example, struggling students in kindergarten or even grade 1 may be more homogeneous in their instructional needs, but in higher grade levels, teachers will likely have to deliver more than one supplemental Tier 2 intervention in reading since students are likely to have differing instructional needs. This need for instructional time on the part of the general education teacher must be part of the planning for implementation of RTI.

What About RTI for Other Subjects?

Experience implementing RTI has demonstrated that other interventions will also be required. Among the twenty-two students in this third-grade scenario, five to six students will likely struggle in mathematics and will require a Tier 2 supplemental instruction to reach benchmarks in that academic area. Again, some of the early promoters of the three-tier pyramid of interventions did not consider this, as reading was the focus of much of the early RTI work. However, the field of learning disabilities has always included some group of students with mathematics disabilities. This group of students with disabilities in mathematics represents as much as 5 to 10 percent of the population currently identified as learning disabled (L. S. Fuchs et al., 2005; L. S. Fuchs et al., 2007).

Unfortunately, in the initial discussions of implementation of RTI, the need to provide RTI for this group of learners was almost wholly ignored, and only much more recently have discussions of RTI in mathematics begun to appear in the literature (Bryant et al., 2008; L. S. Fuchs et al., 2007). Chapter 4 (page 87) addresses the additional issues involved when implementing RTI procedures in mathematics.

Again, the general education teacher will, in all probability, be expected to provide an intensive Tier 2 intervention for these students in mathematics. Thus, that general education teacher would have to allow thirty minutes per day for three days per week to provide this intervention for between three and six students. Of course, there is no guarantee that they will require the same mathematics intervention, but math tends to be a somewhat more linear subject in the early grades than does reading, so for this example, we will assume that they do.

However, to make matters even more logistically complicated for that general education teacher, of the six students who are struggling in math in our scenario, three might also be struggling in reading. Thus, the intensive interventions provided by the general education teacher cannot overlap because some students need both Tier 2 interventions. Clearly, this prevents the third-grade teacher from offering the supplemental instruction in math and reading at the same time, even if that teacher could present those small-group lessons simultaneously.

I should note here that most practicing teachers are acutely aware of the issue of the need for RTI interventions in math. However, many school districts that are currently implementing RTI have decided to implement RTI only in the area of reading/ early literacy initially, and to move into math interventions later. West Virginia is an example of an entire state that chose to implement RTI in reading first and move into math at a later point (Boyer, 2008). That state also chose to implement RTI in elementary schools by July of 2009, in middle schools a year later, and in high schools in the third year (Boyer, 2008).

This phase-in approach seems very reasonable since most of the literature describes RTI in terms of how it might work in elementary schools and not in middle and high schools. Still, this phase in plan doesn't really address this issue of varied interventions; rather, the phase-in plan merely moves the problem for implementing mathematics RTI interventions into future years.

> Phasing in RTI in elementary grades first and middle school/secondary school later seems to be very reasonable since most of the literature describes RTI in terms of how it might work in elementary schools and not in middle and high schools.

Is RTI for Behavioral Interventions, Too?

However, in getting back to our scenario, the grade 3 class will probably need one more type of RTI intervention procedure. Of the twenty-two students, it is quite reasonable to assume that between two and four students demonstrate behavioral problems that are severe enough to warrant a targeted behavioral management intervention for that learning challenge. While positive behavioral supports in general education have been required for almost a decade, these interventions may soon be implemented in the context of RTI procedures for behavior (Sugai, Guardino, & Lathrop, 2007). Teachers must therefore spend some time developing and implementing a Tier 2 behavioral intervention for these students with significant behavioral problems. Furthermore, because behavioral problems are so varied, each of the students with behavioral problems will quite likely require a separate behavioral intervention. Thus, three separate Tier 2 behavioral interventions may be required in this third-grade class.

What Is Really Possible in General Education?

Let's recap how RTI really looks after full implementation in a real classroom setting. A teacher with twenty-two students in grade 3 will have to deliver the following interventions.

- ▶ Tier 1 instruction in reading and math for all of those students
- ▶ One Tier 2 reading intervention for two students on decoding

▶ One Tier 2 reading intervention for two students on fluency/comprehension

▶ One Tier 2 math intervention for six students

▶ Three separate Tier 2 behavioral modification interventions

▶ Any Tier 3 interventions that are required in reading, math, and/or behavior!

How can any educator expect that a single general education teacher could accomplish all this? Clearly, in a typical school classroom, it is not realistic to assume that general education teachers can provide the required Tier 1 and Tier 2 interventions without substantive support in some form. This becomes even more of a critical factor when additional responsibilities are thrust upon the general education teachers for involvement in subsequent Tier 3 RTI interventions.

For this reason, school districts seem to be "exporting" the Tier 3 interventions by making those interventions the responsibility of someone other than the general education teacher. In my experience working with a large number of schools and districts across the nation, I have not yet worked with a single district that expected the general education teacher to actually implement Tier 3 interventions, even when those Tier 3 interventions were based in general education. Most frequently, other educators implement this level of intervention, such as teachers in reading/mathematics support programs, or by instructional coaches, and so on. Still, even with the responsibility for Tier 3 interventions resting with someone other than a general education teacher, finding and making time to complete the Tier 1 and Tier 2 interventions will be a critically important issue, given the number of such interventions required.

An open discussion among the school faculty on the questions of the time requirements for these interventions—and the required progress monitoring—is critical. Faculty should consider together various systems changes, modifications of instructional responsibilities, professional development opportunities, or other school-level changes that would foster effective RTI practices schoolwide. This frank discussion can go a long way toward effective implementation. Given these realities, RTI planners and administrators should openly discuss various ways of providing additional resources and support for those general education teachers in order to assist them in completing this complex mission—not only to provide effective supplemental interventions in a variety of areas, but also to carefully monitor each child's progress during those interventions.

In fact, this single issue is so critical that chapter 3 is devoted to identifying some options that have been implemented around the nation to provide resources and support for the general education teacher to facilitate the necessary Tier 1 and Tier 2 interventions. Of course, many other planning issues should be discussed and decided by individual school faculty, simply because they are the most informed on exactly what schoolwide resources and intervention curricula are available. Facultywide buy-in will be necessary for implementation, and that is much more likely to result from open dialogue. The next chapter and subsequent chapters of this book will address these issues to provide educators with a framework for these frank discussions.

Case Study: RTI for Reading

Within our third-grade scenario, it benefits us to consider what an actual RTI procedure looks like for a single student in a district in which all the tiers are considered functions of general education.

Documenting RTI Procedures

Clearly, documentation of the tiers of intervention and the resulting performance-monitoring data from those intervention tiers are critical, as this record will later help determine the existence of a learning disability. Therefore, the documentation of the early tiers of intervention needs to be thorough and complete to withstand possible challenges from parents and/or their attorneys, who may disagree with a diagnosis of learning disability.

Furthermore, the need to extensively document must be coupled with the fact that when general education teachers begin the RTI process, they cannot know if any particular student will progress to the point of determination of eligibility for special services. In fact, the research on RTI suggests that perhaps as many as 40 to 65 percent of the students who begin a Tier 2 intervention are likely to have their problems alleviated before reaching the point of an eligibility determination (L. S. Fuchs, Fuchs, & Hollenbeck, 2007). Therefore, general education teachers will have to document their early Tier 1 and Tier 2 intervention efforts *for every child* because for any given student, such documentation may be eventually required. Interventions must assume that an eligibility decision may result; if it does, the decision-making procedure will be based, in part, on those Tier 1 and Tier 2 interventions. Accordingly, documentation of what the tiers of intervention involved and how decisions were made in the RTI process is absolutely critical.

> Extensive RTI documentation in every tier is critical because general education teachers cannot know if any particular student will eventually progress to the point of determination of eligibility for special services.

Table 1.3 (page 28) presents a form for documenting an RTI procedure based on several similar forms from the literature on RTI (Bender & Shores, 2007; Vaughn & Roberts, 2007). This form or something like it is recommended for documentation of the RTI procedures for every child for whom a Tier 2 intervention is initiated. To reiterate, general education teachers will not be able to determine ahead of time if the RTI process will lead to an eligibility determination for that particular child. Thus, accurate and detailed documentation of the Tier 1 and Tier 2 interventions and high-quality progress monitoring of the child's performance during those interventions are essential. This form is intended to foster that documentation (see page 194 for a reproducible form, or visit **go.solution-tree.com/rti** to download it).

Table 1.3 Response to Intervention Documentation Form

Student:	Age:	Date:
Initiating teacher:	School:	Grade:

1. Statement of student difficulty and summary of Tier 1 instruction (add supporting evidence and/or progress-monitoring data chart, if available):
2. Tier 2 supplemental intervention plan:
3. Observation of student in Tier 2 intervention:
4. Tier 2 intervention summary and recommendations (must include data chart):
5. Tier 3 intervention plan:
6. Observation of student in Tier 3 intervention:
7. Tier 3 intervention summary and recommendations (must include data chart):

Here is a scenario for one child receiving an intervention in reading skills during the early grades. Note: I will identify a number of issues in this scenario and discuss those within this chapter. However, I urge the reader to realize that there are many more subtle issues embedded herein, and we will discuss each of these later in this text.

In this example, let's imagine a young girl, Tomiko, is having some difficulty with early literacy skills—specifically vocabulary development. Her parents are Hispanic and Japanese, but Tomiko was born in the United States, and while English is her first language, she hears a mix of languages at home. Tomiko showed some difficulty during the first two years of school on various reading skills, and Ms. Robinson, the second-grade teacher, decided to investigate Tomiko's reading problems more closely.

Ms. Robinson used a version of the form presented in table 1.3 to begin the initial stages of the RTI process. Specifically, under the first section of that form—the section labeled "Statement of student difficulty and summary of Tier 1 instruction"—Ms. Robinson wrote the following notes.

> I noticed that Tomiko Takaio was not doing well in her mastery of new vocabulary in late September of this year. She should be decoding new words and learning around ten new words per week, but she was not mastering that much new vocabulary from the second-grade list of vocabulary words. We have stressed phonemic skills in terms of initial consonants, vowels, and final consonants daily this year, as well as multisyllable words. Tomiko should be further along in her decoding skills. I also noticed that on her statewide assessment at the end of grade 1, her scores suggested some difficulty in decoding; she is approximately a year behind at this point. I talked with Ms. Stephens, the lead teacher for grade 2, and we jointly planned a Tier 2 intervention *for Tomiko to build up her decoding skills.* (Ms. Robinson, second-grade teacher, 11/4/07)

Providing all information is critical, and Ms. Robinson did, quite succinctly, address the basic points that this section should cover. These include the following:

▶ Her overall concern with Tomiko's reading skills

▶ The types of decoding activities that had been presented to Tomiko in the general education class that year

▶ Specific comparison data on what Tomiko's mastery of new vocabulary should be

▶ Supporting test scores that also indicate a decoding problem

▶ A consultation with another educator about the problem

Consultation With Other Educators

You may have noted that Ms. Robinson decided to consult with her lead teacher, and the issue of consultation with another educator during the RTI process is important. In some school districts, a general education teacher is required to share his or her concerns and the plan for the Tier 2 intervention with another educator (lead teacher, literacy coach for the school, special education teacher, administrator, or other educator) before implementing a Tier 2 intervention. In other school districts, the teacher is required to bring this information before the student support team— that is, the school-based team intended to support students who are struggling and their teachers. Note that the name of this team changes from state to state (*SAT* or *student assistance team*, or *SWAT* or *schoolwide assistance team*). This is *not* the team that determines eligibility for special education services; rather, it is the school-based team charged with providing prereferral services and support for struggling students.

In some districts, general education teachers can initiate a Tier 2 intervention without any required discussion with anyone. There is wide variation on when general education teachers should bring other educators into the discussion. My recommendation on this question is as follows: a general education teacher should be *required* to share his or her concerns about a student's performance and develop a detailed Tier 2 intervention plan with at least one other educator, or with the student support team, before implementation. In this fashion, a minimum of two educators will collaboratively work out an intervention plan for Tier 2.

> A general education teacher should be required to share his or her concerns about a student's performance and develop a detailed Tier 2 intervention plan with at least one other educator, or with the student support team, before implementation.

I recommend involvement of one additional educator at this level, rather than the entire student support team, simply for ease of implementation (that is, it is easier to call in a consult with a lead teacher or literacy coach than to call together a formal meeting). However, I do believe that the RTI process is on firmer ground if some other educator has been consulted and has signed off on the Tier 2 intervention plan, as Ms. Stephens did for Ms. Robinson.

Ms. Robinson then completed the next section of the form, "Tier 2 supplemental intervention plan," as follows:

> I have four students, including Tomiko, who are struggling with decoding skills and seem to need a more intensive Tier 2 intervention. I intend to begin an intervention concentrating on phonemic skills, phonics, and decoding for those four students. I will do this supplemental intervention three times per week, for a period of 30 minutes each day, using the *Read Well* curriculum (Sprick, Howard, Fidanque, & Jones, 2002). I intend to do this for a period of six weeks, and monitor the students' mastery of new vocabulary terms weekly. I will chart those data on an *x/y*-axis chart for ease of interpretation, and present those data to Ms. Stephens at the end of six weeks. At that point, we will consider what further remediation Tomiko needs. (Ms. Robinson, second-grade teacher, 11/4/07)

Note that this brief paragraph clearly explains the intervention and designates a specific curriculum for this supplementary Tier 2 intervention. Furthermore, it also describes the time frame for the actual intervention. With these notes in the various sections of the RTI documentation form (table 1.3, page 28), Ms. Robinson is providing an excellent documentation basis, and should this case file eventually move to a meeting of the eligibility team, the documentation will be complete for Tier 1 and Tier 2. The same type of paragraph should also be written into the files for each of the other three students who will be participating in this Tier 2 intervention, as any of those students may eventually require a more intensive intervention and thus move to a higher level of the pyramid.

Parental Notification

At this point, one more step should be considered before Tier 2 implementation—parental notification. Many educators have asked when to notify parents about the RTI process. Special education legislation requires parental notification and consent before a referral and/or assessment for an eligibility referral; one could argue that relative to special education placement, the initial Tier 1 and Tier 2 intervention data may become "assessment" data on which such a referral is based. Thus, the question is frequently asked in workshops, is parental notification required before a Tier 2 intervention?

Following are several relevant points. First, the intervention data from Tier 1 and Tier 2 may or may not lead to an eligibility determination, and in that sense, it is similar to the examples of general education classroom work or specialized small-group work that general education teachers have historically brought into discussions of eligibility. Second, general education teachers have always implemented small-group intensive instruction when needed by students in the general education class, without any parental notification. Third, the regulations under IDEA of 2004 recognize that instructional models vary in terms of the frequency and types of repeated assessments that are required to determine accurately a child's progress (Bradley et al., 2007), and clearly, this provides some leeway on this question. Thus, based on these considerations, there is some question on the issue of parental notification before a Tier 2 intervention.

With that stated, I recommend parental *notification* of Tier 2 interventions as one way to increase parental involvement. I do not suggest that educators solicit parental *permission* for a Tier 2 intervention. Rather, educators should contact parents, share the information on the supplemental intervention, and present this as one way to assist the child to catch up on some difficult material.

> I do recommend parental notification of Tier 2 interventions as one way to increase parental involvement, but I do not suggest that educators solicit parental permission for a Tier 2 intervention.

Figure 1.2 presents a sample parent letter informing the parent of the Tier 2 intervention, without requesting parental consent. Of course, after receiving this notification, if parents object to supplemental instruction, I recommend that the general education teacher immediately consult with the administrators and team leaders in the school.

11/5/07

Dear Ms. Takaio,

I have enjoyed teaching Tomiko in second grade this year. She is always very quiet, but is quite quick to participate in subjects such as art, math, and music. I wanted to let you know that over the next six weeks or so, I intend to spend some extra time working with Tomiko to assist her in her reading and vocabulary development. Working with Tomiko and three other students, I will provide them with supplemental practice in decoding new vocabulary words. I plan on pulling this group together three times each week for approximately 30 minutes each session, and I'll continue to work with them for approximately 6 weeks. In these instructional sessions, the students will be presented with new vocabulary terms and asked to identify the initial sounds, any vowel sounds in the word, and the final sound. I'll give every student many opportunities to practice that skill each time we meet, along with practice in identification and correct pronunciation of new vocabulary words. Finally, I'll measure their progress using 10 such items at the end of each week as a performance-monitoring check on how well the student is doing, and I'll share those data with you when we meet again.

If you'd like to see this extra work one day, I'd love to have you come to our class, and you can call me and let me know a day when you can come in. We will typically do this extra work on Monday, Wednesday, and Friday, at 10:30. Please call me at the school (770–421–5821), if you have any questions.

Yours,

Ms. Robinson

Ms. Robinson

Figure 1.2 Sample parent letter about a Tier 2 intervention.

Initiating the Tier 2 Intervention

The next step is initiation of the intervention and working through that intervention for six weeks as described in the intervention plan. In our scenario, Ms. Robinson implemented this intervention and began to chart Tomiko's mastery of new vocabulary words each week. Ms. Stephens chose to go into Ms. Robinson's class and observe this Tier 2 intervention for Tomiko, and she made some observation notes on the RTI form in the section titled "Observation of student in Tier 2 intervention." Having another educator bring his or her expertise to the Tier 2 intervention is always wise and demonstrates a true desire to help Tomiko overcome her decoding skill deficit.

As indicated in the Tier 2 intervention plan, Ms. Robinson monitored Tomiko's performance every week during the six-week intervention, and the chart in figure 1.3 summarizes those data. Because most of the RTI literature presents data in this x/y-axis chart form, and because data presented in this fashion are almost immediately interpretable for parents, students, and other educators, I and many others advocate for presenting Tier 2 and Tier 3 data in this type of chart (Howell, Patton, & Deiotte, 2008). Of course, many assessments and/or computer-based interventions present repeated assessment performance data in other types of charts such as bar graphs and so on, and those are also perfectly acceptable for data presentation at every tier in the RTI process.

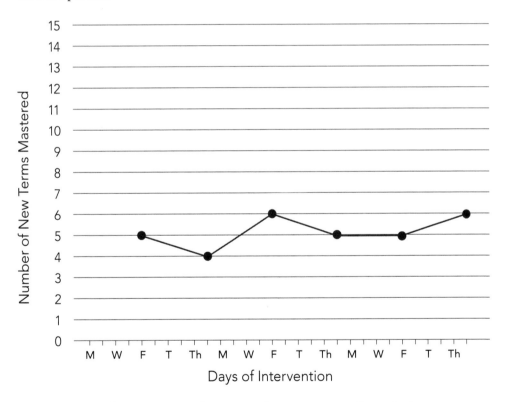

Figure 1.3 Tomiko's Tier 2 performance data: mastery of vocabulary.

> I am a strong advocate for presenting Tier 2 and Tier 3 data summarized in an *x/y*-axis chart since this chart is immediately interpretable to parents, students, and other educators.

As these data indicate, Tomiko is learning approximately five or six new words per week from the second-grade vocabulary list, but the benchmark (as reported by Ms. Robinson in the notes made in the RTI documentation previously) is learning to decode twelve to fifteen new words per week. When Ms. Stephens and Ms. Robinson looked at these data together, it quickly became apparent that a more intensive intervention might be necessary, and they decided to review this Tier 2 intervention data for Tomiko with Ms. Tatnall, the literacy coach for grades 1 and 2, since she was also the chairperson of the student support team at Toccoa Elementary. Thus, these two teachers chose to bring in more expertise at this point in the RTI process to assist with decision making. Ms. Tatnall determined that the entire team should meet and discuss options for Tomiko. In situations in which a Tier 2 supplementary intervention is not successful, I recommend that the entire student support team meet and consider additional options that are appropriate for Tier 3.

> In situations in which a Tier 2 supplementary intervention is not successful, I recommend that the entire student support team meet and consider additional options that are appropriate for Tier 3.

In the case study involving Tomiko, because Ms. Robinson did not consult the entire student support team before the Tier 2 intervention data, she should involve them as a decision-making team at this point. Following are the notes summarizing that meeting, which should be written on the RTI form in the section called "Tier 2 intervention summary and recommendations":

> On January 4, 2008, I met with Ms. Robinson, Ms. Tatnall, our literacy coach for grades 1 and 2, and the student support team to discuss Tomiko's performance in her Tier 2 intervention on decoding and new vocabulary development.

> The weekly progress data presented in her data chart [fig. 1.3, page 33] do not suggest that she was increasing her skill in decoding new vocabulary terms as quickly as she should. Ms. Robinson did state that Tomiko seemed to participate in the *Read Well* curriculum and that she believed this might work for Tomiko, if it could be used with a smaller pupil-teacher ratio since Tomiko seemed somehow intimidated working even in a small group with only three other students.

We determined that a more intensive Tier 3 intervention is necessary for Tomiko, and Ms. Tatnall typically has responsibility for Tier 3 interventions at Toccoa Elementary. She will develop a Tier 3 intervention plan for Tomiko that involves increased use of this same curriculum. (Ms. Stephens, second-grade lead teacher, Toccoa Elementary, 1/5/08)

One consideration in working through the various interventions in an RTI procedure involves how long to continue an intervention. For example, early data for Tomiko suggested that this intervention was not working after only three or four weeks. Still, it is important to provide the child with an appropriate opportunity to respond to the intervention; in some cases, students will only respond after a certain amount of time. Thus, even if the early data points collected in the first few weeks show a lack of positive response, the intervention should be continued, as it was here. With that concern noted, I am not in favor of RTI policies or guidelines that demand extremely long interventions; Georgia, as one example, recently published RTI rules and regulations requiring four data points over twelve weeks. Surely experienced educators can collect sufficient data and make a reasonable determination on the efficacy of an intervention earlier than twelve weeks! In most cases, data can be collected at least weekly. It does not take that many data points to see if an intervention is working, and why should we insist that the child continue to fail for that period of time? Most of the literature on RTI implementation involves weekly monitoring over a period of time ranging from six to nine weeks, so scientifically validated interventions generating at least that many data points within that basic time frame would be considered acceptable. Many schools choose to use a length of intervention that is consistent with their report card grading period (six weeks or nine weeks). For this reason, this example presents a six-week progress-monitoring period for the Tier 2 intervention. I should also note that teachers or school-based teams may choose, after reviewing the data, to extend the same intervention and collect more data before making a recommendation to modify the intervention.

> I suggest an intervention time frame ranging between six to nine weeks since most of the literature on RTI implementation involves weekly monitoring over a period of time, and weekly monitoring during that many weeks generally provides sufficient data on which to base a decision on efficacy of the intervention.

Initiating the Tier 3 Intervention

As indicated in the summary notes on the Tier 2 intervention, Ms. Tatnall, the literacy coach at Toccoa Elementary, typically provides the Tier 3 interventions. Thus, she would typically be responsible for developing a Tier 3 intervention plan and describing that in detail before implementation in the section on the RTI form labeled "Tier 3 intervention plan." Following are her notes on the plan for the Tier 3 intervention for Tomiko:

> As the literacy coach for grades 1 and 2 at Toccoa Elementary, the student support team decided that I should begin a Tier 3 intervention for Tomiko to assist her in her decoding skills. While she did use the *Read Well* curriculum for her Tier 2 intervention, there is reason to believe that with a smaller group this curriculum might result in more success for Tomiko. I will use this curriculum with her, and one other student, conducting five instructional sessions (one per day) with each lasting forty-five minutes during the next four weeks. I will monitor Tomiko's progress weekly during that intervention period, and report those data to Ms. Robinson and Ms. Stephens at the end of that time. (Ms. Tatnall, literacy coach for grades 1 and 2, and chair, student support team, Toccoa Elementary, 1/6/08)

Note that Ms. Tatnall's description of the planned Tier 3 intervention provides considerable detail on the length of time for the intervention, the focus of the new instruction (that is, decoding and vocabulary development), and her plan for monitoring Tomiko's progress. Each of these is an important issue that this text will discuss at length later.

Furthermore, before the implementation of the Tier 3 intervention, many of the other related issues discussed relative to the Tier 2 intervention should be reconsidered here. For example, should Tomiko's parents be informed of this change in their daughter's school activities? Again, I suggest sending a letter detailing the next level of more intensive intervention to the parent. Because this Tier 3 intervention is still a function of general education, I again recommend against requesting parental *permission* for this intervention. However, this level of intervention will presumably involve Tomiko moving into another class for forty-five minutes each day, so parents should certainly be informed about that by the school before hearing of it from Tomiko herself.

Also, during this Tier 3 intervention, I recommend that either Ms. Stephens or Ms. Robinson conduct an observation of Tomiko's work. This keeps various members of the student support team in the loop on Tomiko's progress during the intervention itself. That is why the RTI form includes a section titled "Observation of student in Tier 3 intervention."

> I recommend that an educator other than the teacher conduct an observation of each student's work. This keeps various members of the student support team in the loop on the student's progress during the intervention.

Finally, as with the Tier 2 intervention data, I recommend that data be summarized in a similar *x/y*-axis chart. Eventually, when these educators discuss these interventions with the parent—either in a meeting to determine Tomiko's eligibility for services as learning disabled or in a PTA meeting—using the same type of charted data will make those explanations of the data easier.

Summarizing the Tier 3 Intervention Data

After the Tier 3 intervention is complete, the educators involved should jointly review those data and consider what future actions are necessary. Figure 1.4 presents the data for Tomiko.

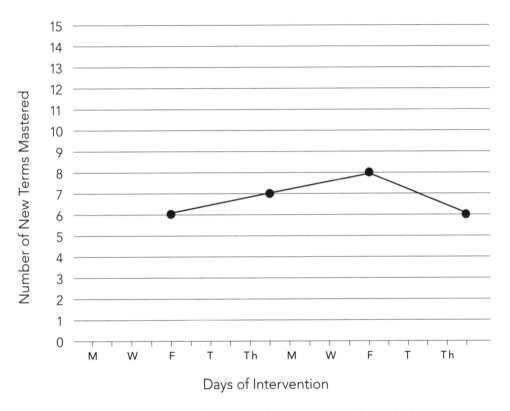

Figure 1.4 Tomiko's Tier 3 performance data: mastery of vocabulary.

As these data suggest, even the more intensive Tier 3 intervention has not succeeded in drastically increasing Tomiko's mastery of new vocabulary terms on the second-grade vocabulary list. In fact, Tomiko still seems to be learning approximately only seven to ten new words per week, and while this is more than she mastered in the Tier 2 intervention, it is clearly not consistent with the benchmark of twelve to fifteen new vocabulary words per week. Thus, these data suggest that even this very intensive supplementary Tier 3 intervention has not remediated Tomiko's decoding and vocabulary problems. Here are the notes that Ms. Tatnall wrote to summarize this Tier 3 intervention for Ms. Robinson and Ms. Stephens:

> Ms. Robinson, the student support team, and I met to discuss Tomiko's Tier 3 intervention data involving Tomiko's progress in decoding skills and mastery of new vocabulary terms from the second-grade vocabulary list. After a four-week intervention, in which I monitored Tomiko's progress weekly, the performance-monitoring data chart showed that Tomiko was not increasing the number of words she learned. Her work continues to suggest considerable difficulty in identification of vowel sounds in the middle of syllables. We believe that these data, coupled with the performance-monitoring data from the previous Tier 2 intervention, suggest that Tomiko might have a significant learning problem, and we recommend that the child study team at Toccoa Elementary review these data and consider the possibility that Tomiko has a learning disability dealing with phonemic awareness, phonemic manipulation, and/or decoding skills. Ms. Tatnall will turn this RTI file over to the child study team.
>
> Signatures:
>
> Ms. Tatnall, chair, student support team, and literacy coach for grades 1 and 2, Toccoa Elementary
>
> Ms. Robinson, second-grade teacher
>
> Ms. Stephens, lead teacher for second grade
>
> Ms. Frattlee, student support team member
>
> Mr. Thomas, special education teacher
>
> Date: 2/14/08

There are several critical points to note about this summary. First, the team recommended that the child study team at the school meet to "consider" the possible eligibility of Tomiko for services as learning disabled. In short, the RTI process does not, in and of itself, demonstrate the existence of a learning disability. By definition, a learning disability involves one of several possible deficits in various cognitive processes, and in many states, some evaluation of those processes is still required to determine the existence of a learning disability. Of course, there is considerable debate about the existence of "cognitive processes" and the necessity to measure them, and states vary considerably in their requirements. Still, in many locales, school psychologists will be expected to evaluate the cognitive processing for students suspected of having a learning disability. Furthermore, in many states, the state RTI plan still stipulates that a psychological be performed (Berkeley et al., 2009). One exception to that is the state of West Virginia, where it is up to the child study team to determine the necessity of an involved psychological (Boyer, 2008).

Next, the data from these interventions, as well as the RTI documentation sheet itself and all of those notes, will be turned over to the child study team as the basis for exploring the existence of a possible learning disability. Thus, the general education teacher will be contributing much more concretely to the eligibility determination than in the past. In the past, the two critical pieces of data to document a learning disability were an IQ score and some achievement score, which were then compared with a general "discrepancy." In the new world of RTI, the most critical pieces of data are the intervention plans for Tier 2 and Tier 3, and the intervention data summary charts—and all of the data for at least one of those charts will be generated by the general education teacher. Clearly, this is an increased responsibility for eligibility than these teachers held formerly.

In my workshops on RTI, I use the question, who talks first? to emphasize the importance of the contribution of the general education teacher in providing Tier 1 and Tier 2 data. Imagine a highly contentious child study team meeting in which parents come, with their attorney, specifically to challenge the diagnosis of learning disability that has been generated by the previously described RTI process. Of course, the presence of a parental attorney will probably result in the presence of an assistant superintendent of schools, the special education director, and perhaps even the school board attorney in that meeting. Clearly, this type of meeting holds the potential to be highly contentious for all involved.

After the introductions around the table that should be used to initiate each meeting, I typically ask, "Who talks first?" The answer is that after the round-robin introductions at this potentially explosive meeting, the meeting facilitator will turn to the general education teacher, Ms. Robinson, and ask her to provide an explanation of her Tier 1 instructional activity, her Tier 2 instructional plan, and the summary of those data! In short, even in the most highly contentious meeting possible, the general education teacher talks first!

Admittedly, such an adversarial meeting is relatively rare; parents who do wish to disagree with the school district typically do not disagree on the existence of the learning disability. Nevertheless, such disagreements can happen, and school personnel are well advised to establish robust RTI procedures that will help prepare them for such challenges, should they arise. I use that rather rare example in workshops with general education teachers to illustrate the increased responsibility they have for eligibility under RTI.

Furthermore, in introducing RTI to general education faculty, I emphasize that the RTI process really empowers general educators. Often in my workshops have I heard the lament from general education teachers that "I referred so and so to the child study team, but nothing happened for six months!" Under the RTI process, this inactivity should not happen; the general education teacher initiates the process that may eventually become the basis for the referral, and the very fact that he or she will "talk first" in the meeting shows how empowered those teachers are in the eligibility process.

> The RTI process both increases responsibility and really empowers general education teachers.

Conclusion

This chapter has presented the basics of the RTI process in terms of the most commonly used model, the three-tier RTI pyramid. I have also highlighted a variety of examples to show how the initial assumptions on how to implement the pyramid were somewhat mistaken. As educators continue to move into RTI procedures, other adjustments will no doubt also become necessary. The next chapter will focus on a number of issues that each school faculty should discuss during the implementation process.

2

RTI Planning and Implementation for the Early Years

Regardless of the level of previous RTI implementation in a particular school or school district, planning for continued implementation is always desirable (Kame'enui, 2007). Even in districts that have implemented RTI procedures for two or three years, planning activities can often streamline the previously implemented procedures, identify additional resources to be used in innovative ways, and generally facilitate improved implementation. Furthermore, as districts move into RTI, the roles of various educators change somewhat (Cummings et al., 2008), and semiannual faculty discussions of the RTI efforts can greatly facilitate these changes. Moreover, an understanding of how other schools and school districts have dealt with various implementation issues can greatly assist school planners during the first years of RTI implementation. Moving through a structured planning process such as the one described in this chapter fosters study and reflective thought about how others have tackled the same problems and concerns.

> Regardless of the level of previous RTI implementation in a particular school or school district, planning for continued implementation is always desirable.

The School-Based RTI Task Force

Some schools across the nation have identified a school-based RTI task force to lead the RTI efforts within the school, investigate interventions that are currently available and used within a school, and assist with planning and implementation during the first several years. Membership on the task force varies considerably from school to school, but might include the school principal or vice principal, team leaders from the various grades, the chairperson of the school resource team, and perhaps a special education teacher. This can be a very effective way to accomplish several things. First, moving into RTI will involve a multiyear process, with initial implementation during year one, and subsequent years dedicated to enhancing the RTI instructional and support effort. Having that multiyear process led by a group of knowledgeable, dedicated faculty can greatly benefit a school. Also, creation of such an RTI task force will tend to create intellectual buy-in for the RTI process. It will facilitate team-based decision making and provide a mechanism for modification of those decisions if certain aspects of the initial plan do not seem to be working.

> I recommend designation of a school-level RTI task force to look into what interventions are currently available and used within a school and to assist with planning and implementation of RTI during the first several years.

The tasks of the RTI task force will vary widely and should be tailored to the needs of the schools. For example, in many Reading First schools, a multitier intervention framework is already in place, and teachers are used to thinking in terms of interventions within the pyramid. In other schools, that may not be the case, and the task force will need to focus the schoolwide RTI implementation initiatives on the needs of the faculty. This text presents a number of informal needs assessments and other tools that the task force may wish to use toward that end. School districts across the nation have used some of these tools, like the planning grid, to assist in RTI implementation.

The Planning Grid

The RTI planning grid, presented in table 2.1, focuses on some of the issues that should be discussed and rediscussed as schools and districts move through the first years of RTI implementation (see page 196 for a reproducible form, or visit **go.solution-tree.com/rti** to download it). This was initially developed to assist schools in their first year of their RTI experience, but some districts have found it useful during the first several years of RTI implementation, for several reasons. First, many of the initial planning decisions warrant revisitation after the first or second year of RTI work, since resources may be shifted after the school faculty has some experience with RTI. Revisiting the RTI procedures during subsequent years also often results in more teacher buy-in and general support for the procedures as well as new suggestions for how to more efficiently handle certain aspects of RTI.

The planning grid itself is fairly simple. I recommend constructing the planning grid on a large sheet of chart paper that will facilitate use of the grid before the entire school faculty. Along the left side of the grid, the planner should place the tiers of

Table 2.1 Response to Intervention Planning Grid

	Person Who Implements	Pupil-Teacher Ratio	Curriculum	Intervention Time and Duration	Frequency of Performance Monitoring	Treatment Fidelity Observation	Notifications
Refer for Special Education							
Tier 3 More Intensive Interventions							
Tier 2 Targeted Supplemental Interventions							
Tier 1 General Education							

intervention used by a school or school district. For our purposes, we will discuss RTI in terms of a three-tier model, as was presented in chapter 1.

> I recommend constructing the planning grid on a large sheet of chart paper that will facilitate use of the grid before the entire school faculty.

Generally, to make the grid similar to the pyramid of interventions, the general education tier, which is typically numbered Tier 1, should be placed at the bottom and the other tiers numbered in sequence up the left side of the grid. In districts that use a four-tier pyramid, Tier 4 is presented at the top and typically deals exclusively with interventions after special education placement. For facultywide discussions of RTI, even that tier should be presented on the left side of the chart and discussed to emphasize that all teachers are responsible for the education of every child.

The top of the grid presents a number of questions and issues that warrant discussion during the implementation of RTI (Bender & Shores, 2007; L. S. Fuchs & Fuchs, 2007; D. Fuchs & Fuchs, 2005; Vaughn & Roberts, 2007). These questions might be appropriate to consider in the first, second, or third year of RTI implementation and may be changed, modified, or eliminated depending on the changing needs of the school. To illustrate the types of planning and discussions that school faculty should have, this chapter will discuss each of these questions in turn. Finally, for students moving through the process, many of the questions on the planning grid should be documented within each student's RTI folder. Thus, if and when a student reaches an eligibility determination, these questions are clearly answered in the documentation for every student, and the RTI procedures are therefore less open to interpretation or potential criticism.

Who Does This Intervention?

As discussed in chapter 1, the first and in many ways the most critical of the questions concerning RTI implementation is who does the RTI intervention? In almost every case, the general education teacher is expected to implement the Tier 1 intervention (L. S. Fuchs & Fuchs, 2007), and perhaps the Tier 2 intervention, and this becomes an issue of time. Faculty creativity may lead to additional ideas on resource management to facilitate RTI. Because this question is of such importance, the next chapter is entirely dedicated to suggestions for additional resources to help the general education teacher in actually completing the Tier 2 interventions.

In fact, the question, who does this intervention? should be discussed for every tier. While general education teachers may be expected to teach the class in general terms and monitor student performance individually against the benchmarks established for that year (Tier 1), they should be provided some resources and assistance to make supplemental interventions possible (Tier 2). However, the question of who does the next level of more intensive supplementary intervention (Tier 3) is still an open question in states where all three of these intervention tiers are considered to be the responsibility of general education. Even when all three tiers are a function of general education, it is rare to find a school district that actually expects the general education teachers to do the Tier 3 intervention.

Consider the scenario of the third-grade class in chapter 1, with five students struggling in reading. Research and experience suggest they will require at least two different types of interventions. Furthermore, research suggests that perhaps three would benefit from the Tier 2 intervention described previously (that is, thirty minutes per day, three days a week); thus, those students' needs would be met at the Tier 2 level. However, research also suggests that two or three of those five students would require more intensive instruction; thus, they would move to a Tier 3 or an increasingly intensive instruction, which may require forty-five minutes per day of additional reading instruction, delivered five days per week. If the general education teacher is struggling to meet the demands of the Tier 1 instruction for the whole class, *and* to provide various supplemental Tier 2 interventions for some class members, is it reasonable to believe he or she can likewise offer the required Tier 3 interventions?

One reasonable option for the Tier 3 interventions is the use of special educators (Cummings et al., 2008). For example, since the passage of IDEA in 2004, 15 percent of federal special education funds received by a school district can now be spent addressing the assessment and instructional needs of non–special education students. While there are some restrictions on use of these funds, special educators may yet play some role in the RTI process at this Tier 2 or Tier 3 level. Furthermore, there is some rationale for using these persons at the Tier 3 level. First, they are highly qualified for implementation of targeted interventions, given their certification in special education. Next, if the Tier 3 intervention is not successful (and research suggests it may not be for perhaps 50 percent of the students that reach this level of the pyramid [Bender & Shores, 2007]), the special education teacher will probably become more involved with those students at the next level anyway, since the next step may involve an eligibility determination for special education placement. Thus, it makes sense to use special educators for some of the Tier 3 intervention responsibilities, with adjustments to their schedules and other responsibilities.

Another option for Tier 3 is use of other educational personnel. For example, many students struggling in reading do so based on a problem with phonemic awareness or phonemic manipulation, and speech language pathologists (SLPs) are the best qualified of all school personnel to address that type of language-based reading problem. For some students, the SLP is the appropriate person to implement a Tier 3 reading intervention, and as the roles of SLPs continue to change, some of those professionals will welcome this direct service provision opportunity.

Discussion of who is responsible for the various RTI interventions is critical for planning and should be revisited during each of the first several years of RTI implementation. One may expect faculty to be quite involved in this discussion, as this directly affects their time. At the very least, determination of who does the interventions at the various levels is sure to be a hot debate among school faculty, and a frank discussion is vital to successful RTI implementation. Again, the next chapter presents many more ideas on this issue.

What Will Be the Pupil-Teacher Ratio for Each Tier?

The RTI implementation literature contains one clear expectation: increasing intensity of instruction as a child progresses up through the pyramid. Tier 2 interventions should be more intensive than Tier 1, and Tier 3 interventions should be more intensive than Tier 2. Furthermore, should parents wish to challenge a diagnosis of learning disability based on an RTI procedure, they will be sure to examine the intensity of the interventions in each tier. However, few guidelines for what "increasing intensity" means have been provided by either the federal government or most state governments. Furthermore, emergent research documents the various possible aspects of intensity that can be manipulated to enhance achievement (Harn, Linan-Thompson, & Roberts, 2008).

To help educators consider the various indicators of intensity, I have collected a number of indicators of "increasingly intensive" intervention from the literature on implementation of RTI, and these are presented in the planning grid (page 43). The first indicator of increasing intensity in the RTI pyramid involves the pupil-teacher ratio in the various intervention tiers. Thus, one way to document that each intervention tier of the pyramid is more intensive than previous tiers is to stipulate increasingly smaller pupil-teacher ratios.

For this reason, many state departments have stipulated specific pupil-teacher ratios to define the various tiers in their states. For example, the Tennessee Department of Education website (www.tennessee.gov/education/speced) provides guidance for Tennessee educators on response to intervention by aligning the RTI procedures to the intervention guidelines for their Reading First program. That website stipulates specific ratios that must be met for an intervention to be considered either a Tier 2 intervention or a Tier 3 intervention. For Tier 2, students must receive instruction in groups of no more than five students (thus a five to one pupil-teacher ratio), while Tier 3 interventions must be delivered to groups of no more than three students (a three to one ratio). Educators in Tennessee must now strive to meet these statewide criteria in their RTI planning, and consequently a pupil-teacher ratio column is not necessary on their planning grid. However, showing that any particular student was instructed in an appropriately sized group (that is, a group with the appropriate pupil-teacher ratio) will be essential in the RTI documentation.

Other educators in other states will need some discussion of what constitutes an appropriate pupil-teacher ratio for Tier 2 interventions and Tier 3 interventions. Should a challenge arise about the accuracy of a diagnosis of learning disability based on any RTI procedure, the parent advocate will question the RTI procedure in every way possible, and documenting that a child had an appropriate opportunity to learn, with an appropriate pupil-teacher ratio in each tier, will be critical.

What Curricula Should Be Used in the Various Tiers?

There are several issues to discuss under curriculum selection for the RTI tiers. What curricula are currently available in the school? What does the phrase *scientifically validated curricula* mean? Should we use any curriculum with scientific support that is available for any students at any level, or should we select specific curricula for discrete tiers and thus try to eliminate any "overlap"?

These curriculum questions may seem somewhat unimportant initially—until, again, one reflects on the possibility of a legal challenge, should an eligibility decision be required later. Imagine a parent who disagrees that his child has a learning disability. It is quite possible that the parent's attorney will challenge the entire RTI process at some point, and setting up one's RTI procedures in a robust fashion to survive that challenge is critical. Or imagine the following scenario. First, a general education teacher notes a reading decoding problem and implements a Tier 2 intervention using a scientifically validated program such as *Language!* by Jane Fell Greene (1998). This particular intervention is not successful, however, and the child progresses into a Tier 3 intervention—an established schoolwide supplemental reading program that also happens to use the *Language!* curriculum. In short, the child would then receive the *Language!* intervention for both Tier 2 and Tier 3 supplemental interventions. The parent's attorney might naturally ask, "Given that this curriculum was not successful for this child in Tier 2, why did the school expect it to be successful in Tier 3?" The attorney could then continue with the logic:

> Since the school implemented a curriculum in Tier 3 that had not worked for this child in Tier 2, we take the position that the child has not received an appropriate opportunity to respond to multiple, increasingly intensive interventions, and we'd like to challenge the LD diagnosis, based on this flaw in the RTI procedure.

In short, by using the same curriculum in multiple tiers, the school opens itself up for this particular legal challenge. Of course, this is not to say that such a legal challenge is likely or would be successful based only on that single issue. Furthermore, there are clearly times when increasing the intensity of an intervention is exactly the correct thing to do and does result in educational improvement. However, why would a school or school district set itself up for such a challenge by using the same curriculum at multiple tiers with all students at all, when reasonable alternatives are available?

Of course, school districts should use only scientifically validated curricula at every stage in the RTI process as required by federal legislation, but I also recommend that students be exposed to *different* scientifically validated curricula at each tier in the RTI process. Thus, schools should identify two or three curricula in reading and two or three in math that will be implemented at each discrete tier within the pyramid to completely cover the essential skills in either reading or math. For example, if a school determines that the special education teacher will complete all Tier 3 reading interventions, and he or she uses the *Read Well I* curriculum (Sprick et al., 2002), other teachers should agree to forgo use of that curriculum in Tiers 1 or 2. Rather, in Tier 2, general education teachers should select from a variety of other curricula available in the school. Thus, if a child progresses through the various tiers and does end up being considered for special education by the child eligibility team at a later point, he or she will have been exposed to the general school curriculum (Tier 1), and a minimum of two supplemental curricula before the eligibility determination. In that case, the parent's attorney will not have a potential challenge to the RTI procedures based on that question of reexposure to the same curriculum in multiple tiers.

> I recommend that students be exposed to *different* scientifically validated curricula at each tier in the RTI process.

Next, consideration should be given to the issue of scientific validation of the curricula used in the RTI process. Unfortunately, when the federal government initially began to emphasize use of scientifically validated curricula several years ago, it provided few guidelines on what constituted "scientific validation" of any particular curricula. Furthermore, the field has not reached general consensus on the question of how much validation is required for a given curriculum.

However, one approach serves to protect the school district on this question. Generally, if a curriculum has received scientific validation, those scientific studies appeared in peer-reviewed journals in education or psychology. Of course, educators with expertise in research design may wish to review actual studies dealing with scientific validation for curricula under consideration, and frequently large school districts do employ educators with such expertise in instruction and/or assessment. However, many educators work in smaller districts that may not have such expertise available.

Fortunately, education experts at several universities have evaluated almost all curricula in reading and mathematics, and those universities established websites for sharing those evaluations of the research supporting particular curricula. For example, both the Florida Center for Reading Research at Florida State University (www.FCRR.org/FCRRReports) and the University of Oregon website (http://reading.uoregon.edu/curricula) provide information on which curricula have received scientific validation. If these websites present a particular curriculum, then it has received some scientific validation, and educators can access summaries of those studies and determine the applicability of the curriculum in their districts. Of course, the number and quality of scientific validation varies widely, but having several studies that provide scientific validation for a particular curriculum will empower the school in the case of a challenge. These two websites provide the best option to document scientific validation for particular curricula, and I strongly recommend against using curricula in the RTI process that are not presented on one or both of these websites.

The site for the RTI Action Network (www.rtinetwork.org) may also be helpful. In fact, a wide variety of additional resources is available online (see appendix B, page 203). Educators working in RTI should investigate these various resources during the RTI implementation process.

Next, schools should select curricula for the various tiers that offer options for instruction. For example, the *Read Well I* curriculum mentioned earlier does an excellent job in teaching decoding skills. However, if one wanted a curriculum that built fluency in reading, one might choose the *Read Naturally* curriculum (Ihnot, Mastoff, Gavin, & Hendrickson, 2001), which is based on repeated readings to increase words read per minute. Thus, including both of these as Tier 2 curricular options makes sense since together they do an admirable job covering the diverse early reading skills. Of course, teachers should then choose the curriculum that most appropriately addresses the specific needs of the individual student during Tier 2 and Tier 3 instruction.

Again, for purposes of planning RTI during the second and third year of interventions, this type of faculty discussion can help hone the skills of teachers as they select curricula for particular students in Tier 2 and Tier 3. At the very least, this discussion will make teachers aware of what other supplemental curricula other teachers in their school are using.

The School-Based RTI Inventory

Of course, to plan effectively for RTI, one needs to know what curricula are currently available at the school. One frequently finds perfectly acceptable scientifically validated curricula gathering dust in the media center. Other times, school faculty find that some teachers have been privately implementing particular supplemental curricula in their classes for months or years. In fact, as an initial step in RTI planning, schools may wish to have the school-based RTI task force conduct an inventory of available scientifically validated curricula currently in the school. In many cases, curricula that can become RTI resources are "found" in back rooms of media centers.

The RTI task force should also look into other resources that are available for RTI within the school or district. I know of one instance in which a license for a technology-based curriculum had been purchased for relatively wide use within the district, but was only being used for a very small number of students in the home-based secondary education program! In that case, the district merely needed to make the curriculum available on some computers in the elementary and middle school, for use as a Tier 2 intervention. Finding such potential resources for RTI can be very helpful work for the RTI task force.

However, the task force should inventory much more than merely the available curricula. The inventory process should note any specialized skills or specialized training teachers have had that can contribute to the RTI process. Have teachers been specifically trained for particular curriculum such as *Read Well*? Are particular curricula more appropriate for use in specific intervention tiers? The task force should inventory the entire school, and then put forth a set of recommendations as to which current interventions are appropriate for Tier 2 or Tier 3. At a minimum, such an inventory should include the following.

1 A check of the media center at the school for unused curricula that are appropriate for individual or small-group interventions at Tier 2 or Tier 3

2 A survey or faculty discussion about curricula that are in use by individual teachers in the school

3 A check of the resources and curricula that are available at the district level, particularly if that district has a curriculum media resource center

4 Consultation with the technology specialists in the district to determine if any computer-based curricula are available

5 Identification of specialized curricular training that teachers have had that can be used for RTI

> I recommend that schools conduct an RTI resource inventory of interventions, available curricula, and specialized training in curricula teachers have had.

Schools can take the inventory either formally or informally, and in the context of this process, identify specific curricula-based interventions that are already tied to specific intervention tiers. For example, if a reading coach in a particular building is using a curriculum such as *Read Well I* (Sprick et al., 2002), and that reading coach is conducting the Tier 3 reading interventions for the school, conducting a school inventory that tags that curriculum directly to Tier 3 is helpful. Table 2.2 presents several questions and a form that may be adapted as the basis for such an inventory of currently used curricula and training (see page 197 for a reproducible form, or visit **go.solution-tree.com/rti** to download it). In most cases, it is helpful to complete the school inventory before conducting faculty meetings based around the planning grid since these inventory assist in completing the planning grid.

Table 2.2 A Sample School Response to Intervention Inventory

Hard Copy Supplemental Curricula Interventions
List all *supplemental* curricula that are "hard copy" (that is, not primarily computerized curricula, for example, various "curricula in a box"). Note the grade range and the areas or subjects for each. Include curricula used by every teacher within the school, including curricula used by particular teachers within specialized programs. Note who is using these and for what group? Also remember to consider any curricula that are unused in the media center or storage areas in the building.

Computerized Supplemental Curricula Interventions
List all *supplemental* curricula software (for example, *Read Naturally, Academy of READING*). Note the grade range and the areas or subjects for each. Include curricula used by every teacher within the school, including curricula used by particular teachers within specialized programs. Note who is using these and for which students.

Hard Copy Assessments for Universal Screening
List all individual assessments that are appropriate for universal screening or repeated assessment for performance monitoring (for example, *Dynamic Indicators of Basic Early Literacy Skills*). Note the grade range and the areas or subjects for each. Include curricula used by every teacher within the school, including curricula used by particular teachers within specialized programs. Note who is using these and for which students.

continued on next page →

Curricula Recommended for Specific Tiers
Are there reasons for recommending particular curricula for specific tiers? For example, a limited site license for a certain computerized curriculum may suggest use of that curriculum only as a Tier 3 intervention. Explain.

Specialized Training
Have teachers received specialized training for particular supplemental curricula (for example, learning strategies training for the *Learning Strategies Curriculum* or training in *Fast ForWord*)? Can or will these teachers be responsible for certain tiers of interventions or prepare other teachers for such intervention? Can other teachers receive such training, as necessary?

What Will Be the Time and Duration of the Interventions?

Another indicator of increasing intensity is the length of time of the intervention. Specifically, schools must determine how many minutes per day of supplemental instruction they will offer, how many days per week the intervention will occur, and how many weeks each intervention will last. Time and duration can each seriously impact the likely efficacy of an intervention; for example, no educator would seriously expect an intervention of thirty minutes once a week or once every two weeks to result in significant educational growth toward benchmarks. However, intensive supplemental interventions involving thirty minutes of instruction per day, three days a week are quite likely to result in significant educational improvement for most students, and interventions of forty-five minutes daily are even more intensive, and thus more likely to result in significant educational growth.

Again, some states stipulate the number of minutes per day and days per week. Tennessee requires that Tier 2 interventions be provided for a minimum of thirty minutes per day, five days each week. Other state RTI procedures stipulate the total number of weeks an intervention must last; for example, Georgia stipulates that an intervention must last at least twelve weeks to be considered an appropriate RTI intervention. Still others (Illinois and California) leave these questions about the time requirements for an RTI intervention to the local school districts or the individual RTI implementation teachers.

In addition to state stipulations, certain curricula make recommendations for implementation. For example, the *Academy of READING*—a scientifically validated, computerized curricula for teaching phonemically based reading (AutoSkill, 2004a)—suggests that the curricula be implemented a minimum of four days per week for at least thirty minutes each day to achieve maximized efficacy. Of course, when the curricula state recommendations or requirements, schools should follow those guidelines in planning the Tier 2 and Tier 3 interventions. Ignoring stated curricular requirements may invalidate the curriculum by diverging from the implementation practices used in the research that supports its scientific validation.

As another consideration, the RTI plan for each student must stipulate the time allocation for each intervention in terms of all three variables: minutes per day, days per week, and number of weeks. Noting this explicitly for every student should be a requirement of RTI documentation (the RTI procedures presented in chapter 1 included such notations for Tomiko). Furthermore, the intensity of Tier 3 interventions compared with Tier 2 and Tier 1 interventions should be clearly obvious. If Tier 2 intervention is offered for thirty minutes a day, three days a week for a grading period of six weeks, then the Tier 3 intervention should clearly be more intensive—perhaps thirty minutes a day, *five* days a week for a six-week grading period.

There is some advantage to providing Tier 2 interventions for three days per week or every other day rather than daily. Obviously, a large number of students can and will have their reading problems alleviated by that level of service (Vaughn & Roberts, 2007), and implementation of Tier 2 for three days each week or every other day allows that teacher to offer some other type of intervention (perhaps a Tier 2 intervention in math) on the remaining days each week. However, the needs of the individual children involved should be the primary decision factor; schools must make certain that the level of intensity provided is sufficient for those students to begin to improve academically and move toward benchmarks for their grade.

In summary, several factors affect the decision concerning how much time should be devoted to an intervention, including the educator's best estimate of what the child requires for success, state guidelines for duration of RTI interventions, recommendations from curriculum publishers concerning duration and intensity, and committee decisions on what intensity is necessary. Again, the overriding emphasis should be on meeting the child's needs, but following state, school district, or school policy is also required.

> Multiple factors should be considered in determining time and duration, including the educator's best estimate of what the child requires, state guidelines for duration of RTI interventions, recommendations from curriculum publishers concerning duration and intensity, and committee decisions on what intensity is necessary.

From the perspective of the planning grid, a discussion among faculty of when and how to provide the time for these interventions can be very beneficial. Some coordination between and among faculty is necessary since they can support each other in making Tier 2 and Tier 3 interventions available. Discussion of when, how long, and how frequently these interventions are provided is often time well spent. Faculty decisions on these questions should be written in the appropriate box on the grid in some detail.

What Will Be the Frequency of Performance Monitoring?

School faculty should also discuss and decide the frequency of performance monitoring. While performance monitoring has always been expected in special education (Etscheidt, 2006), the RTI process requires extensive performance monitoring in general education as well. In some cases, this may increase the level of performance monitoring beyond what teachers are currently doing. Clearly, the literature on RTI is based on frequent performance monitoring, and frequent monitoring of performance is likewise built into the goals and expectations for most state departments of instruction RTI plans (Berkeley et al., 2009; D. Fuchs & Fuchs, 2006; L. S. Fuchs & Fuchs, 2007; Jenkins, Graff, & Miglioretti, 2009). Most of the RTI research literature implemented repeated assessments either weekly or every other week; since many computerized curricula allow for daily performance monitoring, some literature recommended repeated performance monitoring based on either weekly or daily data collection in Tier 2 and Tier 3 of the pyramid (Bender & Shores, 2007). Of course, this recommendation, again, requires time on the part of the general educator. Research is ongoing on this question; work by Jenkins et al. (2009) suggested that less frequent performance monitoring (for example, performance monitoring every three weeks, rather than weekly) may well be as accurate as more frequent monitoring.

> I recommend repeated performance monitoring based on either weekly or daily data collection in Tier 2 and Tier 3 of the pyramid.

The progress-monitoring question for any school or district is twofold: (1) what is right for the student and will facilitate his or her academic growth, and (2) how frequently should student performance be monitored in each tier, given the overall goal of increasing intensity of instruction? For the universal screening and performance-monitoring needs in Tier 1, teachers typically use either statewide assessments, periodic report card grades, or various benchmark-based screening assessments. For example, the *Dynamic Indicators of Basic Early Literacy Skills* (DIBELS; Good & Kaminski, 2002) is frequently used as a benchmark assessment in kindergarten through third grade. It is typically administered three times per year to monitor the Tier 1 reading/literacy performance of all children in those lower grades, and that is sufficient unless the assessment shows some reason for concern for a particular child.

For higher tiers in the pyramid, to demonstrate increasing intensity in the interventions, daily performance monitoring is the most preferable option (Bender & Shores, 2007). Research on curriculum-based measurement has shown that daily monitoring is most sensitive to subtle changes in children's academic performance (Lindsley, 1990, 1992), and thus teachers are able to more quickly modify their instruction to address the specific needs of the child. In fact, daily monitoring of performance is considered the gold standard for intensive instruction, and many commercially available curricula are developed with daily performance monitoring as one repeated assessment option. Furthermore, almost all computer-based intervention curricula are set up to provide daily performance monitoring. For these reasons, daily performance monitoring is preferable for students in Tiers 2 and 3 if the time and resources are available.

With that noted, the obvious problem with daily performance monitoring is that it can be quite time-consuming, and in the RTI environment, teachers will already be quite pressed for time, as discussed previously. In light of this concern, weekly or bimonthly performance monitoring during Tier 2 is recommended (Bender & Shores, 2007). You will recall Tier 2 is the more intensive intervention provided by the general educator, with resources and assistance, for those students struggling in the class. Should Tier 2 not be successful, students progress to Tier 3, where daily monitoring should be the norm (Bender & Shores, 2007). I do not recommend considering students for placement in a learning disabilities class without at least one intensive intervention resulting in high-quality daily performance monitoring. Given that daily monitoring is preferable, and that most educators therefore consider it best practice, school districts should insist on daily monitoring for at least one of the intensive supplemental interventions before considering eligibility for placement. Should additional evidence accumulate that documents efficacy of less frequent performance monitoring (for example, Jenkins et al., 2009), this recommendation may change in the future.

> I recommend that, before consideration for placement in a learning disabilities class, a student should be exposed to at least one intensive intervention with high-quality daily performance monitoring.

How Much Progress Is Enough?

Coupled with the question of frequency of performance monitoring is the question of how much educational progress is enough. What is the appropriate comparison standard to make that determination? Is any positive academic growth enough, or should student achievement be compared to benchmarks or to that of other students in the class?

For this, and subsequent points on the grid, another RTI example is in order. Imagine a second-grader, DeShaun, who is struggling in reading. His teacher, Ms. Carlson, chose to implement a Tier 2 intervention using a repeated reading intervention—*Read Naturally* (Ihnot et al., 2001)—to increase his reading fluency. DeShaun received thirty minutes of supplemental reading instruction three or four times a week, working either individually or in a group of between three and five students for a six-week grading period. Table 2.3 presents a description of such a Tier 2 intervention plan to include in the RTI documentation materials. Again, note the level of detail provided herein; this level of detail will be critical for RTI documentation.

Table 2.3 Tier 2 Intervention Plan for DeShaun Johanson

Student: *DeShaun Johanson*	Age: *7 years, 4 months*	Date: *10/2/08*
Initiating teacher: *Ms. Carlson*	School: *Beaverdam Elem.*	Grade: *2*

In working with DeShaun since the beginning of the year, I've noted that he decodes words fairly well, but has not reached automaticity in that decoding. As a result, his reading is very broken and not at all fluent. I noted that his DIBELS scores likewise indicated some difficulty in that area at the end of the first grade and again at the beginning of this year.
I propose to initiate a Tier 2 intervention with DeShaun, aimed at increasing his reading fluency. I will work with DeShaun along with four other students for thirty minutes per day, four days per week, for the next six-week grading period. I intend to use the curriculum Read Naturally, which uses a repeated reading procedure to enhance reading fluency.
On each intervention day, DeShaun will do a "cold timing" that measures words read correctly per minute on new reading material each day. That dependent measure will be monitored four times a week during this Tier 2 intervention. He will then repeatedly read the same story, along with a computerized reading, until he believes he has improved his fluency. This usually involves three or four practice readings of the same story. DeShaun will then do a "hot timing" in which his words read correctly per minute will again be timed on the same story.
I have requested that Mr. Turner, the literacy coach, be available to consult and to conduct at least one observation during this intervention to address treatment fidelity. I will present a data chart of DeShaun's cold timings to the student support team at the end of the next six-week grading period.
Signed: Jean Carlson

If DeShaun showed progress, his chart of words read correctly per minute on new text would increase during that grading period, as indicated in figure 2.1. However, at the end of one grading period, how can the teacher determine whether to continue the Tier 2 intervention, and what criteria should she employ?

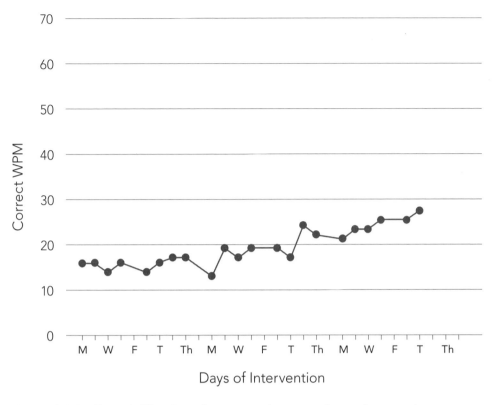

Figure 2.1 DeShaun's Tier 2 performance data: words read correctly per minute (WPM).

In this example, the data show that DeShaun is improving; he is responding to systematic, intensive supplemental instruction. Based on his response to intervention, the teachers can safely conclude that DeShaun does not have a learning disability. In that sense, one question concerning DeShaun has been answered.

However, other questions have not been adequately addressed, such as, what is the appropriate duration of this intervention? Has DeShaun made "enough" progress to indicate he has caught up with his classmates on benchmark assessments? Is this goal of "catching up" with his peers based on a brief intervention even reasonable, and how much progress should teachers expect from targeted intensive interventions directed toward small groups of children? A quick review of the existing research suggests that there are still more questions than answers here (Kavale & Spaulding, 2008; Silberglitt & Hintze, 2007). In this case, the data suggest that DeShaun has not made sufficient progress since most second graders read second-grade words at a higher fluency, typically between forty and sixty words per minute. Therefore, DeShaun would be placed at further risk of failure if the Tier 2 intervention were withdrawn at this point since his reading is not near the benchmark for reading success. He should not be removed from the Tier 2 intervention that is clearly working.

How much progress is enough can be difficult to answer. While researchers are now addressing this question (Silberglitt & Hintze, 2007), no clear guidelines are provided as yet in most state department RTI plans (Berkeley et al., 2009). The issue is finding the most efficient way of presenting data that suggests whether or not DeShaun's performance over time will allow him to catch up with his peers on the various benchmarks.

In some cases it is advisable to actually assess successful readers in the class and record their performance on the chart for a student like DeShaun to provide a comparative indicator of how well DeShaun is progressing. This would provide one measure of how well DeShaun is progressing relative to his peers, though not necessarily of how well he is doing overall. For some students with low motivation, charting their performance compared with others in the class can be quite an effective motivator. Specifically, showing a child his or her progress will, in some cases, motivate that child to increase his or her efforts. Should no progress be noted, the teacher should certainly revise the instruction.

However, I have some reservations on this class comparison measure since it takes additional time to monitor performance on members of the class who are not in need of intensive instruction, and teacher time is already at a premium! In addition, some teachers react negatively to this type of comparative analysis using specific children. While this approach is one way to evaluate DeShaun's progress, other alternatives are not as problematic. First, we should bear in mind that these options for reflecting on progress should only come into play if a student's performance data showed clear indications of *some* progress. If the performance-monitoring data are flat, then clearly the intervention is not working, and some change is necessary. However, when the data do indicate some growth, teachers have several options for interpreting the meaning of that growth:

1   Use existing assessments or periodic reports (for example, statewide assessment typically administered in April of each year or report card grades) to help make a determination about DeShaun's progress. Considering coupling those data with some additional information from the sources that follow.

2   Administer a brief screening assessment at the end of the Tier 2 grading period, and use those data to compare DeShaun with his peers' performance rather than the data gathered during the Tier 2 intervention. This allows educators to determine if DeShaun should remain in the Tier 2 intervention. In many instances, this is likely to be necessary.

3   Use screening data that are built into the intervention curriculum itself. For example, in this scenario, the curriculum *Read Naturally* not only charts daily performance on cold timings, but also includes data on the expected reading fluency levels for various grades; those broad screening data can be used for guidance on continuation of the intervention.

4   Use the consensus judgment of the student support team when they collectively review the positive performance data. Team-based decision making can be critical in determining how much academic growth is enough.

These options noted for comparative assessment will allow the teacher and/or student support team to determine when it is necessary to continue the Tier 2 intervention longer than one grading period. However, in many cases, continuation of the Tier 2 intervention will be necessary, even after the question on eligibility (does this child respond appropriately to well-delivered, scientifically proven interventions?) has been answered. In reviewing DeShaun's performance-monitoring chart in table 2.3 (page 56), it is clear that he is responding positively to this intervention. However, in this scenario, I would recommend that Ms. Carlson use the grade-level comparison data that came with the curriculum; while improving, DeShaun is still far behind his grade-level peers in reading fluency. Clearly, it would be a disservice to DeShaun to discontinue the intervention that is clearly working. Ms. Carlson should recommend continuation of that intervention for at least another grading period.

> I recommend use of screening norms associated with intervention curricula to determine when to extend a successful Tier 2 or Tier 3 intervention. If those data are not available from the curriculum itself, teachers should use other screening data from student records and the student support team to consider the student's level of performance and rate of academic growth.

How Will We Document Instructional Fidelity?

The RTI literature presents several terms to represent the overall quality of instruction in a particular intervention tier. These terms include *treatment fidelity*, *instructional validity*, and *instructional integrity*. *Treatment* or *instructional fidelity* is a critically important concept and perhaps represents the RTI area in which schools and school districts might be more open to challenge.

For example, even if a teacher uses a scientifically validated curriculum in Tier 2 or Tier 3, there is still the question of whether the curriculum was implemented appropriately, resulting in a valid opportunity for the child to respond to instruction. Again, in the few situations in which a parent wishes to challenge the existence of a learning disability, when the school district has used an RTI procedure to document that learning disability, the parent's attorney is sure to inquire, "Did the child have an appropriate opportunity to learn from the curricula used in Tier 2 and Tier 3?"

In short, schools will need to document that not only was a scientifically valid curriculum used but also that it was used appropriately. That is, the school must show that the teacher implemented the curriculum the way it was implemented in the research supportive of that curriculum. This frequently boils down to whether the teacher followed the instructional lesson and/or instructional guidelines provided in the instructor's manual for teaching each daily lesson.

> To address the question of instructional fidelity, schools will need to document not only that a scientifically valid curriculum was used but also that it was used appropriately.

Unfortunately, most RTI guidelines presented on the various state department of education websites do not address this issue at all (Berkeley et al., 2009), and thus many districts are open to this type of challenge to their RTI procedures. However, schools have two methods to address this issue, and though they should use both methods, only the second really protects the school legally.

The first option is professional development; teachers should receive some degree of training on use of the curricula that they intend to use as Tier 2 or Tier 3 interventions (D. Fuchs & Fuchs, 2005). Of course, many commercial companies will provide training in their curricula at no cost as a service with the purchase, while other companies charge for training. Still others maintain that teachers who read and study the instructor's manual will be able to effectively implement the curriculum based on the teacher's certifications and previous training.

With that stated, the most effective way to address the issue of treatment fidelity is actual observation of the Tier 2 or Tier 3 instruction for at least one instructional period during those interventions (Bender & Shores, 2007). These observations can be conducted by the principal, a literacy coach, another teacher on the grade-level team, another member of the student support team, or any other certified educator in the building. Preferably, the observer is someone who has received training on implementation of the specific intervention used.

Notes should be made that address two points during that observation. First, the observer should make some statement that the teacher was following the instructional procedures as outlined in the teacher's manual for the curriculum implemented; for example, "I noted that Ms. Jones followed the lesson outline on page 28 of the teacher's manual when I observed DeShaun receive Tier 2 supplemental instruction on 9/18/07." Such a written observation note will put to rest any possible challenge relative to the quality of instruction DeShaun received in Tier 2.

Second, the observer should also make some notes about DeShaun's performance during the observation, to contribute to future discussions of DeShaun's work. These should be based on hard data when possible, but even informal observation notes such as, "I noted that DeShaun was attentive to his work, and seemed to read the story quite fluently," may help in subsequent discussions of DeShaun's performance. These observation notes should be signed, dated, and added to DeShaun's RTI file.

When Will We Notify Others?

The issue of notification should be placed on the planning grid and discussed by the school faculty. Most educators tend to think of *parental* notification first, and that is one aspect of notification, as discussed in chapter 1. However, notification of other educators within the school is also important.

School faculty, as a group, should consider what types of involvement are recommended for general education teachers who believe that a Tier 2 or a Tier 3 intervention may be necessary. Of course, some state and district websites have policies relative to involvement of other educators in the RTI process (Berkeley et al., 2009). Georgia's four-tier RTI process, as one example, allows teachers to implement Tier 2 interventions in general education without the mandatory involvement of other educators, but before implementing a Tier 3 intervention, teachers must consult the student support team. Other states and districts mandate the involvement of the student support team before even a Tier 2 intervention.

Involvement of other educators often results in the pooling of intervention ideas, so as noted in chapter 1, I recommend that any general educator who chooses to implement a Tier 2 intervention involve at least one other educator. I do not support the policy of automatic involvement of the entire student support team since that becomes quite cumbersome. Also teachers have been shown to be quite effective in remediation efforts at Tier 2; research has shown consistently that approximately 50 percent of children who begin a Tier 2 intervention in reading do respond positively to that intervention (Denton et al., 2006), so any extra requirements for the student support team seem merely overkill. Of course, should a teacher wish to have the input of the entire team, then such involvement should be encouraged.

One final word on that notification/involvement of other educators before a Tier 2 intervention: in my workshops around the country, many principals have expressed support for having at least one other educator involved before any Tier 2 intervention. In that fashion, both the general education teacher and the other educator (that is, the lead teacher) can be jointly responsible for any intervention decisions that were made, and should the principal receive a phone call from an angry parent ("Why is my child singled out for extra reading and more assessment?"), the principal can then rely on both documentation of performance data and the joint judgment of two educators rather than one. Of course, in that instance, an invitation to meet with the parents relative to these interventions should be extended to alleviate any further concerns.

In both cases involving the entire student support team as well as cases managed by one teacher, in conjunction with a lead teacher, a well-written intervention plan for Tier 2 is critical. Thus, the teacher would prepare a brief set of notes on the planned intervention and present that to either the team or the other educator.

A Multiyear Implementation Plan

The RTI task force should take the lead in the long-term planning process. Using the tools presented in chapter 1 and in this chapter, the task force should consider how to move the school forward toward effective implementation of RTI as a systems-change school improvement process. Implementation will be a multiyear process, and the RTI task force should consider developing a set of yearly RTI implementation goals. These yearly goals will then help guide the RTI task force in implementation efforts. Of course, some states, such as West Virginia, have stipulated such goals on a statewide basis, with targeted dates for RTI implementation in different curricular areas and different grade levels, and any goals set locally by an RTI task force should certainly be consistent with state or district goals. However, schools can also state goals for year-to-year implementation of RTI. While these will vary from one locale to another, or even among schools in the same district, the implementation goals presented in table 2.4 indicate the types of multiyear planning schools may wish to undertake during the early years of RTI implementation.

Table 2.4 Multiyear RTI Implementation Plan, Toccoa Elementary School

RTI Goals for Academic Year 2008–2009

1. All teachers will receive three hours of in-service on each of the following topics:
 	
  (a) RTI procedures for our state—in that meeting, the RTI planning grid will be introduced as our primary planning mechanism. This will be completed during the first month of school, and an outside expert (perhaps from the state department of education) will be used to introduce RTI to our faculty.
 	
  (b) The use of various screening assessments for performance monitoring in reading and mathematics
 	
  (c) Computerized interventions available in our county school in reading and math

2. Members of the school-based RTI task force will select specific professional development opportunities at various state and national conferences, and various members will attend these to bring back additional information on RTI implementation.
3. The school-based RTI task force will develop and present an RTI implementation plan for RTI implementation in reading to the school faculty. It will be discussed at one meeting, modified as suggested, and adopted. Current recommendations for the RTI implementation timeline are presented herein.

4. The school-based RTI task force will work with the principal on necessary resources for RTI on an ongoing basis. These may include the following:
 	
  (a) Additional professional and/or support staff for RTI interventions
 	
  (b) Purchase of intervention curricula in various areas
 	
  (c) Discussions of reallocations of job responsibilities for RTI implementation

5. The school-based RTI task force will implement a needs assessment among the faculty on RTI.

6. The school-based RTI task force will conduct a school-based inventory to identify assessments, curricula, and specialized staff training at Toccoa Elementary to assist in RTI implementation.

7. Items on the schoolwide planning grid will be discussed at the end of the year to note any changes from the initial planning session.

8. Data on student referrals to special education will be collected at the end of this year as a comparison measure on efficacy of RTI.

RTI Goals for Academic Year 2009–2010

1. Toccoa Elementary will implement universal screening in reading literacy for all students (kindergarten to grade 3) three times each year, and use those assessments to determine which students are not on benchmark for reading growth.

2. Toccoa Elementary will provide Tier 2 interventions in reading for all students requiring more intensive instruction by providing a minimum of thirty minutes of small-group supplemental instruction four times each week.

3. By January of 2010, Toccoa Elementary will provide Tier 3 interventions in reading for students requiring them. These will be provided five days per week for a minimum of thirty minutes per day.

4. The school-based RTI task force will be expanded to include all former members as well as all grade-level team leaders.

5. Various teachers will be invited to attend professional development opportunities that address RTI implementation in mathematics, writing, and behavior.

6. Screening instruments in mathematics, writing, and behavior will be collected and discussed by the school-based RTI task force. Ultimately, one or more screening instruments in mathematics will be identified and recommended to the school faculty.

7. The schoolwide planning grid will be used again, in May of this year, specifically to note any changes from the initial planning session.

8. Data on student referrals to special education will be collected at the end of this year as a comparison measure on efficacy of RTI. These data will be compared with data from the previous year to determine the impact of RTI in our school.

RTI Goals for Academic Year 2010–2011

1. Toccoa Elementary will implement universal screening in mathematics and reading for all students (kindergarten to grade 3) a minimum of twice a year, and use those assessments to determine which students are not on benchmark in mathematics.

2. Toccoa Elementary will provide Tier 2 interventions in mathematics and reading for all students requiring more intensive instruction by providing a minimum of thirty minutes of small-group supplemental instruction four times each week.

3. By January of 2010, Toccoa Elementary will provide Tier 3 interventions in reading and mathematics for students requiring them. These will be provided five days per week for a minimum of thirty minutes per day.

continued on next page →

4.	Screening instruments in behavior will be collected and discussed by the school-based RTI task force. Ultimately, one or more screening instruments in behavior will be identified and recommended to the school faculty. The faculty has previously implemented a schoolwide positive behavioral supports system, and articulation of those efforts with the RTI process will be the focus of the school-based RTI task force.
5.	The schoolwide planning grid will be used again, in May of this year, specifically to note any changes from the initial planning session.
6.	Data on student referrals to special education will be collected at the end of this year as a comparison measure on efficacy of RTI. We will compare these data with data from previous years to determine the impact of RTI in our school.

Conclusion

As shown in this discussion, virtually every decision concerning how to implement RTI can be a source of considerable discussion. Who should do the RTI interventions? Who should evaluate them for treatment fidelity? What curricula should be used? How frequently should performance be monitored, and how much progress is enough? All of these questions can be either problem areas for a school faculty or alternatively, sources of resource reallocation that can strengthen the overall RTI effort. Furthermore, in particular schools, additional questions will arise that the faculty should consider placing on the grid for discussion.

Still, the overall purpose of these planning recommendations is to facilitate a faculty working through these questions together. A school-based RTI task force can be of great benefit in that regard and can take the lead not only in creating the school RTI inventory but also in future planning for RTI. Working through these discussions may take several faculty meetings; as decisions are reached, they should be written down on the grid and identified as final decisions. These decisions will then guide the student support team and the school leadership team as well as every teacher in the school.

Of course, even final decisions can be revisited at the end of the year, or the beginning of the next year, and the school-based RTI task force can take the lead in coordinating that faculty meeting. This grid has proven to be quite helpful for schools and task forces across the nation, including schools who are just initiating RTI as well as schools that have been doing RTI for two or more years.

3

Teacher Time and Resources for RTI

As mentioned previously, one of the most critical issues affecting RTI implementation is how to find or create the time for the general education teacher to complete the initial tiers in the RTI procedure (Vaughn & Roberts, 2007). While the RTI implementation models vary from state to state (Berkeley et al., 2009), virtually all RTI plans involve the general education teacher conducting general education activities for the entire class (including differentiated activities) as well as either conducting the Tier 2 interventions outright or playing some role in those interventions (Torgesen, 2007). In most RTI plans in the literature, as well as the examples I've worked with in schools, the general educator is expected to conduct *all* Tier 1 and Tier 2 interventions (L. S. Fuchs & Fuchs, 2007; Vaughn & Roberts, 2007; Torgesen, 2007). Of course, this expectation is likely to result in considerable demands on that teacher's instructional time.

As indicated in the scenarios presented in chapters 1 and 2, the preliminary three-tier pyramid suggested that a general education teacher would conduct instruction for all students (Tier 1) and do some type of small-group pull-out intensive instruction for perhaps four to six students struggling in reading (Tier 2). However, as discussed previously, general education teachers are likely to be required to conduct many more interventions than were indicated in the early presentations of the RTI pyramid. Preliminary experience has shown that in many instances, several different reading interventions are required (for example, an intervention in decoding for some students, and an intervention in reading comprehension for others), along with interventions for students struggling in math as well as students with behavioral problems. Thus, even in situations where the Tier 3 interventions are conducted by someone other than the general education teacher, the general education teachers will, in virtually every grade level, require some assistance to make the various RTI Tier 2 interventions available for the students needing them. Clearly, creatively supporting those teachers can make or break a school's RTI efforts, and one critical focus of the school-based RTI task force should be the designation of resources to support them.

> Most general educators will require some assistance to make a variety of RTI Tier 2 interventions available for students with a variety of different needs.

However, the time demands on the general educator may be even greater. Some RTI models—the Reading First approach, for example—originally suggested that general education teachers would be required to conduct not only the necessary Tier 1 and Tier 2 interventions but also the Tier 3 interventions as well. While that has proven to be at least possible in Reading First schools when RTI procedures were limited exclusively to reading interventions, the need for RTI procedures in math, behavior, and perhaps other areas (such as writing skills) precludes having the general education teacher conduct all interventions in all three tiers. In short, if a general education teacher needed to conduct only three supplemental intervention instructional activities daily, and each took thirty minutes, that general education teacher would "miss" ninety minutes of instructional time daily with his or her class! Clearly, that situation is neither optimal nor desirable.

In every district in which I have worked, someone other than the general education teacher conducts the Tier 3 interventions, even when those interventions are considered functions of general education. However, this still leaves the general education teacher with a heavy time demand for supplemental instructional interventions. This chapter presents options for creatively supporting general education teachers in that regard.

Initially, rather than focus exclusively on the demands that RTI makes on a general education teacher's time, I recommend that the school-based RTI task force and the school faculty in general tackle this difficult problem in terms of schoolwide resources that can be developed or reshuffled to address the expectations of RTI. In short, what resources are available already at the school, and what additional resources might the school need? Of course, while some districts make certain types of additional funding available for RTI, other districts may not have that option. Thus, this question concerning resources devoted to RTI is critically important, since some schools have found that few additional funds can be made available.

> Rather than focus on time demands inherent in RTI, I recommend that faculty work together to tackle this difficult problem in terms of schoolwide resources that can be developed or reshuffled to assist general education teachers with RTI.

By addressing the demands on teacher time as a *general* resources question, various options that can facilitate RTI become apparent. For example, does the school have paraprofessional educators who can be reassigned to assist teachers with Tier 1 or Tier 2 interventions? Are after-school remedial programs an option for Tier 2 or Tier 3 interventions? Is the school practicing inclusive educational programming by coupling a special educator and general educator together in the same class for any time period each day, and can that inclusion practice help facilitate RTI? How can other educators be used in these intervention roles?

This chapter discusses the basic requirements of the RTI procedure to shed light on the types of time requirements that teachers confront, and thus, on the types of resources that they need. Next, I describe some resource options that, for many schools, should not require additional revenues. While not all schools have the resources available that are described, many schools do, and for those schools, it may be a matter of adapting an existing program or educational initiative to meet the requirements of RTI. Finally, I make some recommendations that require additional funds.

Of course, any of these options can be implemented with supportive funding. Furthermore, options that I suggest require additional funds may not require them in a particular school. Still, consideration of both no-cost options and cost-based options can assist schools in planning for the ongoing RTI process during the first three to five years.

Additionally, this chapter focuses on resources to complete Tier 2 academic interventions since in my experience, this has been the single most difficult problem for schools. For Tier 1—general education activities for all students—teachers are already experts, in that they have been delivering effective education for years. Likewise, since educators other than the general education teacher frequently conduct Tier 3 interventions, the resource needs associated with Tier 3 are not, in most cases, as critically pressing as those for Tier 2—at least in my experience.

Finally, this chapter focuses on *academic* interventions. While all teachers should expect to conduct various behavioral interventions within the broader positive behavior supports and RTI process, these interventions are most frequently conducted while class is ongoing, and typically do not require a separate pull-out instruction time for the students and the teacher. For example, teachers frequently conduct interventions, such as a token economy or behavioral contract, by merely documenting inappropriate behaviors while they lead class instruction. More information and ideas on behavioral interventions within the RTI framework are presented in a later chapter. Still, implementation of Tier 1 and Tier 2 behavioral interventions typically does not make demands on the general education teacher's time, and these will not be discussed in this chapter. Again, the most critical issue is how to make resources available to conduct Tier 2 academic interventions.

Which RTI Requirements Affect Teacher Time?

As indicated previously, neither the federal government nor most state governments provide highly specific requirements for RTI in any intervention tier (Bradley et al.,

2007; Kemp & Eaton, 2007). However, some state departments of education stipulate specific requirements, and those requirements do vary (Berkeley et al., 2009). Teachers should check the state department of education website for specific guidelines for their state or school district.

Given the relative lack of guidelines, the best explanation of what RTI requires is the research literature itself; chapter 1 summarized these general requirements as follows:

▶ Universal screening

▶ A pyramid of increasingly intensive interventions

▶ Implementation of a research-based curriculum

▶ Frequent monitoring of each child's progress

▶ Data-based decision making

While some of these requirements are probably determined at the district level, prior to any teacher's involvement with a student's RTI process—for example, what universal screenings are administered, how the pyramid is structured, or what research-based curricula are purchased—others do inform us as to what teachers are actually expected to do in the various tiers. Based on the preceding list, and the general literature on RTI, general education teachers are expected to:

1 Conduct intensive Tier 2 interventions with small groups of students, targeted directly toward each child's documented academic needs

2 Conduct up to three separate Tier 2 academic interventions (that is, two different types of interventions in reading and one in math)

3 Monitor each child's performance on those interventions using frequent repeated assessments appropriate for the RTI process and subsequent decision making

Using the suggestions and recommendations made previously in the scenario described in chapters 1 and 2, we will assume that a Tier 2 intervention must be conducted a minimum of every other day, and that each child's academic growth should be monitored weekly, at a minimum. These parameters can provide guidance on the types of resources (both time and money) that are necessary for facilitating Tier 2 interventions. While some states (for example, Tennessee and West Virginia) mandate that Tier 2 interventions be undertaken daily, most states provide some decision-making leeway to the school districts, so Tier 2 interventions that take place every other day or three days per week are certainly a possibility in most instances. In short, each of the following examples will be described in terms of meeting these requirements for RTI.

No-Cost Tier 2 Intervention Options

Under the assumption that schools will not be provided with additional funds to facilitate RTI interventions, school faculty and administrators must jointly seek ways to redistribute resources that are already available to support the general education teachers in making RTI procedures available for struggling students. The first set of resource options are no-cost options based on real-world solutions that have been put into practice and have worked in various school districts around the nation. These include using paraprofessionals for RTI, coupling RTI needs with inclusive education, class sharing, scheduling an "intervention" period, using existing remedial classes for Tier 2, and other types of creative teacher scheduling.

Scheduling Paraprofessionals to Assist

Most schools have some paraprofessionals (or *paras*) available at various educational levels in the district. While some paras are specifically assigned to certain legally required duties (for example, some paras are assigned to work with one student with a severe disability all day), others have more leeway in their assignments, and reassignment of these persons can provide one option for facilitating RTI.

On examination, some educational administrators have found that certain paras were underutilized in their current assignments. Almost every educator has seen paras who were working in the back of a classroom on nonessential tasks while a teacher led a whole-group lesson with little regard for appropriate use of the paras. Clearly, this does not represent optimal use of the paras' time, and in that type of situation, reassignment of the paras into situations where Tier 2 interventions are required is in order.

Of course, school district administrators should initially consider where most Tier 2 interventions are likely to be required. History has indicated that most students identified for learning disabilities have traditionally been identified in grades 3 or 4, though the implementation of RTI procedures in early literacy kindergarten programs may push that down a bit in the next few years. However, schools should acknowledge that much of the RTI effort is likely to take place in kindergarten through grade 6, and assign paras accordingly. Furthermore, for RTI purposes, it may be more effective to assign paras to grade-level teams, and then to allow those teams to monitor their RTI workload and make specific daily para assignments appropriately. Nevertheless, a senior-level professional educator—perhaps a grade-level team leader or an instructional coach—should always take responsibility for monitoring the paras' time, work responsibilities, and for setting the schedule.

> History has indicated that most students identified for learning disabilities have traditionally been identified in grades 3 or 4, though the implementation of RTI procedures may push that down a bit in the next few years. Paras with a role in RTI should be assigned accordingly.

For the following example, let's assume that a large number of RTI procedures are needed in second and third grade at a K–5 elementary school. Imagine that there are three second-grade teachers, three third-grade teachers, and two paras assigned for the mornings to this second/third-grade team in this particular school. Therefore, each one of those six teachers will need some support for conducting three separate types of Tier 2 interventions (reading—decoding; reading—comprehension, and math).

In this case, it would be simpler to establish Tier 2 interventions that require thirty minutes of intensive instruction every other day rather than three days per week to facilitate the scheduling of the paras. Next, the paras' time should be allocated in terms of ninety minutes to each teacher, every other day, since that will allow each teacher to conduct three thirty-minute small-group interventions (that is, two different reading interventions and one intervention in math). This allocation of time will have to be established in such a way that does not conflict with the whole-class reading and math lessons since it serves little purpose to schedule a Tier 2 intervention in the place of the Tier 1 instructional time. Therefore, the paras have to be in the general education classes when the teachers are not conducting the whole-class (Tier 1) reading or math instruction.

To facilitate these scheduling needs, the second-grade teachers in this example (Ms. Smith, Stampler, and Strooker—note that these teachers' last names begin with s for second grade, as a memory technique to aid the reader) should agree to conduct their reading and math instruction each day after the schoolwide recess (that is, after 10:30 AM each day). The third-grade teachers (Ms. Toony, Thompson, and Trayner—all names here begin with t for third grade) should agree to conduct their reading and math instruction between 8:10 and 10:00 AM. Thus, as long as the paras are not scheduled in those general education classes during those time blocks, the Tier 2 interventions they facilitate will not result in pulling students out of the Tier 1 instruction in reading or math.

Given these scheduling agreements, the schedule for the two paras presented in table 3.1 will allow each teacher to conduct the three separate required interventions. Those teachers may elect to use their paras by either having the paras work with small-group instruction for the Tier 2 students or teaching the paras to monitor the work of the whole class while the teacher conducts the Tier 2 interventions.

Here are several final thoughts on the use of paraprofessionals for RTI. First, note that every teacher in this second/third-grade teacher team is supported by a para for ninety minutes every other day. This will allow those teachers to conduct three separate academic interventions of thirty minutes each (that is, a reading/decoding intervention, a reading comprehension intervention, and a math intervention) for three subgroups of struggling students. However, teachers should realize that because some students will be struggling in both reading and math, these supplemental interventions cannot be allowed to overlap; some students will need both a reading intervention and a math intervention. The schedule in table 3.1 provides for this contingency.

Table 3.1 A Two-Week Schedule of Paraprofessionals' (Paras') Time to Facilitate Response to Intervention in Six Elementary Classrooms

Teacher	Mon	Tues	Wed	Thurs	Fri	Mon	Tues	Wed	Thurs	Fri
Paras work in second-grade classrooms from 8:15 AM to 10:00 AM.										
Smith	Para 1		Para 1		Para 1		Para 1		Para 1	
Stampler		Para 1		Para 1		Para 1		Para 1		Para 1
Strooker	Para 2		Para 2		Para 2		Para 2		Para 2	
Paras work in third-grade classrooms from 10:30 AM to 12:15 PM.										
Toony	Para 2		Para 2		Para 2		Para 2		Para 2	
Thompson		Para 2		Para 2		Para 2		Para 2		Para 2
Trayner	Para 1		Para 1		Para 1		Para 1		Para 1	

Next, as indicated previously, paras, if provided with appropriate training, can be used in several ways, including monitoring ongoing whole-class instructional activities while a teacher gives a Tier 2 intervention to a small group of students or leading Tier 2 instruction in many cases, while working under a teacher's supervision. For example, many scientifically validated curricula are based on scripted direct instructional lessons, and paras can undertake the responsibility of leading instruction in that type of Tier 2 intervention—as long as training is provided on that specific curriculum and they follow the prescribed lesson. In fact, many supplemental instructional curricula are created with exactly that option in mind, and the teacher's manual will typically provide guidance on the question of who may lead instruction with that particular curriculum.

> When provided with appropriate training, paraprofessionals can undertake the responsibility of leading instruction in certain types of Tier 2 interventions.

One significant advantage is that this schedule does not require all of the para's time each day. In fact, this schedule does not require any para's time in the afternoon after 12:30, and thus, some of that time is left over for other paraprofessional responsibilities, or perhaps other RTI duties, in other grade levels. Two paras, appropriately used, can assist in facilitating Tier 2 interventions for RTI in a fairly large number of classes.

Next, the advantage of presenting Tier 2 interventions every other day, or three days per week, is obvious in the schedule presented in table 3.1. Planning the Tier 2 interventions for every other day makes available a wider variety of scheduling options. In particular, many struggling students can have their needs met by interventions of this intensity, and thus I recommend planning Tier 2 interventions for three times a week or every other day. Again, however, certain states (such as Tennessee) have decided that Tier 2 interventions must be presented daily, and clearly all teachers will have to follow state policy.

Finally, while this discussion has focused on implementation of scheduled paraprofessional time, the same type of creative scheduling can be applied to other adults working within the general education class. Schools with structured adult-mentoring programs that focus on academic support can implement the same type of schedule for adult mentors who could lead instructional lessons and/or tutoring lessons. While a mentor's instructional talents are likely to vary considerably, most schools that undertake adult mentoring to assist with academics find that many mentors are, in fact, retired teachers who want to "keep a hand in" even after retirement. Schools across the United States have employed such persons for Tier 2 instruction with extremely positive results.

Scheduling Inclusive Educators to Assist

Many schools have put another scheduling solution into practice—scheduling special education inclusive education services in a manner that facilitates RTI interventions (Cummings et al., 2008). Chapter 2 briefly mentioned this idea, but because this is a critically important option, it deserves a bit more attention here.

Today, many schools practicing inclusion or inclusive education establish schedules that place a special education teacher in a general education teacher's class on a daily basis for one educational period or more on each school day. In other cases, special educators are in the general education class for a period of time every other day. In either case, a bit of creative scheduling can create the possibility of the special educator and general educator teaming up to provide the required Tier 2 interventions. In fact, by substituting "special education teacher" for "para" in table 3.1 (page 71), educators can get a sense of the types of time and resource support that are possible using the inclusive educator to facilitate RTI.

When a special educator is in a general education class co-teaching or conducting targeted individual assistance for students, that educator is typically assisting students who have been previously identified as having special needs. However, in many co-teaching models, special educators are encouraged to facilitate group instruction for mixed groups of students—some with special needs and others without. Thus, inclusive instruction lends itself to the option of having either the special educator or the general educator undertake a Tier 2 intervention with a number of students in need, while the other teacher leads instruction for the others in the class for twenty to thirty minutes.

> In many co-teaching models, special educators are encouraged to facilitate group instruction for mixed groups of students—some with special needs and others without, and this can lend itself to providing Tier 2 RTI support.

For example, the special educator might lead the majority of the class in a subject such as math, while the general educator devotes some time to small-group supplemental reading instruction. In that example, students with learning disabilities in math would have their inclusive instructional needs met by the whole-group activity led by the special education teacher, while students struggling in reading would work with the general educator in a Tier 2 group for targeted reading instruction. Of course, for those students with special needs in mathematics, their individualized education plan (IEP) should stipulate how to deliver their specialized instruction, and in the preceding example, it should state that students will receive such instruction in the whole-group inclusive setting.

I should also note that certain changes in federal policy have facilitated this option. The federal government included a rather unusual provision that bears directly on the use of special educators for RTI intervention support when RTI was first passed into law in 2004 through IDEA (Bradley et al., 2007). For the first time in history, the government allowed up to 15 percent of the federal funds devoted to special education to be used for meeting educational needs of students who were *not yet identified* as students with special needs. One nationwide survey of special education administrators indicated that in 52 percent of the districts in the survey, some portion of those funds were indeed allocated to the RTI early intervention process (Spectrum K12/CASE, 2008). Thus, change in funding options seemingly provides some new options for implementing RTI.

Of course, there are provisions limiting the use of these funds, and many districts designate these funds for other expenditures. Educators should inquire about these financial restrictions from the district director of special education to investigate use of these funds for RTI purposes. Also, it should be quite clear that special education teachers in inclusive classes have responsibilities other than RTI, and they must continue to meet those obligations. However, the use of inclusion special education teachers for implementing some Tier 2 interventions is certainly one option given this change in legislation, and schools should consider it for provision of some Tier 2 interventions.

Sharing Classes

In some districts with limited funds and few or no paraprofessionals, teachers have banded together in groups of two or three teachers to create intervention options along grade-level lines. This idea involves a sharing of one's class with another teacher in the same grade level. I've chosen to refer to this idea as *class sharing*, specifically to differentiate it from the broader idea of team teaching; however, there clearly are similarities.

Here is how this no-cost class-sharing idea might work. In most schools, classes in the same grade level are situated near each other or side by side; such proximity will facilitate class sharing. For example, in two third-grade classes that are located across the hall from each other, each class may be expected to have twenty-two students, resulting in forty-four students whose RTI needs may be shared. Specifically, among those forty-four students, perhaps six to eight will require a phonemically or phonics-based Tier 2 reading intervention (that is, three or four students from each class), while another four to six students require a Tier 2 reading comprehension intervention (two or three from each class).

Using the class-sharing idea, one of those third-grade teachers—Ms. Lovorn—might agree to conduct *all* the Tier 2 interventions during the months of September, October, and November, while the other teacher—Mr. Whiten—instructs the remaining students in science, social studies, or enrichment activities unrelated to reading. Thus, on Monday, Wednesday, and Friday of each week, Ms. Lovorn would first pull the eight students needing a Tier 2 phonics/decoding intervention for twenty-five minutes, while Mr. Whiten did an enrichment activity with the remaining students. For the next twenty minutes on the same days, Ms. Lovorn would pull the four to six students requiring a Tier 2 reading comprehension intervention. Meanwhile, Mr. Whiten would continue the enrichment lesson for the whole group. Thus, these two teachers have "shared" the RTI intervention needs between these two classes.

To provide quality instruction for the students not receiving a Tier 2 intervention, Mr. Whiten would have to plan three forty-five-minute enrichment lessons each week on some topic other than reading and math, since RTI should not result in targeted students missing reading and math instruction. These enrichment lessons should extend the students' understanding in various curricula areas and may involve a variety of subject areas. Mr. Whiten would teach those lessons to students from both classes, while Ms. Lovorn conducted the two separate reading interventions.

Depending on scheduling and the needs of students in the class, on alternative days, Mr. Whiten might conduct a Tier 2 math intervention, while Ms. Lovorn taught the remaining students in the shared class. To make this work and to truly share the RTI responsibilities, teachers have generally agreed to shift these instructional responsibilities, such that in this example, at the end of November, Mr. Whiten might do the Tier 2 reading interventions during the next three months of the school year, while Ms. Lovorn taught the larger group.

Sharing the RTI responsibilities in this fashion does require that teachers work closely together, and that each feels comfortable in conducting both intensive interventions and lessons for larger groups of students. In fact, some teachers have expressed concerns with the idea of teaching anything to a group of thirty-six students! However, I should point out that a large group is typically more homogeneous in educational need than the whole class since students with demonstrative needs in reading and/or math are selected for the small-group Tier 2 intervention work. Furthermore, teachers who have tried this idea have repeatedly indicated to me that they had no difficulty in managing instruction for the larger group of students, since those students were more highly skilled academically. Again, this is an option for schools and teachers to consider in instances in which resources for RTI are limited.

Scheduling Targeted Intervention Periods

One of the common concerns about time to do Tier 2 interventions focuses on how much time can be "taken away" from other subjects. Teachers frequently share this concern in terms of the need to address all the state standards in all subject areas: "How can I expect students to meet standards in science, history, and health if I pull them out for a Tier 2 intervention in reading—particularly when I'm not supposed to pull them out of the reading class for the intervention?"

Students and teachers today are held responsible for meeting all state standards in all subjects, and pulling students from any subject area for supplemental Tier 2 instruction in any area becomes a serious concern. This has led administrators across the nation to one creative scheduling option—building an "intervention" period into the school day. This option has been implemented in a variety of schools, including many middle schools and even secondary schools, and for those departmentalized schools (schools in which students change classes for different subjects). In fact, it is the RTI option of choice.

> For many schools, particularly middle and secondary schools, schools in which students change classes for different subjects, creating an intervention period is the RTI option of choice.

In most elementary-level examples of these intervention periods, a general education teacher works with more intensive small-group instruction with a limited number of students, perhaps at the back of the classroom, while the majority of the students in the class reviews an enrichment video or holds a student-led group discussion on a topic of interest.

While most of the national attention on RTI has focused on early reading in the lower-grade levels (Spectrum K12/CASE, 2008), there will always be some need to provide Tier 2 and Tier 3 interventions in higher grades (Vaughn & Roberts, 2007). In many districts, administrators in the middle and secondary grades, with the support of the faculty, have scheduled an intervention period into the school day, during which students receive supplemental Tier 2 interventions. In those departmentalized schools, scheduling such interventions is merely a matter of creating a semester-long course (for example, "Reading in the Content Subject" or "Mathematics Preparation for Statewide Assessment").

Course designations such as "Remedial Reading" should be avoided when creating such Tier 2 intervention courses, since that could entail embarrassment for many middle and high school students. Of course, that issue is not eliminated by the creative terms used in the sample course titles, but it is diminished somewhat.

> Course names such as "Remedial Reading" should be avoided when creating Tier 2 intervention courses in middle and high schools since that could entail embarrassment for many middle and high school students.

Using Existing Academic Programs

One of the most frequently asked questions about RTI is how this set of procedures interfaces with existing programs: "Can we use our Title I, or tutoring, or other supplemental program for Tier 2 interventions?" The answer depends on several factors, but certainly educators should consider this option.

In fact, many educators across the nation have begun to use existing supplemental instruction programs as their Tier 2 intervention. Depending on what types of existing supplemental programs the school has, these programs may include, for example, federally funded Title I reading programs, Reading First programs, early intervening services, after-school tutoring programs, and/or other types of academic support programs.

Existing programs should certainly be considered as one option for providing Tier 2 interventions. In one example, a creative faculty in an elementary school in a southeastern state determined to use an existing after-school tutoring program to provide time for Tier 2 interventions! In that situation, an after-school general tutoring program had been offered for some time, with little support from the students and community. However, when that program was revamped into a more structured, intensive reading enhancement program with weekly performance-monitoring requirements, teachers at that school determined that the program could meet their need for Tier 2 interventions in reading. Furthermore, once the revamped program was presented and explained to parents as a reading enhancement program, parents became much more supportive and even assisted with transportation for the program. Almost all the students lived within a mile of this urban school (assisting with transportation would be more challenging in a rural area), but parents still made the effort to rearrange home and work schedules to accommodate the program.

> In one small city school, the faculty chose to use an after-school tutoring program to provide extensive Tier 2 interventions.

In a workshop in West Virginia, I heard the question, "Can our Title I reading program meet our needs as our Tier 2 intervention?" A member of the state department of instruction indicated that while the federal perspective was unclear, this idea was certainly possible according to West Virginia authorities, provided that the school met eligibility for Title I funding and that the Title I program was structured to generate the types of intervention and performance-monitoring data that are necessary under RTI (Boyer, 2008). During the subsequent presentation on RTI, multiple options for teachers in that state were discussed such as implementing Tier 2 interventions within the Reading First program, which, as discussed in chapter 1, is already structured as a three-tier intervention program anyway!

The advantages of using existing programs as Tier 2 interventions are obvious— these programs are already in existence and thus are already funded. Likewise, these programs will alleviate many of the time demands relative to the general education teacher's time since they tend to be pull-out programs, whereby students are pulled from the general education class, moved into another classroom, and then taught by other educators. Because of these advantages, I encourage educators to explore the use of existing programs as one option to deliver Tier 2 interventions—as long as existing data reflect the efficacy of those programs.

With this noted, educators should clearly understand what is required of the RTI process. For an intervention program to function, participation should not exclude a student from receiving Tier 1 instruction in the general education classroom—and participation in some existing programs does. In those cases, other arrangements for Tier 2 supplemental interventions must be created.

Next, the program intended to serve as a Tier 2 intervention must be *more intensive* than the general education instruction. The intensiveness of a program is typically indicated by the factors presented across the top of the planning grid in chapter 2 (page 43; that is, such factors as pupil-teacher ratio; number of minutes per day, days per week, and weeks; use of a scientifically validated structured curriculum; see Vaughn & Roberts, 2007). It does little good to place a struggling child in a Title I class with twenty-two other students when his or her needs dictate the requirement for highly intensive instruction founded on a pupil-teacher ratio of four to one. In fact, in almost all of the existing RTI literature, most Tier 2 interventions involved intensive instruction with pupil-teacher ratios ranging from four to one up to about twelve to one (Bender & Shores, 2007). These indicators should serve as a general guide on the level of intensiveness of the Tier 2 instruction required. Again, some states have stipulated these factors explicitly, and educators should make certain that the existing program meets those requirements before using it.

> I encourage educators to explore the use of existing programs as one option to deliver Tier 2 interventions in their school, but these programs must meet the requirements of the RTI process.

Finally, the proposed Tier 2 program must be structured to generate the types of frequent performance-monitoring data required by Tier 2 RTI procedures. While the RTI literature varies on how frequently such data should be generated during Tier 2 interventions, proponents of RTI interpret "frequent performance monitoring" as meaning daily, weekly, or every other week (Bender & Shores, 2007; Vaughn & Roberts, 2007). Educators should carefully monitor the academic performance of each child repeatedly during each Tier 2 intervention. Performance monitoring on a weekly or every-other-week basis should be a minimum, and when possible, daily progress monitoring is recommended (again, this is quite possible in computerized curricula when the software is designed to provide daily performance monitoring; Bender & Shores, 2007).

With these requirements of the RTI process noted, we can again approach the question of using existing supplemental programs for Tier 2 RTI purposes. Some existing programs (for example, Reading First) probably meet these general requirements, and can with relative ease serve as the Tier 2 interventions offered by a particular school. However, even in existing programs that do not meet these general requirements, school faculty may wish to consider restructuring those existing programs to meet them. For instance, many Title I classes have smaller pupil-teacher ratios than the general education classes in the school. In that case, simply instituting a slightly more rigorous performance-monitoring system in the Title I class may meet the requirements for Tier 2 intervention. However, one overriding concern should guide a school's planning and RTI implementation efforts: what is in the best interest of each individual struggling child?

Other Creative Scheduling Options

In some schools, creative scheduling offers a way to provide some Tier 2 intervention time. In working through the requirements of RTI, teachers in one elementary school decided to compare their daily schedules and see if any "extra" time was apparent. This is a good exercise for faculty at the school level, and I sometimes do this in RTI workshops with a single school.

Begin by listing time slots on a dry-erase board—say every thirty minutes through the school day. List these down the left side of the board. Next, list the teachers' names at the top, and inquire of each teacher as to their exact task for each time slot. In one case, after only five teachers in grades 3 and 4 had completed this task, it became apparent that between 10:00 and 10:25, all teachers in grades four and five (in this case, ten teachers!) were on the playground monitoring their class at recess. One teacher in that group suggested sharing that responsibility among a more limited number of teachers, and thus freeing up some teachers each day to do Tier 2 interventions.

> When working with a single school faculty on RTI, I will often have teachers compare their daily schedules to see if any "extra" time is available for Tier 2 interventions.

The next problem was quickly apparent; the teachers did not want students to miss their recess to participate in the Tier 2 intervention. However, they solved that problem by breaking up the assigned recess time, by having fourth-grade students go to recess from 9:45 to 10:10, and fifth-grade students from 10:10 to 10:35. Thus a bit of creative scheduling created some daily intervention time for both teachers and students, which could then be devoted to supplemental Tier 2 interventions.

Tier 2 Intervention Options Requiring Financial Resources

When conducting RTI workshops, I've told educators across the nation that it is quite easy for me to recommend spending *their money!* With unlimited financial resources, schools could easily meet every RTI need for every child. However, most educators neither live nor teach in those types of school districts, so such thinking is not really relevant to most teachers. While funds are limited in almost every school district, many districts do make available some funds for RTI implementation, and judicious spending can more easily address the requirements for Tier 2 interventions (and even Tier 3 interventions). Several options follow that may involve some expenditures, technology, and use of additional certified personnel.

Using Technology-Based Instructional Programs

Technology-based instructional programs should be considered as an option for Tier 2 RTI procedures whenever possible; I strongly encourage use of technology for RTI implementation in general. While the use of computerized instructional programs may entail some expense on the part of the school or district, it offers a number of distinct advantages. Foremost among these advantages, the use of computerized instruction and performance monitoring saves time for the general education teacher, and as this discussion has shown, that single concern is often the biggest issue in RTI implementation. If a class of twenty-six students includes seven who need a Tier 2 reading intervention, the general education teacher would use the assessment tools that are typically built into the computerized program to accurately place each individual child within the program. Then, that teacher would let the computer do the actual daily instructional work, leaving the teacher free to conduct instruction for the remaining students in the class. This, of course, is a critical advantage.

> Technology-based instructional programs should be considered as an option for Tier 2 RTI procedures whenever possible.

Next, many computerized programs include not only an instructional component that can be used as a Tier 2 or Tier 3 intervention but also weekly or even daily assessments. This can certainly be very significant. While districts use many assessment tools for RTI purposes, I urge them to spend their funds wisely by spending limited funds on a technology-based intervention *curriculum* that *includes* assessment rather than merely an assessment tool. In short, why should a district purchase a stand-alone assessment program when they could purchase an instructional program that includes a built-in reliable and valid assessment tool?

Of course, when negotiating a site license for any computerized program, schools should consider actual use of the program. Specifically, in a K–5 school with six hundred students, a site license for all six hundred students often represents wasted funds since one might anticipate that only 20 to 25 percent of that population actually needs a Tier 2 supplemental intervention program. In that case, the school administrators should consider a site license for 100 to 150 students. Of course, if an *entire* school population requires assistance, then a site license for a particular technology-based program may be in order.

Software-based instruction holds a key advantage on the issue of treatment fidelity, as discussed in chapter 2. In computerized instruction, there is little likelihood of mistakes in instruction since the technology delivers the instruction required by the child at any given time. Therefore, the treatment fidelity concerns discussed previously are not an issue in this context.

Finally, because of the engaging nature of educational software today, students who have a difficult time paying attention in both whole-group and small-group instructional sessions will frequently become engaged with the lessons presented by high-quality educational software. In some cases, students with attention deficit disorders have engaged with software programs for thirty to forty-five minutes without their attention wandering! Today's software is, in many ways, more engaging than a teacher conducting a small-group instructional lesson since the instruction presented on the computer demands very frequent individual responses for each question, whereas in some small-group instructional programs, one student out of four or five is called on for reading or providing an answer. Of course, computers will never replace qualified teachers since teachers must be active in the selection and assessment processes, and make determinations as to the placement of the child within the program. Still, many software programs do result in actively engaged students, and that is critical for many struggling readers.

Many high-quality, highly engaging computer-based instructional programs are available today that will meet the need for Tier 2 interventions. For example, the reading program *Read Naturally* (Ihnot et al., 2001) is a computer-based program that focuses on both fluency and reading comprehension, and is applicable throughout the elementary and middle school grades. Using a repeated reading intervention, this research-supported program requires students to repeatedly read a selected passage daily. Initially, the teacher will assess student's fluency on a *cold timing* by having the student read a new reading passage, while the teacher listens and counts the words read correctly. This generates a score on *words read correctly per minute*. Next, students are required to retell the reading passage, resulting in a measure of reading comprehension based on a single reading of the passage.

At this point, the student is exposed to choral reading exercise in which he or she is required to complete the same reading passage several times, while reading along with the computer program. Of course, the teacher is free to work with other students on other activities when students are reading with the computer, and in that fashion, this computer-based program helps to address the teachers' overriding concern, "When can I find time to do RTI interventions?" In this scenario, the software is teaching the struggling student while the teacher continues to teach the rest of the class!

Finally, after the student has read the same passage three or more times using the choral reading software, the teacher sits again with the student and again checks reading fluency. This score is referred to as the *hot timing*. The student then retells the reading selection, providing a final measure of comprehension for that passage.

In almost every case, the student's fluency and comprehension will increase from the cold timing to the hot timing, and thus students feel rewarded by their reading progress. However, something much more important and fundamental likewise takes place; over time, the student's fluency will increase on the cold timings, thus indicating an overall improvement on reading fluency on material to which the student has not been exposed.

Again, this program effect has been thoroughly documented in the research (Denton et al., 2006), and thus this program works for the child and facilitates a daily measure of fluency and reading comprehension. However, in the context of this discussion, this type of computerized program also works for the teacher since the teacher is free, almost all of the time, to be working with other students or teaching the whole class, even while a specific highly engaging Tier 2 intervention is taking place.

Another example of a computerized reading program that facilitates RTI is the *Academy of READING*, coupled with the *RTI Toolkit*, both published by AutoSkill (2004b, 2008). These programs are specifically structured to provide intensive phonemically based reading instruction across a wide range of grades, and to facilitate high-quality performance monitoring, resulting in data that can be charted daily or weekly for RTI purposes. Research on this program is somewhat limited, but the initial research was quite positive, and many school districts have reported impressive increases in reading achievement using this program with struggling readers from kindergarten through high school.

There is a related program in mathematics, *The Academy of MATH*, available from the same company, and when teachers gain experience using one program they likewise gain some familiarity with the other. This can be an important advantage since RTI will be necessary in both areas in almost every class. Finally, these programs are a bit more affordable than other comparable instructional software programs, and the savings in teacher time make this type of instruction advantageous for RTI implementation.

Of course, high-quality computer-based instructional programs abound, and this text cannot present all of them. Teachers should consider a variety of programs for RTI and then make an informed selection about which best meets their needs and the needs of the students. Also, teachers should inquire about programs already in use in their school or district. If a school is already using a strong research-supported software-based program for another purpose (for example, Reading First, or Title I), that school should investigate extending the site license and using the same software for RTI since this may be less expensive than purchasing a new software program. However, implementation of these software-based intervention programs within the RTI framework is highly recommended whenever possible because of the numerous advantages described here.

Using Technology for Performance Monitoring

In addition to the use of technology for providing interventions, commercial programs are now available to assist with performance monitoring, and a recent survey indicated that 50 percent of the districts in the nation currently use software to track student performance (Spectrum K12/CASE, 2008). Furthermore, 49 percent of those survey respondents indicated that their district used software to manage or monitor the RTI process.

AIMSweb (www.AIMSweb.com) is one commonly used example of software that can be beneficial in performance monitoring. *AIMSweb* (a trademark of NCS Pearson, Inc.) is an integrated progress-monitoring system based on continuous student assessment in a variety of specified areas. The system includes assessment measures in reading (including a version in Spanish), early literacy, curriculum-based measures in mathematics, early numeracy, spelling, and other areas. It facilitates presentations of data at three levels:

Tier 1: Facilitates benchmarking student performance three times per year

Tier 2: Strategic monitoring of student performance monthly

Tier 3: Individual monitoring more frequently for students in more intensive intervention tiers

This system does not include specific instructional software, and thus, will not save as much time for the general education teacher as some of the technology-based curricula discussed earlier. However, computerized systems such as this will provide educators with good documentation and performance monitoring for all tiers in the RTI efforts, and unlike individual performance monitoring, this type of system allows administrators to compile performance-monitoring data across groups of students. Of course, that feature can be beneficial in reporting progress relative to state and local educational standards.

Another computerized performance-monitoring system is the *EXCEED/RTI Program*, trademarked by Spectrum K12 School Solutions (see www.spectrumk12.

com/exceed/exceed-overview/). This system was designed specifically for the RTI process. It is highly configurable, and thus flexible enough for addressing the needs of large or small school districts. Included within this system are four capabilities that directly tie to the RTI process: (1) student-centered progress monitoring, (2) differentiated instruction, (3) a highly effective intervention, and (4) fidelity assurance.

Again, there are many advantages to the use of software or Internet-based progress-monitoring tools, and schools are well advised to implement such a system, if their funding allows. This will enhance the RTI efforts in many ways, not the least of which involves saving the time of the educators involved.

Using Certified Teachers for Tier 2

Some school districts have chosen to implement RTI using certified teachers for the Tier 2 interventions, and if the funds are available, this approach to RTI should certainly be considered. In some cases, districts have employed retired teachers on a part-time basis, and those personnel are expected to conduct instruction for three or four targeted reading or math interventions per day, for Tier 2 intervention purposes. Of course, every administrator realizes that it is economically advantageous to use part-time certified personnel rather than full-time teachers for this role, as part-time persons typically cost a school district less (savings come in the form of not having to pay benefits for part-time persons, and so on). The main advantage of using certified teachers for Tier 2 instruction is obvious—the student receives perhaps the highest quality instruction available since certified teachers are delivering that instruction.

In an interesting variation on the last two ideas presented, some districts have employed a part-time certified teacher (or in some cases, a full-time teacher), and placed that teacher in charge of an intervention computer lab with twelve to fifteen computers. That teacher can then conduct Tier 2 interventions specifically targeted to each student's needs, for up to fifteen students every thirty minutes. While both the computer software and the teachers represent real costs to the district, one teacher in such a situation can facilitate numerous Tier 2 and Tier 3 interventions, thus alleviating the time concerns for some of the Tier 2 responsibilities of the general education teacher.

In another variation, some schools have chosen to redistribute the workload for certified personnel who are already in the school. For example, in some cases, teachers who serve as "instructional coaches" or "grade-level lead teachers" have been used to conduct some RTI Tier 2 interventions. These are exactly the types of educators who are frequently used for Tier 3 interventions, and the time demands on the instructional coaches and lead teachers then become a pressing issue. Furthermore, like all other school persons, these individuals most often already have extensive responsibilities; care should be taken to avoid overloading any teacher or other instructional personnel with RTI responsibilities. Still, with those cautions stated, some districts have found ways to make this option work.

The main advantage of using certified teachers for Tier 2 instruction is obvious—the student receives the highest quality instruction available since certified teachers are delivering that instruction.

Conclusion

In seeking options for assisting general education teachers with Tier 2 interventions, the list of possible options is almost endless. Many schools have various educational programs and/or personnel that can be used to assist general education teachers in conducting Tier 2 interventions that have not been considered here. School faculty, working together, should be able to create options for themselves, and the planning grid and the potential resources discussed in this chapter can facilitate that type of creative planning. Of course, issues such as availability of funding and/or use of existing support personnel will frame faculty discussions, but encouraging creativity from all involved faculty will be critical to generate ideas for implementing RTI successfully.

Combinations of these options should be considered whenever possible. For example, the class-sharing option can provide the basis for Tier 2 math interventions in a school that is using a Reading First program as the basis for Tier 2 interventions in reading. Furthermore, while some schools can reassign some paraprofessionals and/or special education inclusion teachers, others will not have that option. Again, flexible creative thinking should provide the basis for faculty discussion of how to make RTI happen in an effective and efficient manner.

One additional point should be stressed with school faculty. Faculty should consider how resources might become available during the first year or two of RTI implementation within a given school. For example, successful RTI implementation during a period of two or three years is quite likely to reduce the number of students in need of special education services, according to the preliminary research on RTI (Abernathy, 2008; Bender & Shores, 2007). In that situation, there would presumably be some special education teacher time available for RTI interventions, as RTI begins to take root in that school.

Likewise, as more reading and math difficulties are successfully addressed in lower grades, instruction in the general education class in those grades and subsequent grades should become a bit easier. No veteran educator would ever believe that teaching is "easy," but alleviating significant educational deficits for most of the struggling students will positively affect the general education teacher's workload. In short, educators should realize that RTI does have positive benefits in terms of reducing academic deficits, and those benefits show up within two years of successful implementation of RTI (Abernathy, 2008).

Finally, the major focus should always be provision of the interventions necessary to facilitate learning progress for each individual student. While school faculty should consider all of the ideas and recommendations presented herein, the gold standard should always be, what strategies, techniques, and ideas will work for the students struggling in our classes? These are, after all, the students we have all chosen to serve.

> The gold standard for RTI implementation should always be, what strategies, techniques, and ideas will work for the students struggling in our classes?

4

The RTI Process in Mathematics

Discussions of RTI implementation in mathematics are somewhat preliminary, because the recent literature on RTI as a diagnostic tool to identify students with learning disabilities focused initially on reading and literacy (Ardoin, Witt, Connell, & Koenig, 2005; L. S. Fuchs et al., 2007; Jordan, Kaplan, Locuniak, & Ramineni, 2007). In a nationwide survey of special education administrators in March 2008, 84 percent indicated that they had implemented RTI in reading, whereas only 53 percent indicated RTI procedures had been implemented in mathematics (Spectrum K12/Case, 2008). This is understandable since approximately 90 percent of students diagnosed with learning disabilities display a reading deficit, and most remediation efforts for students with learning disabilities focus squarely on phonemically based reading/literacy interventions. In fact, some states and school districts have determined to implement RTI exclusively in reading/literacy for the first year or two, placing mathematics on the back burner until the implementation issues can be worked out. In West Virginia, as one example, the thirty-six pilot RTI schools implemented RTI for reading initially, and only later did they move into RTI for mathematics (Boyer, 2008).

While that is advisable in certain schools that are moving into RTI cold—for example, schools that have little or no experience with multitiered intervention programs such as Reading First or other similar programs—in schools that have some experience with multitier interventions for struggling students, I suggest that RTI be implemented in both reading and mathematics as soon as possible. In fact, I would argue that the needs of our students demand that such multitiered interventions in both of these core subjects become available. Simply put, RTI should now be considered best practice and should be used as a definitive educational approach.

> Schools that have some experience with multitiered intervention programs such as Reading First or similar programs should implement RTI in both reading and mathematics as soon as possible.

As early as 2005, many researchers began to realize that RTI procedures would likewise be critical in mathematics since some students present a disability in mathematics but not a disability in reading (Barberisi, Katusic, Colligan, Weaver, & Jacobsen, 2005; L. S. Fuchs et al., 2005). As the United States moves into implementation of RTI as the primary way to support struggling students in general education as well as the primary diagnostic tool to determine eligibility for learning disability services, we cannot simply overlook students with math disabilities; that would be tantamount to denial of necessary services for those students (Baskette et al., 2006). Furthermore, the evidence suggests that many students need assistance in mathematics throughout the school-age years.

For example, Barberisi et al. (2005) indicated that between 6 and 10 percent of young children experience early math disabilities—quite similar to the number of young children who experience reading disabilities. Jordan and her colleagues have documented that young students with difficulties understanding basic number relationships, regardless of the existence of reading disabilities, perform less well on timed math achievement calculation exercises (Jordan et al., 2007; Locuniak & Jordan, 2008). Mabbott and Bisanz (2008) indicated that many older students—grades 5 and 6 in that particular study—demonstrate serious mathematics disabilities. Indeed, the evidence suggests that some children experience math disabilities that are independent of reading disabilities (Barberisi et al., 2005; L. S. Fuchs et al., 2005; Locuniak & Jordan, 2008). Furthermore, there may be a number of other children with math disabilities whose difficulties go unrecognized or are overshadowed by reading disabilities. At the very least, math disabilities have not yet received the research attention that they should, and clearly, some RTI procedures in math will be necessary in almost every general education class (Spectrum K12/CASE, 2008).

> As we move into RTI as the primary diagnostic tool to determine eligibility for learning disabilities services, we cannot simply overlook students with math disabilities, as that would be tantamount to denial of necessary services for those students.

While research on multitier intervention in reading is becoming fairly common, research on RTI procedures in mathematics is very limited. Ardoin et al. (2005) did an early investigation of the impact of a targeted, intensive intervention on fourteen students struggling in grade 4 mathematics. In that study, general education teachers were responsible for Tier 1 instruction, and the researchers themselves implemented an intensive tier of supplemental instruction for students showing difficulty in mathematics. In the intensive intervention, nine of the fourteen target students made improvements, but five showed little or no progress. However, with the addition of increasingly intensive intervention, those five students also began to show limited progress. While this study involved only a limited number of students, the results indicate that in this instance, an RTI procedure in mathematics can alleviate math difficulties for almost two-thirds of the students struggling in mathematics.

This chapter presents information to facilitate RTI procedures in mathematics. We anticipate that such procedures will be necessary across the mathematics spectrum, from the development of early number sense to more sophisticated mathematics skills. General education teachers will certainly need preparation to conduct RTI procedures in mathematics as well as in reading, and even in states or districts that have prioritized reading as an initial RTI emphasis, the need for RTI procedures in math is readily apparent. Teachers should anticipate addressing those needs either immediately or within only one or two years. This chapter presents a discussion of several issues affecting RTI in math, and then presents an example of an RTI procedure in mathematics.

Universal Screening and Early Intervention for Number Sense and Early Math Skills

As mentioned in chapter 1, an essential component of the RTI process is universal screening to identify students who require a multitier RTI process, and this RTI requirement presents several additional difficulties in the area of mathematics. For example, the availability of appropriate screening instruments is much more limited than in other areas. To discuss this issue, it is necessary to compare the research basis, assessment tools, and interventions available in early reading to the available tools in early mathematics.

In the area of reading and literacy, one universal screening measure has emerged that is being widely implemented for RTI purposes across the nation, the *Dynamic Indicators of Basic Early Literacy Skills* or DIBELS (Good & Kaminski, 2002). This instrument assesses prekindergarten literacy and early reading skills and can be administered as early as the first month of kindergarten. This assessment presents four subtests, though typically only two or three are administered for any one student, depending on that student's grade and overall literacy. Table 4.1 shows those subtests.

Table 4.1 DIBELS Subtests for Reading Skills

Initial Sounds Fluency	Ability to pick a picture that begins with the same sound as a model picture (used in grades K–1)
Letter Naming Fluency	Ability to name letters (used in grades K–1)
Nonsense Word Fluency	Ability to decode nonsense words (used in grade 1)
Oral Reading Fluency	Words read correctly per minute (used in grades 2–3)

Norms are presented in ranges indicating *at risk*, *some risk*, or *low risk* for each subtest. Generally, this instrument should be used three times in the kindergarten year as a screening tool for all students, and since it takes only three to eight minutes to administer per child, this type of universal screening is relatively easy to do very early in a child's academic career. DIBELS has, in some states, become the major universal screening assessment tool. In West Virginia, for example, the discussion of RTI on the state department of education website is built on implementation of RTI using DIBELS (Boyer, 2008).

> The fact that DIBELS takes only three to eight minutes to administer makes this universal screening relatively easy to do very early in a child's academic career.

One can easily see how the initial subtests can assess literacy as early as the beginning of kindergarten. Unfortunately, only a few commercially available, quick-screening assessments have emerged in the area of number sense or early mathematics literacy, though various researchers are in the process of developing math screening assessments. While many assessments are available to assess math skills from grade 1 and higher, the RTI emphasis has stressed universal screening as early as possible—in kindergarten—to detect early threats to educational achievement in reading and mathematics. Most of the available math assessments deal with math skills that students typically *acquire* in kindergarten and grade one, and thus, unlike DIBELS, those assessments are not appropriate for screening during the first month of kindergarten. In short, educators need universally applicable screening instruments that include a focus on prekindergarten number sense and early number skills, and only a few are currently available. This presents a significant problem in planning RTI in early mathematics, and this distinguishes prekindergarten mathematics literacy from math achievement during kindergarten and the early school years.

> Few commercially available quick-screening assessments have emerged in the area of number sense or early mathematics literacy, and this presents a significant problem in planning RTI procedures in early mathematics.

What Are These Early Math Skills?

Educators should be aware of the types of number sense knowledge and skills that do seem related to early mathematics achievement as well as the early math screening instruments that are available. Most children acquire many of the number sense abilities and early math skills before kindergarten. L. S. Fuchs et al. (2007) completed a review of literature on early math screening measures and created a catalog of the types of screening measures used by researchers to document number sense and early math skills in kindergarten and grade 1. Across a series of nine research articles, the following provide the best indication of the number sense and early math skills students in kindergarten and grade 1 should demonstrate. Table 4.2 lists these measures.

Table 4.2 Measures of Number Sense and Early Math Skills

Repeating digits backward	Writing dictated numbers	Comparing magnitudes in sets
Counting orally	Identifying numbers	Discriminating between quantities
Noting missing numbers	Knowing basic addition facts	Counting by 2s, 5s, or 10s
Writing numbers	Reading numbers	Producing numbers
Selecting numbers	Writing reversible numbers	Circling numbers

> Most children acquire many number sense abilities and early math skills before kindergarten.

As table 4.2 shows, both number sense and early math skills are included in the types of mathematics variables that researchers measure during the early years. While most students seem to acquire some of these before kindergarten (such as comparing magnitudes in sets, counting orally, identifying numbers, or circling numbers), others are usually acquired during kindergarten (such as knowing basic addition facts or counting by 5s or 10s). Also, while some mathematics assessments include some of these skills, few existing assessments include the majority of them. With that said, early math assessments intended for universal screening are in development, and research has shown that the skills in table 4.2 do relate to later success in mathematics (Locuniak & Jordan, 2008). Clearly, as more of these assessments become available, they will greatly facilitate the RTI process in math for young children.

Early Math Screening Instruments

While a complete compendium of the early math screening assessments that are available is beyond the scope of this text, we can mention several such assessments. The early number readiness assessment tool available through *AIMSweb*, a technology-based performance-monitoring system that was described in chapter 3, is called the Early Numeracy General Outcome Measure. This performance-monitoring tool assesses a child's ability to count orally, identify numbers, identify bigger numbers from a pair, and identify missing numbers from a number line. Thus, this is an appropriate performance-monitoring tool for early kindergarten and grade 1 that does assess several of the number sense measures in table 4.2.

Ginsburg and Baroody (1990) published an early mathematics screening assessment called the *Test of Early Mathematics Ability, Third Edition* (TEMA-3). This assessment is normed for children from ages two through eight and is one of the only such assessments available that includes such young children. The TEMA-3 assesses students on both school-based math skills (for example, reading and writing numbers) and intuitive mathematics and related early math concepts such as those in table 4.2 (counting, quantity, and magnitude judgments). Some research has reported high reliability for this instrument (Murphy, Mazzocco, Hanick, & Early, 2007), and given the implementation of RTI in mathematics, this assessment will probably become more widely used in the immediate future.

Early Math Skills Curricula

In addition to the relative lack of a quick effective screening measure for early math skills, the implementation of RTI procedures in mathematics during kindergarten seems to be further complicated by relatively limited supplemental curricula in mathematics. Of course, supplemental mathematics curricula abound, in terms of both "hard copy" curricula and software-based curricula. Furthermore, some of these curricula do include instructional aspects directed toward number sense and early math skills. Nevertheless, the possibilities in mathematics are considerably more limited when compared with the number of supplemental curricula available in reading, literacy, or language arts in general. Early mathematics curricula that more fully address number sense are in development, however (Chard et al., 2008).

For these reasons, planning a tiered intervention in math early in the kindergarten year is a bit more challenging than planning such an intervention in reading or early literacy since neither appropriate screening instruments nor appropriate curricula are as readily available. While these limitations do not exist for later mathematics achievement, they do affect early RTI procedures in mathematics. Educators should be aware of these issues as they move into planning for RTI in mathematics.

Case Study: RTI for Early Math Skills

This section presents an example of a response to intervention for early math skills to serve as a basis for discussion of the RTI issues discussed in chapters 1 and 2. For this scenario, let's imagine a young boy in the first grade, known by his initials—TJ—who is having some difficulty with early math. Ms. Goodwin, the first-grade teacher, has noted that TJ doesn't seem to "understand numbers," so she talked with TJ's kindergarten teacher. The kindergarten teacher reported that TJ was never terribly successful in most math exercises, but that he did manage basic counting up to approximately 20. However, when he was presented with pattern numbers and asked to say the next number in the pattern (for example, "3, 5, 7, 9 . . .") he could not. Also, TJ had great difficulty comparing sets of items ("Which has more?"). Skip counting by 2s and 5s was another problem that his teacher noted. Finally, Ms.

Goodwin noted that TJ hadn't developed the idea of "counting on" to assist with simple addition problems (*counting on* involves beginning with the largest digit and then "counting on" from that point to add the number represented by the second digit). Table 4.3 presents a completed RTI form in mathematics for TJ.

Table 4.3 Response to Intervention in Mathematics for TJ

Student: TJ	Age: 6	Date: 9/12/08
Initiating teacher: Ms. Goodwin	School: Baker Elem.	Grade: 1

1. Statement of student difficulty and summary of Tier 1 instruction (add supporting evidence and/or progress-monitoring data chart, if available):

TJ has not succeeded in mathfacts addition problems in math this year, and while I've worked with him a bit informally, he is still having difficulty. He doesn't seem to understand that numbers represent quantity, even when I use manipulatives to illustrate mathfacts problems.

After I noticed that TJ was having difficulty in math, I talked with his kindergarten teacher, who reported that TJ was never successful in math. She reported that he did manage basic counting up to approximately 20. However, last week, when I asked him to do a few number exercises and identify the next number in a number sequence, he could not do that. He had great difficulty comparing sets of items ("Which has more?"). Finally, he hasn't developed the idea of "counting on" to assist with simple addition problems, while most students have mastered that idea for early mathfacts problems in addition.

Ms. Goodwin, 9/12/08

2. Tier 2 supplemental intervention plan:

I will provide TJ and two other students with supplemental practice in early math skills three times each week for twenty minutes each session. I'll continue to work with them for approximately four weeks. TJ and the other students will be presented with pattern numbers exercises; practice in counting by 2s, 5s, or 10s; and other math problems taken from the first-grade mathematics curriculum textbook. Finally, I'll use fifteen questions at the end of each week as a performance-monitoring check on how well TJ is doing, for RTI purposes. I have developed this plan in conjunction with Mr. Stager, our assistant principal, and he has agreed to observe TJ during these exercises from time to time.

Ms. Goodwin, 9/12/08

3. Observation of student in Tier 2 intervention:

I observed the Tier 2 instruction in Ms. Goodwin's class on 9/24/08. TJ participated in a lively fashion throughout the twenty-five-minute intervention period, while TJ and the other students completed number pattern work such as presenting the next number in the sequence when a series of five numbers were written down.

continued on next page →

This exercise came from the math text, and Ms. Goodwin presented the material in a clear, straightforward manner. I also noted that TJ answered several questions correctly and got only one incorrect. While only two indicators of weekly assessment data were available for review, that indicated some level of success, and the data suggest that this is the right intervention for TJ at this point.

Mr. Stager, 9/24/08

4. Tier 2 intervention summary and recommendations (must include data chart):

I implemented the Tier 2 intervention described above for TJ and two other students for five weeks. The accompanying data chart summarizes TJ's performance-monitoring data. During Week 3, TJ was absent on Friday, so he was assessed twice the next week.

While TJ seemed to be progressing somewhat, he should have been able to grasp all of these skills (pattern work in 2s, 5s, and 10s and simple math problems). On the data summary chart, I charted the work of one of the other students who did master these skills during that five weeks for comparison purposes.

TJ is not moving forward quickly enough to have a realistic opportunity to "catch up" with the other first-grade students on number patterns or early mathematics skills by the end of the year. He is making most of the progress shown here on number pattern work, but does not seem to grasp the various strategies, such as counting on, that I have demonstrated for early math addition problems. I believe that a more intensive intervention is necessary for TJ in order to assure that he does not fall further behind.

Ms. Goodwin, 10/22/08

5. Tier 3 intervention plan:

Based on a Tier 2 intervention conducted by Ms. Goodwin in September and October of 2008, the student support team met, reviewed the intervention data from the Tier 2 intervention, and considered various options for providing a more intensive intervention for TJ. Team members for this meeting on 10/23/08 included Ms. Goodwin, Mr. Stager, Ms. Strompton, as the lead teacher for first grade, Mr. Sosebee, the special education teacher, and Mr. Thurston, the school principal. I was given the task of summarizing that meeting and then designing and describing a Tier 3 intervention for TJ based on those discussions.

After reviewing the Tier 2 data (see the intervention description and charted performance-monitoring data herein), this group concurred with Ms. Goodwin that TJ was not making appropriate progress to meet his curriculum goals in math this year. We agreed that a Tier 3 intervention would be necessary.

Mr. Stager suggested the possibility of having TJ come and join a small group of students in my class who receive individual software-based instruction in number sense exercises, pattern number prediction exercises, and early mathematics skills such as counting on for addition. This software program generates charted data on each student's daily performance, and that will serve as a running assessment of how TJ is performing.

TJ will work in my class each day from 11:15 until 12:00 noon. Thus, TJ will receive forty-five minutes of supplemental math instruction with me daily, while still participating in math with Ms. Goodwin daily. The software selected for TJ assures one-to-one instruction using a research-proven curriculum, and the instructional problems will be specifically targeted to the specific skills TJ needs, in the areas listed above.

Ms. Strompton, 10/24/08

6. Observation of student in Tier 3 intervention:

I made certain that I had the chance to observe the Tier 3 instruction offered to TJ by Ms. Strompton, beginning on 10/24/08 through 11/30/08. TJ is a happy student, and seemed to enjoy the computer-based work; he participated in a lively fashion throughout the intervention period, and never seemed to waiver in his attention to the problems presented on the computer. The software program presented problems that were at exactly the correct level for TJ. During this observation, I noted that TJ answered almost all of the questions correctly, but did get four incorrect, and each of those dealt with an example of addition skills that involved the "counting on" strategy. At the end of TJ's work, Ms. Strompton praised him for a great job, and then reviewed those four problems.

Mr. Thurston, 11/05/08

7. Tier 3 intervention summary and recommendations (must include data chart):

On 12/18/08, the student support team met to consider TJ's academic performance on the Tier 3 intervention. That team consisted of Ms. Goodwin, Ms. Strompton, Mr. Sosebee, the special education teacher, and, Mr. Thurston, the school principal. Mr. Stager was absent on that date.

Ms. Strompton completed a four-week intervention with TJ, as described above, and the software program generated a data chart of his academic performance. These charted data indicate that TJ mastered prediction of the next number in number patterns (2s, 5s, and 10s), within three weeks. While it took a bit longer, the data show that he has now mastered use of the counting-on strategy for computing basic addition facts. Ms. Strompton indicated that his timed performance on basic addition facts does not indicate automaticity with these facts. In short, he is now successfully using the counting-on strategy, which should be viewed as a significant stepping stone for TJ, but clearly automaticity with those facts is essential. For that reason, Ms. Strompton recommended continuation of TJ in the Tier 3 mathematics intervention for at least one more grading period.

The student support team concurs with that recommendation and will review this student's performance at the end of the next grading period.

Mr. Thurston, 12/18/08

Identifying a Need for Intervention

Overall, the array of early math problems suggested to Ms. Goodwin that TJ needed additional remedial work on early math skills. She decided to summarize those problems on the RTI form, as shown in the section titled "Statement of student difficulty and summary of Tier 1 instruction" in table 4.3. Note that Ms. Goodwin summarized her concerns and her previous work with TJ. She then noted TJ's specific deficits in mathematics. She also documented that she had consulted with other educators about TJ, and that information should indicate to TJ's parents that this teacher is concerned and committed to TJ's success.

Her next step was to plan and provide a Tier 2 intervention on number sense and basic math skills for TJ and two other students in the first grade. She planned to work with those three students three times each week, while her paraprofessional supervised the class in other learning activities. Ms. Goodwin decided to use a set of instructional activities that focused specifically on number sense, pattern recognition, and skip counting activities from the grade 1 edition of the mathematics textbook used at the school, since that curriculum had received research support, and was carefully matched with state standards in her state.

Ms. Goodwin also devised a set of fifteen assessment questions that featured pattern completion, counting by 2s, counting by 5s, comparing sets of items to find larger and smaller sets, and mathfacts addition problems. She intended to use that assessment each week to carefully monitor the performance of the students. After planning that intervention, Ms. Goodwin sent a letter to the parents of the three students informing them of the planned intervention, a portion of which follows:

> Working with TJ and two other students, I will provide them with supplemental practice in early math skills. I plan on pulling this group together three times each week for approximately twenty minutes each session, and I'll continue to work with them for approximately four weeks. In that work, the students will be presented with patterns of numbers they need to complete, practice in counting by 2s, 5s, or 10s, and other math problems. The students will not be pulled out of their ongoing math class, so they should be able to keep up with their other mathematics work. Finally, I'll use fifteen questions at the end of each week as a performance monitoring check on how well TJ is doing. I have discussed this intervention with our assistant principal, Mr. Stager, and of course, I'll share all of these intervention results with you at the next parent/teacher meeting.

Note that this letter does not mention the possibility that this intervention may eventually serve as a Tier 2 intervention in a possible consideration of TJ's eligibility for special education services. At the point of instituting a Tier 2 intervention, no general education teacher knows which specific intervention for any given child may eventually become part of an eligibility discussion, and research suggests that most such interventions will not become part of an eligibility discussion. Thus, at this point in the procedure, the parental information letter does not typically discuss that possibility.

> At the point of instituting a Tier 2 intervention, no general education teacher knows which specific intervention for any given child may eventually become part of an eligibility discussion, and research suggests that most such interventions will not.

Finally, as the letter indicates, before beginning the intervention, Ms. Goodwin shared her plan and the proposed activities with her assistant principal, Mr. Stager. Mr. Stager was an administrator who was also a certified math teacher. While not indicated in the parent letter, Ms. Goodwin did invite Mr. Stager to come and observe when TJ and the other students were receiving the Tier 2 math instruction, and they scheduled an observation time during the second week of the intervention.

Tier 2 Intervention Planning

Chapter 2 presented a number of issues that are important in planning any multi-tier intervention process, and this RTI in mathematics appropriately addresses these concerns. As you recall, these included intensity of the intervention, selection of appropriate curricula, and instructional fidelity, among other issues.

Scientifically Validated Curriculum

One overriding issue in planning a Tier 2 RTI procedure is the issue of implementing a scientifically validated curriculum (Bender & Shores, 2007). Of course, teachers realize clearly that interventions should be based on scientifically proven instructional tactics, and in most cases, teachers will probably use a commercially available curricula that has received scientific support, as Ms. Goodwin did in this example. Furthermore, Ms. Goodwin solicited and received Mr. Stager's affirmation that the activities selected from the approved curriculum directly target TJ's specific math deficits; he concurred with Ms. Goodwin that these activities were appropriate for alleviating the math problems of TJ and the other students.

Initially the issue of a scientifically proven curriculum may seem really a non-issue since most curricula today have some scientific validation. However, as I work on RTI implementation in schools across the nation, this issue comes up in several different ways. First, some curricula that are commercially available do not have supportive research published in scientific journals, though most of those curricula do have some supportive research—which may have been funded and published by the publisher of the curriculum. Clearly, the standard for "scientifically proven curricula" should involve independent scientific research with experimental and control groups that is subsequently published in peer-reviewed journals. While teachers moving into RTI are not really expected to consult individual research articles, educators should consult the summaries of research, such as those provided by university-affiliated websites, as discussed in chapter 2 (page 48). Teachers should also be extremely careful about using curricula that have been supported only by scientific research published by a single publishing company (rather than in scientific journals).

Next, a more subtle curricular issue arises continually—the use of scientifically validated instructional *practices* rather than scientifically validated *curricula*. While federal legislation such as No Child Left Behind and the 2004 IDEA stipulates use of scientifically validated curricula, that provision may not be wise or preferable in some cases. For example, I worked in a charter school in North Carolina on RTI implementation, and unlike most schools, that faculty had chosen to teach kindergarten through grade 6 without a designated basal reading or mathematics curriculum. Thus, for all Tier 1 interventions, and many Tier 2 interventions, they could not demonstrate the use of a scientifically validated reading or math curriculum. Of course, some teachers had used curricula that had received scientific validation, while others had not, opting instead for a plethora of scientifically validated *instruction procedures.*

As one example, one teacher was using a repeated reading procedure, based on the research supportive of repeated reading practices, and she was coupling those instructional procedures with reading the daily newspaper! That was a wonderfully creative way to teach reading, and while the instructional procedure—repeated reading—has received wide scientific validation as an effective instructional procedure, one cannot state that this particular teacher was using a scientifically validated curriculum.

When asked if such instruction was acceptable as a valid RTI procedure, I discussed the use of that procedure with the teacher. She indicated her awareness of the research support for repeated reading interventions, and indicated that she was using those procedures as described in that body of research. She also indicated that at least one subsequent intervention tier *would* involve a scientifically validated curriculum.

Based on that information, I indicated that I believed those procedures were acceptable as an RTI intervention tier. To restate, in some cases, *scientifically validated instructional procedures* may be used for an intervention rather than a *scientifically validated instructional curriculum*, and those procedures should be considered acceptable as one intervention tier within a broader RTI. However, if teachers choose to implement an intervention that is not based on a particular scientifically validated curriculum, the burden will clearly be on that teacher to demonstrate research supportive of that particular instructional procedure.

> In some cases, I believe that scientifically validated instructional procedures may be used as an intervention tier rather than scientifically validated instructional curricula, and that those procedures should be acceptable as one intervention tier within a broader RTI.

Increased Intensity

As discussed in previous chapters, another major issue involves the intensity of the intervention. A multitier intervention presupposes that each intervention is more intensive than the previous tier; thus, Tier 2 must be more intensive than Tier 1, and Tier 3 must be more intensive than Tier 2. Only through such increasing intensity can teachers hold a realistic hope for the success of the remediation effort.

In our earlier scenario, in her letter to the parents, Ms. Goodwin outlined a variety of indicators that stress intensity of the intervention. First, she described exactly what types of mathematics activities the intervention involves. Furthermore, since this intervention should be more intensive than the general instruction offered to the whole class, Ms. Goodwin stated explicitly that this would be *supplemental* instruction and that participating students will not be removed from their other math instruction. Next, Ms. Goodwin noted the intensity of the instruction explicitly by stating how many students would participate and stipulating exactly how many minutes per day, how many days per week, and how many weeks the intervention would require.

Should TJ progress all the way through the intervention tiers without success, it is possible that this Tier 2 intervention will become a significant piece of information for a later eligibility determination. Thus, documenting the intensity of the Tier 2 intervention before and during that intervention is critical.

Accordingly, the level of performance monitoring should also be noted, and again, it should reflect a more intensive performance monitoring than other students receive. So Ms. Goodwin indicated exactly how she would monitor progress for TJ in this Tier 2 intervention. While math performance is monitored for all students using student grades every grading period, TJ and the other students receiving this Tier 2 intervention would be additionally assessed each week, resulting in more intensive performance monitoring. In summary, to document an intensive Tier 2 intervention, each of these indicators of intensity must be described.

Instructional Fidelity

Another issue to consider in implementing a Tier 2 intervention in mathematics is the issue of instructional fidelity (Bender & Shores, 2007). As discussed in chapter 2, this issue addresses the question, was the instruction offered appropriate for, and of sufficiently high quality to, provide a student with an appropriate opportunity to learn? This is particularly critical when a teacher chooses to use scientifically validated instructional procedures rather than a particular scientifically validated curriculum.

In our scenario, Ms. Goodwin chose to implement some instructional activities from a scientifically validated instructional curriculum. Therefore, as long as she implemented those activities as described in the instructor's manual, she implemented the curriculum with fidelity, and TJ would therefore receive high-quality instruction tied directly to his learning needs.

However, chapter 2 also discussed the issue of *accountability* for treatment fidelity; how can teachers assure parents that they used the instructional activities with fidelity? To address that question, Ms. Goodwin did several things. First, note that she shared her instructional intervention plan with Mr. Stager, a certified mathematics instructor, and solicited his suggestions. Next, while she was conducting the instruction for TJ and the other students, she invited Mr. Stager to visit the class and observe her conducting the instruction. Thus, should this intervention become part of a later eligibility determination, Mr. Stager can attest that Ms. Goodwin selected appropriate instructional activities for TJ and implemented them with fidelity. Note that in table 4.3 (pages 93–95), Mr. Stager wrote a few notes in the RTI form that indicated his support of these activities and his observation that Ms. Goodwin did implement the Tier 2 intervention with fidelity.

Tier 2 Data Review

As Ms. Goodwin progressed through this intervention over the next few weeks, she noted that the other two students were moving toward increased success with this supplemental assistance in math. However, TJ was not progressing as quickly as she would have liked, and she began to suspect that TJ needed more intensive instructional assistance.

After five weeks in the intervention, Ms. Goodwin wrote some informal notes and summarized her intervention efforts for TJ (table 4.3, pages 93–95). She also created a data chart to summarize his progress. She then took that summary report and

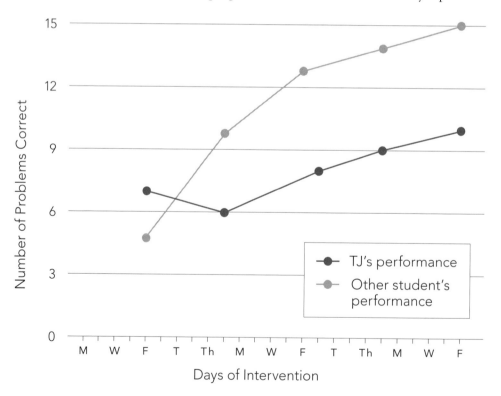

Figure 4.1 TJ's Tier 2 performance data: mastery of early math skills.

the data chart to the student support team in her school, and along with Mr. Stager, she used those data to recommend a Tier 3 intervention for TJ.

Tier 3 Intervention Planning

Based on the notes about the Tier 2 intervention and the data chart presented in figure 4.1, Ms. Goodwin and Mr. Stager met with other members of the student support team to discuss TJ's educational needs. These members included Ms. Strompton, the lead teacher for first grade, Mr. Sosebee, the special education teacher, and Mr. Thurston, the school principal. Ms. Goodwin presented the data summarized in figure 4.1 and discussed her intensive instruction with the team. She noted that while TJ seemed to be progressing somewhat, he was not moving forward quickly enough to have a realistic opportunity to catch up with the other first-grade students by the end of the year since most of her other students, including the others in this Tier 2 intervention, had mastered these early number sense and early math skills.

Next, Mr. Stager told the team that he'd participated in selection of the instructional activities that Ms. Goodwin had used with TJ as well as reviewed the assessment data each week. He then stated that he had observed one class period when TJ received the supplemental instruction. Finally, Mr. Stager indicated that the instructional activities were the correct type of activities for TJ, but that he concurred with Ms. Goodwin that TJ needed more time on those types of early math activities to catch up with the other students. Both he and Ms. Goodwin recommended that the team consider a Tier 3 intervention that would address the same early math skills but would offer a more intensive supplemental intervention program for TJ. After all team members concluded that such a Tier 3 intervention seemed reasonable, Mr. Stager suggested one possibility for such an intensive intervention program.

Because she was team leader, Ms. Strompton typically had a somewhat smaller class than the other first-grade teachers, and she was also provided with a number of computers for use in computer-assisted interventions. She received these resources to allow her to do extra duties such as model teaching for other teachers on the team or support for students with academic or behavioral problems in the classroom. With that extra support, she could also conduct various Tier 3 intensive instructional groups. She indicated that she was currently teaching such an intensive small group of four students for forty-five minutes daily in a computerized math curriculum, *The Academy of MATH* (AutoSkill, 2004a; www.autoskill.com).

That software-based supplemental math curriculum presented a wide variety of tasks individually to each student in the area of number sense and early math skills, and in TJ's case, Ms. Strompton set parameters that specified work on pattern numbers and pattern number prediction, and math addition problems when each addend is 9 or less (so TJ could use a counting-on procedure). While four students were included in this small group, the use of a computerized instructional program assured that each student received academic work targeted specifically to his or her needs. Thus, each student received essentially one-to-one instruction.

Furthermore, that curriculum generated a daily report of progress for each student that could be used to summarize a child's academic progress in a Tier 3 intervention; this is a significant strength for most computer-based curricula. Thus, Ms. Strompton indicated that that curriculum would be a good intervention for TJ. Under that plan, TJ would receive math instruction with Ms. Goodwin daily as well as forty-five minutes of intensive software-based supplementary instruction in Ms. Strompton's class daily on the specific skills he needed (see table 4.3, pages 93–95). Note that this description of the planned Tier 3 intervention addresses the issues of scientifically validated curriculum, instructional intensity, and instruction fidelity.

> Many computerized curricula generate daily reports of progress for each student that can be used to summarize a child's academic progress in a Tier 2 or Tier 3 intervention; this is a significant advantage for computer-based programming.

The team decided to go with that recommendation and meet at the end of the next grading period in six weeks to consider TJ's progress. Ms. Goodwin and Ms. Strompton then worked out the time that TJ would come into Ms. Strompton's class daily.

Critical Decision-Making Points

There are several important points to consider when implementing a Tier 3 intervention. First, note that in describing the Tier 3 intervention, the team attended to the RTI expectation that higher tiers provide more intensive instruction. The indicators of increased intensity were all described in the decision-making process and the notes about the meeting, and a comparison of the Tier 2 and Tier 3 interventions documents that the interventions did increase in intensity. Table 4.4 presents a direct comparison of the intensity of the Tier 2 and Tier 3 interventions provided for TJ.

As this comparison shows, the Tier 3 intervention was considerably more intensive than the Tier 2 intervention in every respect. Thus, it was reasonable to believe that providing this supplemental program could realistically address TJ's problems in math. The document also addresses instructional fidelity, in addition to the intensiveness of intervention. *The Academy of MATH* is a computerized individualized curriculum, and with implementation of a computer-based curriculum of this nature, one can be relatively comfortable that the curriculum will be taught in an appropriate fashion, consistent with the instructions of the curriculum developers since most of the actual teaching will be delivered in an electronic environment.

Table 4.4 Comparison of Intensity of Tier 2 and Tier 3 Mathematics Interventions

Indicator of Intensity	Tier 2	Tier 3
Supplemental program	Math textbook exercises	*The Academy of MATH*
Time commitment	Twenty minutes, three times per week	Forty-five minutes, daily
Program length	Four weeks	Four weeks
Performance-monitoring frequency	Every week	Daily
Pupil-teacher ratio	Three to one	One to one

Also, as is frequently the case, implementation of the Tier 3 intervention in this example actually became the responsibility of another teacher, Ms. Strompton. The export of Tier 3 interventions is the norm in most cases where both Tier 2 and Tier 3 interventions are considered to be functions of general education. Thus, when multiple intervention tiers are required prior to consideration for special education, someone other than the general education teacher usually administers the Tier 3 intervention.

> The export of Tier 3 interventions to an educator other than the general education teacher is the norm in most cases where both Tier 2 and Tier 3 interventions are considered to be functions of general education.

Tier 3 Data Review

After the Tier 3 intervention, Ms. Strompton prepared a summary of TJ's performance, as presented in table 4.3 (pages 93–95). That intervention summary accompanied the data chart of TJ's performance, as presented in figure 4.2 (page 104). Finally, the student support team met again to consider the student's performance and the overall impact of this intervention for TJ.

These data indicate that implementation of *The Academy of MATH* was exactly what TJ needed. As the data indicate, TJ's weekly performance showed impressive progress on both pattern number exercises and early addition skills. Thus, TJ was receiving instruction at the intensity level he needed to make progress and catch up with his classmates by the end of the year. At the end of the grading period, after reviewing the data, the team determined to keep TJ in the intensive Tier 3 intervention with Ms. Strompton for at least another grading period, while Ms. Goodwin continued to work with him on math in the general education class.

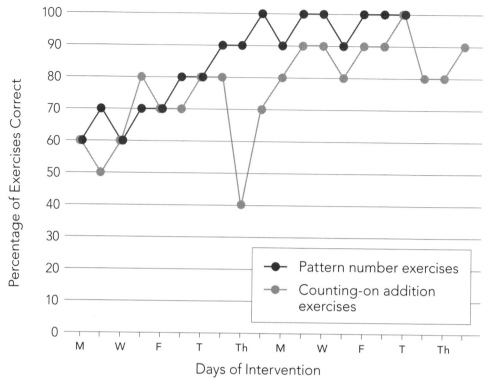

Figure 4.2 TJ's Tier 3 performance data: mastery of pattern number recognition and counting-on.

Critical Implementation Issues

This math RTI demonstrates several additional points. First, as noted throughout this book, in almost every case, the general education teacher will typically conduct the Tier 1 instruction and subsequently initiate the Tier 2 supplemental intervention. In this case, a paraprofessional was available to assist Ms. Goodwin, but in reality, the general education teacher often has to do without extensive support. Despite the lack of support, in most states, general education teachers will be responsible for both the Tier 1 and Tier 2 interventions for students struggling with reading and math (Bender & Shores, 2007; D. Fuchs & Deshler, 2007).

However, that does not necessarily mean that those general education teachers must implement those interventions alone. The time pressures for all Tier 1 and Tier 2 interventions in the typical general education classroom would become unbearable in most cases, and as discussed in chapter 2, it is usually unrealistic to expect general education teachers to teach all students in all subjects for an entire day *and* to implement a variety of Tier 2 interventions in reading and math. Adding the responsibility for delivering Tier 3 interventions into that mix is highly problematic. General education teachers should request and receive some type of support to implement these interventions.

In most states, general education teachers will be responsible for both the Tier 1 and Tier 2 interventions for students struggling with reading and math.

Note that though Ms. Goodwin could offer TJ a seemingly appropriate intervention, she could not provide it as intensively as he needed, as demonstrated by the progress-monitoring data in figure 4.1 (page 100). Therefore, in this instance, a Tier 3 intervention was necessary. However, in many cases, a Tier 3 intervention will not be necessary since Tier 2 interventions do alleviate many problems in mathematics. Research has demonstrated that between 25 and 75 percent of students who receive a Tier 2 intervention in math have their problems alleviated by that intervention and do not require a more intensive intervention (Bender & Shores, 2007; L. S. Fuchs et al., 2005). In one summary, L. S. Fuchs, Fuchs, and Hollenbeck (2007) indicated that the number of students who were unsuccessful in mathematics fell from 9.5 percent to 5.14 percent of the school population as the result of a Tier 2 intervention. Thus, only 5.14 percent of students should require an intensive Tier 3 intervention. Clearly, RTI procedures in mathematics can alleviate many problems in mathematics for many students.

Research has demonstrated that between 25 and 75 percent of students who receive a Tier 2 intervention in mathematics have their problems alleviated by that intervention and do not require a more intensive Tier 3 intervention.

Simultaneous Interventions

In various workshops around the nation, I have been asked in how many separate interventions a student should participate at any given point. Specifically, should a student participate in more than one supplementary math intervention? For example, the *Georgia Pyramid of Interventions* presented on the Georgia Department of Education website (http://public.doe.k12.ga.us) specifically states that students may participate in Tier 1, Tier 2, and Tier 3 interventions all at the same time! Hence the question, when a student is receiving Tier 1 instruction in general education and the data suggest that the student's Tier 2 intervention is not working, should that Tier 2 intervention be continued even while the student moves into a Tier 3 intervention? Alternatively, I've been asked, should a child continue to participate in Tier 1 (whole-class instruction) while participating in a highly intensive Tier 3 intervention? The assumption behind this question seems to be that if a child's need is intensive enough to require a Tier 3 intervention, participation in general education may not have any benefit at all for that child.

All students should always continue in Tier 1 instruction, but I strongly recommend against multiple supplemental interventions at Tiers 2 and 3. In most of the RTI literature, if a Tier 2 intervention was not successful, that intervention was terminated at the beginning of a Tier 3 intervention. Thus, no student would participate in more than one supplemental intervention at any given time (Bender & Shores, 2007; Kemp & Eaton, 2007). Participation in multiple supplemental interventions should not occur unless a child is participating in interventions in different subject areas (for example, a child in a Tier 2 reading intervention might also participate in a Tier 3 math intervention).

> I strongly recommend against having any student participate in more than one supplemental intervention at a time in any subject area, but participation in any Tier 2 or Tier 3 intervention should always be supplemental—in addition to—participation in Tier 1 instruction.

In the preceding example, TJ participated in traditional class instruction with Ms. Goodwin and for several weeks also received a Tier 2 intervention from her. Once the data demonstrated that the Tier 2 intervention was not working, however, that intervention ceased, and TJ moved to a Tier 3 intervention in Ms. Strompton's class. TJ never participated in Tier 2 and Tier 3 interventions at the same time.

Documentation

Note, too, that this is a first-grade mathematics scenario, and yet, even in a subject other than reading and in a relatively early grade, this RTI in mathematics could easily have led to a diagnosis of learning disability. While traditionally most students with learning disabilities were diagnosed based on reading deficits in grades 3 or 4, I suspect that the "age of onset" for learning disability diagnosis will eventually be considerably lower since many assessments, both informal and formal, are now available to assess early literacy in reading or math. In fact, given the early education assessments associated with RTI procedures (for example, DIBELS), it is possible to diagnose a learning disability in the first half of the kindergarten year. While concerns about overidentification and early labeling are still important, it is perhaps more important to ensure that struggling students receive the assistance they need as soon as possible—and RTI should facilitate that. Under RTI, students with learning disabilities will receive more intensive instruction much sooner than in the past, in both reading and mathematics.

Finally, this example, like the previous case studies, demonstrates the increased responsibility that general education teachers have in the eligibility process when documenting a learning disability. Of course, general education teachers have always participated in determining the eligibility of students for learning disability services;

they have historically participated in meetings, brought in work samples, and done error analysis and/or task analysis of student learning skills. Under RTI, general education teachers have an increasingly serious responsibility. They are responsible for providing one of the two most critical pieces of data in that learning disability determination: the performance-monitoring assessment data chart for the Tier 2 intervention. General education teachers should be made aware of that increased responsibility and the need to understand the intricacies of RTI and in particular, the intricacies of performance monitoring.

Data-Based Decision Making

In TJ's case, his teacher and others made multiple decisions at various points, but their educational decisions were always based on the student's academic performance data. As chapter 1 explained, a major emphasis in RTI is the concept of data-based decision making—using student performance data to determine what type, extent, and intensity of intervention is right for the *student*.

> A major emphasis in RTI is the concept of data-based decision making—using student performance data to determine what type, extent, and intensity of intervention is right for the *student*.

Data should be used to make the determination as to future educational interventions when either a Tier 2 or Tier 3 intervention is completed. Table 4.5 (page 108) presents the possible data outcomes and the decisions that may result from them.

Intervention data should make the decision on a child's educational future relatively clear, and the educational option that provides the child with the best opportunity to catch up to his or her classmates should be the option of choice. However, sometimes the data are difficult to immediately interpret. It is relatively rare for an intensive intervention to result in no improvement. Usually the data will reveal some improvement, and then the issue is whether the child's progress is sufficient.

> Intervention data should make decisions on a child's educational future relatively clear, and the educational option that provides the child with the best opportunity to catch up to his or her classmates should be the option of choice.

Some authors have recommended relatively complex procedures such as benchmarking a child's performance, based on aim lines or trend lines, to determine how a student's performance is related to expected performance or performance of others (Howell et al., 2008). This issue has been discussed earlier, and again, I generally encourage more simple procedures for addressing the question, how much progress is enough?

Table 4.5 Data-Based Decision Making in Response to Intervention

Possible Data Outcomes	Possible Decisions on Future Interventions
Data chart shows great success, and child is now on grade level or meeting benchmarks.	Discontinue the intervention; child continues participation in general education.
Data chart shows some success, but child is not yet on grade level or meeting benchmarks.	Continue the intervention for an additional grading period; child continues participation in general education. *or* Modify intensity of the current intervention without otherwise changing it. *or* Move child to a more intensive intervention and continue participation in general education.
Data chart shows little positive growth on targeted skills.	Move child to a more intensive intervention, and continue participation in general education. *or* Consider moving the child forward toward a child study team meeting to consider eligibility for special education services.

In some instances, showing a student's limited progress in comparison to others within that intervention will let teachers know how to proceed. For example, figure 4.1 (page 100) presented performance for the target student and for another student in that Tier 2 intervention in math, and those data make a simple direct case for moving TJ into a more intensive intervention, even though he's demonstrated some progress.

Another option for data-based decision making when the data show only limited progress is rooted within team-based decision making. The student support team should consider the data and then choose any of the educational options presented in table 4.5. In short, when a teacher is uncertain of the meaning of the intervention data, the team should collectively consider the data and then determine the future educational program for that child.

> If student performance data show some progress, but the teacher still has questions about the child's overall skills in the target area, that teacher should bring the data before the student support team.

Diagnosing a Learning Disability Using a Math RTI

At this point, we should consider how an RTI in mathematics fits within a diagnosis of learning disability. For this discussion, we'll need to modify the results from our case study. Specifically, let's imagine that the data on the results of the Tier 3 intervention indicated either a lack of progress for TJ or very minimal progress. In that case, the student support team should review the Tier 2 and Tier 3 intervention data and would presumably conclude that TJ's math difficulties had not been adequately remediated—that is, he had failed to respond to two separate tiered interventions in mathematics. Based on those data, the student support team should consider recommending that the schoolwide child study team or student eligibility team convene and consider the possibility that TJ has a learning disability in mathematics.

As discussed previously, the student support team should not *state* that TJ has a learning disability. Rather, they should document the exposure to multiple targeted mathematics interventions and present performance monitoring indicating that TJ failed to respond positively to those interventions. At that point, a psychological assessment to examine TJ's auditory and visual processing skills, his memory skills, and other psychological processes that may underlie a learning disability would presumably be necessary. However, since the advent of RTI procedures, not every state mandates a psychological for students suspected of having a learning disability (teachers should check local district and state requirements on that question). In addition, the eligibility team should consider medical, home, and other factors stipulated in special education law that might have impacted TJ's performance (assuming the student support team had not already investigated those factors).

I do suggest weighing RTI procedures in mathematics equally with RTI procedures in reading or literacy in determination of the existence of a learning disability. In other words, after a student has not succeeded in two mathematics interventions (that is, Tier 2 and Tier 3), a learning disability should be suspected, based on that work in mathematics, even in the absence of reading or early literacy difficulties. I thus recommend that we consider this type of intervention-based evidence for deficits in mathematics to be as influential as intervention evidence in reading when determining if a learning disability exists.

> I recommend that we consider intervention-based evidence for deficits in mathematics to be as influential as intervention-based evidence in reading when determining if a learning disability exists.

However, as in reading and literacy, even several unsuccessful RTI mathematics interventions do not prove the existence of a learning disability. That determination is the responsibility of the eligibility team's evaluation of the data from Tiers 1, 2, and 3, coupled with their interpretation of the underlying psychological processes, as presented in a psychological report, and other relevant data.

Conclusion

This chapter has presented a model of how a response to intervention can be implemented in mathematics. Because many students experience difficulties in mathematics, teachers may well anticipate initiating math RTI procedures fairly often. In fact, RTI procedures in mathematics may be necessary in the general education class for students who are already receiving learning disability services for reading and/or language arts. While it is likely to be relatively rare that an RTI procedure in mathematics results in a diagnosis of learning disability (historically, more than 90 percent of students identified with a learning disability were identified based on a disability in reading [Bender & Shores, 2007]), all teachers should expect to implement Tier 2 math interventions fairly frequently. Subsequent chapters will focus on RTI procedures in areas such as behavior and secondary classes.

5

The RTI Process and Behavior Problems

As indicated in chapter 1, the multitier pyramid described in the RTI literature is not new, and one earlier application of that powerful multitier instructional pyramid concept was in the area of positive behavioral supports for appropriate student behavior (Horner & Sugai, 1999; Simonsen, Sugai, & Negron, 2008). Direct applications of the multitier concept to children with specific behavior problems have shown this model to be quite effective in reducing or eliminating many problem behaviors in the classroom (Fairbanks et al., 2007; Hughes & Dexter, 2008; Sugai, Simonsen, & Horner, 2008). Thus, it is no surprise that RTI is being used fairly frequently for behavioral interventions. The March, 2008 survey of special education administrators indicated that 44 percent of the respondents were implementing RTI procedures to deal with behavioral problems (Spectrum K12/CASE, 2008).

Of course, the basis for the behavioral orientation that undergirds the RTI model has been around much longer than RTI and has been used in education for several decades. As one example, the precision teaching paradigm developed several decades ago by Ogden Lindsley (1990, 1992) and associated with the concept of repeated daily assessment of student behavioral progress has been recommended for use in RTI procedures (Bender & Shores, 2007). Thus, both the history of behavioral psychology and the positive behavioral supports initiative of the last fifteen years have built a solid foundation for using multitier interventions to alleviate behavior problems, and districts across the nation are using the RTI process to address behavioral issues.

> Direct applications of the RTI concept to children with specific behavior problems have shown this model to be quite effective in reducing or eliminating problem behavior in the classroom.

The Split Pyramid

In applying RTI to behavioral problems, a number of researchers have presented a version of the multitier pyramid that is slightly different from the three-tier pyramid discussed previously in this text (Horner & Sugai, 1999; Kemp & Eaton, 2007). In the pyramid shown in figure 5.1, the vertical split emphasizes that multiple tiers of intervention are required that focus on academic skills on one hand and behavioral problems on the other. To distinguish this from the more common depiction of the three-tiered pyramid, I have chosen to refer to this as the *split pyramid*.

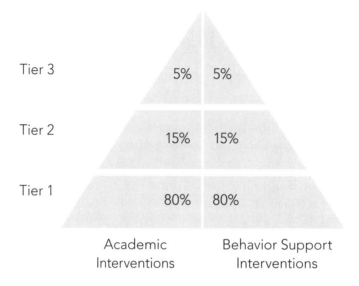

Figure 5.1 The split pyramid of behavior and academic RTI procedures.

Good Teaching Habits for Behavior Management

Before discussing intervention tiers within the split pyramid, we should note that general education classes also involve a host of teaching behaviors or actions that are not in the strictest sense "behavioral interventions" since they are not based on a specified behavioral intervention plan and do not result in data collection on any specific behaviors for any specific child (Bender, 2003). Rather, these behavioral management actions should be considered "good teaching habits" that teachers use to foster positive behaviors in the class.

For example, many teachers recognize that the teacher's movement around the classroom provides increased opportunity for using *proximity control* (that is, moving toward a student who is mildly misbehaving), and most veterans develop this habit as well as certain other subtle behavior management habits they use all the time. General education teachers are experts in managing most problem behaviors in the classroom, and teachers at every level of experience beyond the first year of teaching can and do manage a wide array of mild behavior problems in the class without a formal behavioral intervention using merely this array of good teaching habits (Bender, 2003). Furthermore, research has indicated that these habits do effectively manage behavior for a majority of students (Conroy, Sutherland, Snyder, & Marsh, 2008; Lohrmann, Talerico, & Dunlap, 2004; Simonsen et al., 2008).

> Teachers at every level of experience beyond the first year of teaching can and do manage a wide array of mild behavior problems in the class without a formal behavioral intervention merely by using good teaching habits.

When working with teachers in general education, I am often struck by the differences in what the research literature presents as a classroom behavior problem and the real-world behaviors that veteran teachers consider significant. The literature on behavioral management often refers to fairly mild behaviors such as blurting out answers, off-task behavior, or talking out of turn as serious behavioral problems in the classroom. However, most veteran teachers do not see those behaviors as extremely serious and can manage them as a matter of course using informal proactive management tactics such as proximity control, planned ignoring, a pointed look, or a quiet word (Bender, 2003). Other good teaching habits that positively affect student behavior include:

- ▶ Establishing a positive classroom climate
- ▶ Setting clear, fair behavior standards
- ▶ Personally greeting students each day
- ▶ Teaching class rules
- ▶ Consistently enforcing class rules
- ▶ Closely supervising transitions
- ▶ Visually monitoring behavior
- ▶ Increasing praise
- ▶ Requiring frequent student responses
- ▶ Offering frequent feedback
- ▶ Providing frequent help

In contrast to the research, general education teachers typically consider only more serious behaviors as problematic, including behaviors such as verbal or physical aggression, cursing in class, disruptive behavior, or noncompliance with teacher directions (Bender, 2003). Of course, the severity of behavioral problems comes into play when conceptualizing RTI for behavior, given the fact that general education teachers do manage a large array of mild behavior problems with no overt strategy whatsoever! Thus, when implementing RTI for behavioral change, educators must be cognizant of this discrepancy between what teachers and the literature consider a serious behavior problem. Furthermore, during the next years, we should anticipate that RTI procedures will be implemented for those more serious types of behaviors, and not terribly frequently for more mild behavior problems.

> We should anticipate that RTI procedures will be implemented for those more serious types of behaviors, and not terribly frequently for more mild behavior problems.

Intervention Tiers Within the Split Pyramid

The tiers within the split pyramid, as described by Sugai and his colleagues, are extremely similar to the tiers in the original three-tier pyramid presented in chapter 1 (Fairbanks et al., 2007; Horner & Sugai, 1999; Sugai et al., 2008). Tier 1 represents the universal interventions for behavior that all students receive within the general education class (Simonsen et al., 2008). For example, any classwide behavioral interventions that are routinely applied to reinforce positive behavior or reduce negative behaviors and result in some data collection are considered Tier 1 interventions. Data on a specific child's behavior that result from these Tier 1 interventions could and should be used in making educational decisions about that child during an RTI process. Many schools use schoolwide computerized record-keeping systems such as *AIMSweb* to compile data on anecdotal reports from the teacher on office referrals or office disciplinary referrals during a single grading period.

The classwide, Tier 1 behavioral interventions may include tactics such as the use of a token economy to support positive behaviors or posting class rules and recording rule infractions. Like the more common three-tier pyramid, the split pyramid indicates that 80 to 90 percent of students will succeed in behaving appropriately, based on both good teaching habits and the behavioral interventions applied within the context of the general education class (Kemp & Eaton, 2007).

> Tiers within the split pyramid are extremely similar to the tiers in the original three-tier RTI pyramid.

Tier 2 behavioral interventions include all interventions that target small groups of students or specific students who have not responded positively to the initial classwide interventions (Fairbanks et al., 2007; Simonsen et al., 2008). Thus, as in the more common three-tier pyramid, this split pyramid likewise involves a set of interventions—described as Tier 2 behavioral interventions—that are targeted at specific students or groups of students and implemented to help them develop and manifest more positive classroom behavior. Again, as in the three-tier RTI model, this tier is most often described as addressing the needs for perhaps 15 percent of the students in school (Bender & Shores, 2007). Several possible Tier 2 interventions are discussed later in this chapter.

Tier 3 behavioral interventions are highly detailed and individually targeted interventions that are reserved for those students—perhaps 2 to 5 percent of all students—whose behavioral problems are so involved that neither the general education behavioral interventions nor the more targeted small-group behavioral interventions in Tier 2 can alleviate them (Fairbanks et al., 2007; Kemp & Eaton, 2007; Simonsen et al., 2008). At this level, most researchers recommend conducting a formal functional behavior assessment (FBA) and initiating an individually targeted intervention to assist the student in managing his or her behavior (Eber, Breen, Rose, Unizycki, & London, 2008; Fairbanks et al., 2007; Fairbanks, Simonsen, & Sugai, 2008).

Functional Behavior Assessments

A functional behavior assessment or FBA involves measurement and documentation of a problem behavior and its antecedents and previous consequences, in an effort to determine how that behavior functions to provide reinforcement or emotional support for the child (Eber et al., 2008; Fairbanks et al., 2008). Once the function of the behavior has been determined, teachers can usually identify antecedents that will result in more acceptable behaviors. Teachers then develop an intervention to produce those desired behavioral consequences.

A full description of the FBA process goes well beyond the scope of this book, but it is important to note that the FBA should be undertaken as the Tier 3 behavioral intervention is developed, particularly if an FBA has not been conducted previously for the Tier 2 intervention. Functional behavior assessments undergird the RTI process for students in a fundamental way for students with serious behavioral problems since these assessments foster high levels of teacher and/or student reflection on the purpose of the student's behavior.

> A functional behavior assessment should be undertaken as the Tier 3 behavioral intervention is developed, particularly if an FBA has not been conducted previously for the Tier 2 intervention.

The good news is that most teachers have been implementing FBAs for students with behavior problems in general education for a number of years now since many students who are already identified as emotionally or behaviorally disordered require them. Thus, this procedure is fairly routine in schools today.

However, teachers should be encouraged to undertake FBAs in general education whenever a behavior problem is noted since this procedure allows the teacher to focus on the exact antecedents and consequences that support and maintain inappropriate behavior. A number of resources available to general education teachers provide assistance in positive behavioral support planning and/or functional behavior assessment (see appendix B, page 203).

Behavioral Interventions for RTI

As noted earlier, many minor behavioral problems do not require specific management techniques other than good teaching habits, and as we discuss RTI procedures for behavior, we should assume that the general education teacher is an effective veteran teacher who routinely displays these good teaching habits.

Tier 1 Behavioral Interventions

Assuming the teacher is experienced, a number of specific interventions can be conceptualized as Tier 1 interventions for behavior in the general education classroom (Arter, 2007; Bender & Shores, 2007; Cruz & Cullinan, 2001). In particular, a number of researchers have recommended level systems for behavioral management in general education. Cruz and Cullinan (2001) described a leveled system that delineated a hierarchy of several *contingency arrangements* (that is, levels) that link student privileges and behavioral responsibilities: the closer a child is in compliance with all behavioral expectations, the more privileges he or she has. To develop a level system, a general education teacher should first define the levels within the system, describing each in terms of the student's behavioral responsibilities and associated privileges. Table 5.1 presents an example of such a description.

Note that under this system, all students keep a record of each time the teacher had to speak to them. For example, if a student called another student a name, the teacher, using a neutral voice tone, might say, "Billy, that name calling is not showing respect for all students, as indicated in responsibility Number 2. Please mark your index card for a failure to comply with that responsibility on Tuesday at 9:45 AM."

The teacher would then visually monitor Billy to assure that he marked his record, which she could consult later when awarding rewards. While this level system is described here as an example of a Tier 1 classwide intervention, it could also be used as a Tier 2 intervention since individual student performance data could easily be collected and charted for any target student. In that sense, it is often the case that classwide interventions can lend themselves to both Tier 1 and Tier 2 applications because teachers can collect individual data on how specific students respond to the intervention, if they so choose.

Table 5.1 An Individual General Education Level System

Level	Behavioral Responsibilities	Reward Options
	The student must complete all within a given level to receive a reward.	*The student may select only one reward.*
Blue	1. Pays attention in class at all times 2. Treats teacher and all others with complete respect 3. Obeys all teacher instructions 4. Completes all homework	• Automatic permission for a three-minute break (limit of one per day) • Extra five minutes at beginning of lunch or recess • Opt out of one homework assignment per week • Extra five minutes at beginning of lunch or recess for the entire class (limit of one per month)
Green	1. Pays attention in class most of the time 2. Treats teacher and all others with respect almost all of the time 3. Obeys almost all teacher instructions 4. Completes most homework	• Automatic permission for a three-minute break (limit of one per day) • Extra three minutes at beginning of lunch or recess
Yellow	1. Needs more than one reminder to pay attention 2. Treats teacher and all others with respect sometimes 3. Needs reminders to obey teacher instructions 4. Only completes some homework	• Extra two minutes at beginning of lunch or recess
Red	1. Needs more than two reminders to pay attention 2. Treats teachers and all others with respect sometimes 3. Needs reminders to obey teacher instructions 4. Only completes some homework	• No privileges associated with this level

Rules for the Level System

1. At the beginning of each grading period, all students will begin at the yellow level.
2. Students may request consideration for a level change once per week.
3. All students will keep an index card (tally card) on their desks and will mark their cards as instructed by the teacher to keep track of responsibility infractions.
4. The teacher will also keep a record of responsibility infractions for some students, including students at the red level.

However, the possible use of behavioral data in an RTI procedure, in my opinion, precludes the use of self-monitoring behavioral data for RTI purposes. I strongly recommend that if a teacher comes to believe that he or she will need data on student behavior in an extended RTI process, that teacher should start recording those data directly (in addition to the student self-recording). At a later point in the RTI process, the existence of a behavior disorder or other disability might be linked to these behavioral data, and therefore, use of self-monitoring data exclusively in a series of multitier behavioral interventions is unwise. Of course, with that caution noted, self-monitoring is a very effective intervention procedure for behavioral change (Bender, 2007) and should be included as one option within the broader RTI process. However, teacher data should be used for most, if not all, of the data on which subsequent placement determinations are made.

> I strongly recommend that if a teacher believes he or she needs data on student behavior for a Tier 2 intervention, that teacher should record those data directly and not depend on student self-recording for RTI purposes.

In most classwide level systems and other classwide interventions, teachers are not required to compile data on each student's performance. However, should the teacher identify a specific student such as Billy who has consistent behavior problems, that teacher could record Billy's behavior problems during the implementation of the level system. The teacher would then compile that behavioral data on Billy's behavior as a record of his behavioral infractions, and that charted data could serve as an excellent performance-monitoring record for Billy. In short, while the level system may be applied classwide, compiling data on a specific child also makes this an option for a Tier 2 intervention. Again, classwide options frequently lend themselves to data collection on a specific child's behavior, and thus, even though the intervention is provided to everyone in the class, performance is monitored for only target students—thus these interventions may be considered Tier 2 interventions for those specific students.

> While many classwide interventions do not require collection of behavioral data on a specific child, compiling data on a specific child makes these interventions an excellent option for a Tier 2 intervention.

Tier 2 Behavioral Interventions

Because behavioral problems have long been a concern of educators, researchers have documented the effectiveness of a variety of targeted interventions to improve students' behavior over the years. In fact, large lists of behavioral interventions for more serious behavioral problems have been compiled (Bender, 2007; Sousa, 2009). However, only more recently have researchers placed these interventions into the specific RTI context (Bender & Shores, 2007; Fairbanks et al., 2008; Sousa, 2009).

Sugai and his colleagues, as one example, have recommended a "Check In, Check Out" (CICO) procedure as a Tier 2 intervention for students with mild to moderate behavior problems (Fairbanks et al., 2008; Fairbanks et al., 2007). In this procedure, students used a self-monitoring sheet to record their own behaviors and/or compliance with classroom rules (Fairbanks et al., 2008). The student's self-recording of behavior was typically done on a daily report card—an index card that includes specific behaviors to be counted—and that daily report card served as a basis for the intervention (Fairbanks et al., 2007).

In the CICO procedure, students are required to check in with the teacher each day by holding a brief individual conference at the beginning of the instructional period, when they pick up their daily report card. During that check-in conference, the teacher and student review the explicit behavioral expectations for the student and set a daily goal in terms of the individually targeted behaviors on the CICO card. The daily report card also notes this daily goal. Table 5.2 presents a sample for such a CICO daily report card.

Table 5.2 A CICO Daily Report Card as a Tier 2 Intervention

Name:			Date:						Points earned:								
My goal for today:																	
Behaviors Desired	8:30 to 9:30			9:30 to 10:30			10:30 to 11:30			11:30 to 12:30			12:30 to 1:30			1:30 to 2:30		
Respect others	2	1	0	2	1	0	2	1	0	2	1	0	2	1	0	2	1	0
Use your quiet voice	2	1	0	2	1	0	2	1	0	2	1	0	2	1	0	2	1	0
Manage yourself	2	1	0	2	1	0	2	1	0	2	1	0	2	1	0	2	1	0
Solve problems responsibly	2	1	0	2	1	0	2	1	0	2	1	0	2	1	0	2	1	0
Rating scale: 2 = Great behavior; 1 = Acceptable behavior; 0 = Goal not met (no points earned)																	
Did I meet my goal? Comments:																	

Using this particular daily report card, a student could earn up to 48 points per day, with various levels of reinforcement for identified point ranges. The CICO intervention also involves frequent teacher monitoring during the instructional period or day. At regular intervals, the teacher awards the student points for good behavior, offering either praise or correction based on how well the student followed classroom rules. At those brief meetings, the student notes these comments on the daily report card.

At the end of each day, the teacher "checks out" by holding a brief conference with the student to review his or her behavior that day. The student is then instructed to share the daily report card with his or her parents to solicit their assistance and generally facilitate parental involvement in the intervention process.

This intervention procedure, therefore, involves providing the student with explicit examples of behaviors, increased structure and prompts for appropriate behavior, additional instruction on specific positive behaviors, increased feedback on inappropriate behavior, and parental review of the child's behavior on a daily basis (Fairbanks et al., 2007).

Based on these daily report cards, coupled with the CICO conferences, teachers could review these behavioral data on a weekly basis to determine the efficacy of the intervention and/or the necessity of a more intensive Tier 3 behavioral intervention (Fairbanks et al., 2008). In that sense, this CICO procedure is a perfect fit as a Tier 2 intervention within a broader RTI procedure.

Research on this intervention as a Tier 2 intervention in an RTI paradigm has shown that the CICO procedure is effective in reducing problem behaviors (Fairbanks et al., 2008; Fairbanks et al., 2007). For example, Fairbanks et al. (2007) implemented the CICO procedure as a Tier 2 intervention for ten students between the ages of seven and eight, in grade 2, who were nominated by their second-grade teachers as having serious behavior problems such as increasing office disciplinary referrals and disruption in the classroom. Based on input from the teachers, the researchers identified a set of problem behaviors to monitor including inappropriate touching, talk-outs, out-of-seat behavior, noncompliance, and nondisruptive off-task behavior. The researchers then observed in the classrooms, noting each interval during which any of these problem behaviors occurred for each target student, and those observational data were used to monitor behavioral improvement.

The CICO report cards for this study stipulated three simple goal statements— "respect others," "manage self," and "solve problems responsibly." A point scale similar to the point scale shown in table 5.2 (page 119) was used. Thus in this study, students had the opportunity to earn up to 36 points daily, based on these three behaviors, across six discrete periods each day. The general education teachers taught those behaviors to the entire class, but only targeted students who completed the CICO intervention and used the daily report card. Students with the CICO cards were identified as "leaders" of the class and all other students were identified as "coaches." It was stressed that the coaches should assist the leaders in staying on task and following behavioral expectations. Also, in this study, improved behavior by the leaders resulted in reinforcement for the entire class, so all class members had an interest in fostering good behavior.

After a week of collecting baseline data, the CICO intervention began for all ten target students. Within only two weeks, the data indicate that four of the ten students had responded positively to this Tier 2 intervention. While these results stem from only one study, data suggest that perhaps as many as 40 percent of students with serious behavior problems respond positively to a structured Tier 2 intervention provided in the general education class (Fairbanks et al., 2007). This is very similar to the number of students that respond positively to academic-based Tier 2 interventions for reading in the general education classroom. Furthermore, in a continuation of this same study, these researchers also showed that four of the remaining students responded positively to a more involved intensive Tier 3 intervention! The remaining two students served as controls for the study and were not exposed to a Tier 3 intervention. Overall, these are impressive results, as these data document the power of multitier interventions to curb behavioral problems.

> Data suggest that perhaps as many as 40 percent of students with serious behavior problems respond positively to a Tier 2 behavioral intervention!

Tier 3 Behavioral Interventions

The positive behavioral supports literature for Tier 2 and Tier 3 interventions has recommended a number of intervention ideas (Bender, 2007; Bender & Shores, 2007; Eber et al., 2008; Sousa, 2009).

To serve as a Tier 3 intervention in a behavioral RTI procedure, an intervention must be a research-proven intervention that is targeted for a specific child, and result in repeated assessment on specific behaviors—typically daily assessment. I also recommend daily assessment for behavioral RTI procedures at Tier 3 (Bender & Shores, 2007).

The intervention must also be sustained long enough to show efficacy; behavioral interventions administered for only four to ten days are probably not long enough to modify behavior over the long term. Most of the literature describes behavioral interventions that continue from two to six weeks or more (Bender, 2007; Fairbanks et al., 2007; Sugai et al., 2008).

Targeted individual behavioral interventions that have received research support include an array of options.

- ▶ Level systems
- ▶ Token economies
- ▶ Individual contingencies
- ▶ Peer-mediated anger management
- ▶ Peer confrontation
- ▶ Social story interventions
- ▶ Adult-mentoring programs

▶ Video monitoring

▶ Dialog journals

▶ Self-talk strategies

▶ Relaxation techniques

Implementation guidelines for these strategies are likewise available in a variety of contexts (Bender, 2007; Eber et al., 2008; Fairbanks et al., 2007; Sousa, 2009; Sugai et al., 2008).

This list is not exhaustive, and some interventions involve or require group or full class participation. A detailed description of all possible behavioral interventions is beyond the scope of this book. However, as pointed out previously, even in classwide interventions such as token economies or CICO, charting data for individual children is possible, and thus these interventions can be appropriate as either Tier 1, 2, or even 3 interventions. Educators familiar with these interventions can readily see how these individual behavioral interventions can fit within either Tier 2 or Tier 3 in a behavioral RTI, and in the behavioral arena, that is frequently the case, as it is in the academic arena. You may recall that some supplemental reading curricula discussed in previous chapters are perfectly appropriate for either Tier 2 or Tier 3 interventions, depending on the context.

However, as mentioned previously for academic interventions, when a particular behavioral intervention has not resulted in improved behavior at one tier in the RTI pyramid, educators would be wise to implement a different intervention for the next intervention tier to demonstrate active commitment to alleviating the student's behavioral problems.

> When a behavioral intervention has not resulted in improved behavior at one tier, educators would be wise to implement a different intervention for the next intervention tier.

Additional Tier 3 Considerations

The literature does suggest several unique considerations when teachers are conceptualizing a behavioral intervention for Tier 3.

Self-Monitoring

First, many Tier 3 interventions involve self-monitoring of behavior since students can be taught to exercise some control over their own inappropriate behaviors (Fairbanks et al., 2008). While many Tier 2 interventions also stress self-monitoring, by the time a child's behavior requires a third intervention tier, self-monitoring of behavior should be an absolute *requirement* since research has shown this intervention to be so very effective, and the self-monitoring procedure does promote the student's immediate awareness of his or her own behavior problems (see Bender, 2007, for a brief review of research on self-monitoring).

> By the time a child's behavior requires a third intervention tier, self-monitoring of behavior should be an absolute requirement to promote a student's immediate awareness of his or her own behavioral problem.

Sousa (2009) provided an example of a Tier 3 self-monitoring intervention in a behavioral RTI framework. In that example, a student had been exposed to a Tier 2 intervention aimed at curbing her "blurting out" answers in class. The Tier 2 intervention was based on a weekly opportunity for a student to be a class leader and to coteach (with the teacher) lessons on computer networking sites. This reinforcement was coupled with daily reinforcement for raising her hand and reducing inappropriate talking. Data did not indicate much effect for this Tier 2 intervention. However, combining that same intervention with a self-monitoring requirement drastically reduced the inappropriate talk-outs. In that case, the self-monitoring requirement had the effect of making the student aware of her own behavior, and that awareness led to a reduction of inappropriate behavior—a result that has been demonstrated repeatedly in the behavioral literature (Bender, 2007; Sousa, 2009).

Wraparound Supports

Next, when conceptualizing a Tier 3 intervention for an RTI in behavior—unlike academic RTI procedures—educators should give some consideration to *wraparound* supports for positive behavior (Eber et al., 2008). Because social behavior is context dependent and highly related to the multiple social situations in which a child lives, when addressing extreme behavioral problems, educators should consider all of the environmental factors that affect a student's behavior. Wraparound behavioral support is individualized planning that focuses the efforts of all concerned on the student's overall development, including parents, teachers, the student, and others in the student's community (Eber et al., 2008).

For years, educators have recognized that a large number of factors in the environment of the student can either impede behavioral improvement or support positive behavioral change (Eber et al., 2008). The wraparound approach acknowledges the stakeholders in a student's life and pulls them together to focus their collaborative efforts across all the environments in which the student functions. As both a philosophy and an educational planning process, wraparound supports the positive development of the student by emphasizing family, student, teacher, and interagency planning to enhance both behavior and academic performance. While the wraparound planning process is unique for any particular child, this emphasis in planning for students with significant behavior problems does differentiate the behavioral RTI process from merely planning a Tier 3 educational intervention in reading and/or math since many more individuals become involved in RTI procedures that address behavioral problems. Particularly, at the Tier 3 level in the RTI process, educators should be cognizant of, and actively solicit, the direct involvement of the student, the student's parents, teachers, others in the child's community, and other agency personnel for planning and implementation of interventions. The wraparound process works to foster long-term behavioral improvement. More information on the wraparound process is available from the website for the National Wraparound Initiative (see appendix B, page 203).

Case Study: RTI for Behavior

As an example of an RTI procedure designed to address a behavioral problem, let's imagine a young student, Alphonso, in grade 4, who has been demonstrating aggression by calling other students names, cursing, and demonstrating other types of extreme verbal aggression. Within only the first couple of weeks of the academic year, the teacher, Ms. Nelson, considered Alphonso's behavior to be problematic and began to document these instances using a procedure called an "ABC log." *ABC* refers to documentation of problem behavior in terms of *antecedents*, *behaviors*, and *consequences*. By identifying the relationship between these factors, teachers can understand how a student's behavior serves his or her needs, and thus an ABC log can serve as an FBA.

> The ABC log represents an excellent way for a general education teacher to glean an understanding of how a student's behavior serves that student. Thus, this is another way to initiate an FBA.

To initiate an ABC log, after a behavioral infraction occurs, the teacher deals with the overt behavior problem through appropriate disciplinary means. Then, the teacher makes notes on the behavioral infraction, including notes in three areas:

1 The antecedents—what was happening immediately before the behavioral problem

2 The behavior itself

3 The consequences applied as a result of that behavior

In our example, the ABC log for Alphonso included twenty-three instances of misbehavior and the antecedents and consequences of each, as presented in table 5.3. Ms. Nelson also reflected on those behaviors, antecedents, and consequences after continuing the ABC log for a couple of weeks.

Table 5.3 ABC Log for Alphonso

Name: Alphonso Jacobs	Grade: *Four*	Teacher: *Ms. Nelson*	Date: *Aug. 24–Sep. 4, 2009*
Date	**Antecedents**	**Behavior**	**Consequence**
Aug. 24	*Transition to math at 9:15*	*A. saw another student drop a book and said, "You're an idiot!"*	*I spoke to A. in class and told him we did not call others names.*
	Walking in the hallway back from lunch	*A. pushed the student in front of him.*	*I spoke to A. again and told him not to push.*
	History class, 1:45, middle of class	*A. called another student "stupid" when that student got an answer wrong.*	*I took A. to hallway and reminded him not to call others names. I told him he could get a treat from the treat bag the next day if he behaved well.*
Aug. 25	*Before first bell*	*A. shouted to another student, "Leave me alone!"*	*I told A. not to shout in class and that he'd lost his treat for that day.*
	At morning recess	*A. called another student "You ***hole" when the other student caught the fly ball A. had just hit during a softball game.*	*I sent A. in for the rest of recess and reminded him that he'd lost his daily treat.*
Aug. 26	*Morning transition*	*A. called the same student "***hole" again (student that caught the ball on Tuesday).*	*I told A. he would lose 10 minutes of his recess for calling others names.*
	When class left for recess	*A. said to me, "I don't like being in your class. You're a real turd."*	*I talked with A. about his name calling and took the rest of his recess to send him to the office.*

continued on next page →

Name: Alphonso Jacobs	Grade: *Four*	Teacher: *Ms. Nelson*	Date: *Aug. 24–Sep. 4, 2009*
Date	**Antecedents**	**Behavior**	**Consequence**
	12:15, leaving the class for lunch	*A. ran to get in front of the line, bumped past another student, and said, "Get out of my way, you turkey!"*	*I moved A. to the back of the line and told him I was going to talk with his mom about his behavior.*
	1:15, transitioning to science class	*A. could not find his book in his desk and shouted, "Some idiot stole my book. When I find out who, I'll kill 'im!"*	*I took A. outside the room and cautioned him about shouting and accusing others.*
	*Note: Alphonso's mom did not come. She telephoned and said she could not make it, but we talked a bit on the telephone about Alphonso's behavior problems. She said she'd speak to him at home about this.*		
Aug. 27	*9:30, transitioning from reading to math*	*A. said, "I hate math! I don't want to do it."*	*I asked A. to come outside the room and told him he needed to keep those thoughts to himself.*
	At recess	*A. got mad in the softball game when a player tagged him out at second base.*	*I sent him in for the rest of recess, having him sit in the office. I also talked with him.*
	Going to lunch in the hallway line	*A. shouted, "I was there first. Get out of my way!"*	*I reminded him not to be rude to others and sent him to the back of the line.*
Aug. 28	*Before first bell*	*A. came in just behind another student and said, "Get out of the way, you idiot!"*	*I reminded A. of our previous discussions and said I intended to call his mom for a discussion again. Seems to have worked for the rest of the day.*
Aug. 31	*Transitioning to science, 11:20*	*A. called another student a name again.*	*I spoke to A. and said this had to stop or I'd have to involve his mom again.*

Name: Alphonso Jacobs	Grade: *Four*	Teacher: *Ms. Nelson*	Date: *Aug. 24–Sep. 4, 2009*
Date	**Antecedents**	**Behavior**	**Consequence**
	Walking out to recess	*A. pushed the student in front of him.*	*I made him miss 10 minutes of recess and decided to speak to the principal. I sent another note to his mom.*
Afternoon of Aug. 31: I spoke to Mr. Daggley about Alphonso and shared the ABC log. He indicated that we should try to talk with his mom again and that I should continue the log.			
Sept. 1	*At lunch in cafeteria line*	*A. pushed the student in front, trying to make him trip. A. said it was "just a joke."*	*I told him not to push and didn't punish him.*
	Health class @ 2:10	*A. called another student "stupid" when she got an answer wrong.*	*I took A. to hallway and told him his behavior had to change. I penalized him 10 minutes of recess again on the next day.*
Sept. 2	*Before first bell*	*A. shouted to another student, "Hey, ***hole. Leave me alone."*	*I told him I had to call his mom again.*
	At morning recess	*A. called another student a name.*	*I sent A. in for the rest of recess.*
	2:30, transitioning from science to history	*A. said, "I don't like history! I hate everything in school!"*	*I asked A. to come outside the room and told him he needed to keep those thoughts to himself.*
Sept. 3		*A. was absent.*	
Sept. 4	*Morning transition*	*A. said his mom spoke to him and that he'd behave well all day! May be progress!*	
	Going to lunch	*A. was lining up and called a student a name.*	*I talked with A. and decided to talk with his mom again by phone.*

continued on next page →

Name: Alphonso Jacobs	Grade: *Four*	Teacher: *Ms. Nelson*	Date: *Aug. 24–Sep. 4, 2009*
Date	**Antecedents**	**Behavior**	**Consequence**
	When bell rang to dismiss school	*A. said again, "I don't like school."*	*I talked with A. about his behavior and told him we'd have to do something. I decided to speak to Mr. Daggley again, and perhaps the student support team.*

Overall Reflections: *A. seems to have a number of problems at transition times, between subjects, or going to recess or the cafeteria. Students are interacting more at those points, and many students don't manage transitions well. He is demonstrating a serious behavior problem that I have to address over twice daily, and most of these are aggressive. However, only one instance here involved physical aggression, so that is not a great problem. I punished him for name calling some by not letting him earn a treat from my treat bag, but that didn't work. I intend to request some assistance from the student support team.*

The log indicates that Ms. Nelson talked with Alphonso about his aggressive behavior and verbal aggression on a number of occasions. She punished him and called his mother several times, and sent home two notes describing his behavior. Ms. Nelson also referred Alphonso to the office more than once. At the end of two weeks, she referred his problem of verbal aggression to the principal, Mr. Daggley, and requested a meeting of the student support team for the school. She had by then determined that further assistance was required—perhaps a more intensive intervention. Table 5.4 presents the RTI form that summarizes the various steps in this behavioral RTI procedure for Alphonso.

Table 5.4 Behavioral RTI Summary Report for Alphonso

Student: *Alphonso Jacobs*	Age: *10*	Date: *9/9/09*
Initiating teacher: *Ms. Nelson*	School: *Tobruk Elem.*	Grade: *4*

1. Statement of student difficulty and summary of Tier 1 instruction (add supporting evidence and/or progress-monitoring data chart, if available):

In my fourth-grade class, while working with Alphonso, I noticed a large number of aggressive behaviors and began to make notes on these within the first couple of weeks of school. The ABC log (attached) included verbal aggression and various name calling instances that I noticed between 8/24/09 and 9/4/09. Twenty-three separate instances are noted, and this far exceeds the level of verbal aggressive behavior of any other student in that class. I've also noted the consequences I used with Alphonso to try and curb this behavior.

For example, I tried ignoring the behavior initially, which didn't work. I also used a "treat bag" in my class to reinforce correct work and appropriate behavior. To use that idea, I first compliment the child and then hold the bag out for individual students to select a small treat such as a piece of candy or small item such as a colored pencil, and so on. I made of point of using that at least once each day when Alphonso had participated well in an activity and not demonstrated aggression. Even that did not curb these problems.

Finally, during that two-week period when I noticed the problems were not decreasing, I talked twice with Alphonso's mother and once with Mr. Daggley, the school administrator, about these behavior problems.

Mr. Daggley noted that Alphonso's previous teachers indicated certain behavior problems, and he recalled a number of office disciplinary referrals for Alphonso over the years. However, Alphonso's third-grade teacher resigned at the end of last year and was not available for consultation.

I believe these problems warrant further attention, and probably some type of intervention to alleviate this verbal aggression, so I've requested a meeting of the student support team and Mr. Daggley to address these concerns.

Ms. Nelson, 9/7/09

Ms. Toulieu, the chairperson of the student support team, created a subcommittee of three teachers from that team to meet with Mr. Daggley and me concerning Alphonso's behavior. Ms. Thompson, lead teacher for grade 4, Ms. Pope, the guidance counselor, and Mr. Jefferies, a fifth-grade teacher, met with Mr. Daggley and me on 9/9/09. This group concurred that Alphonso was demonstrating high frequencies of verbal aggressive behavior, and instructed me to develop a Tier 2 intervention plan and submit that plan to Mr. Daggley for approval prior to implementation. They further agreed to review the data resulting from that intervention within six weeks.

Ms. Nelson, 9/9/09

2.   Tier 2 supplemental behavioral intervention plan:

Based on the input from the student support team, I developed a Tier 2 intervention plan for Alphonso. The intervention involves continuation of the reinforcements I offer in the class, coupled with daily meetings with Alphonso in which I discuss his behavior. I will also offer targeted specific reinforcement exclusively for Alphonso. On any specific day in which he is able to reduce his verbal aggressive behavior from his average of two per day (see the ABC log), he will earn ten minutes of computer time at the end of the day since he enjoys computer time as much as any student I've ever worked with. After Alphonso establishes this reduced level of verbal aggression, we anticipate setting a goal for further reduction, perhaps during the final two weeks of this four-week intervention.

To develop a daily measure of his aggressive behaviors, I will count (using an index card on my desk) his aggressive comments. I will also note specific days on which he meets his goal.

continued on next page →

At least once per week, Mr. Daggley will meet with Alphonso and me while we review his daily behavior to stress for Alphonso that everyone in our school is trying to support him as he reduces his name calling and verbal aggression. We will begin this Tier 2 intervention immediately, and continue it for four weeks, at which time the student support team will meet and consider the performance data from this intervention.

Ms. Nelson, 9/9/09

3. Observation of student in Tier 2 intervention:

On three occasions (Sep. 11, Sep. 18, and Sep. 24), I had the opportunity to meet with Ms. Nelson and Alphonso during the Tier 2 intervention. In each instance, I also visited that class for approximately twenty minutes to observe Alphonso in his class work. During those observations, I noticed that Ms. Nelson took many opportunities to praise Alphonso for good behavior (an average of three such instances in each observation), so she was following correctly the intervention plan. At no point did I see Alphonso display aggression, though it is not uncommon for students to behave more appropriately when the principal is in the classroom.

In each of the meetings, we three discussed the fact that Alphonso was continuing to display some name calling and verbal aggression periodically. On one occasion (Sep. 24), Alphonso earned his computer time, and Ms. Nelson praised him and emphasized that success. While he earned his computer time reinforcement on some days, he did not earn it on others. Perhaps this intervention will take effect within the next week or so, though Ms. Nelson will discuss the possibility of talking with the student support team within the next day or so about Alphonso's behavior.

Mr. Daggley, 9/24/09

4. Tier 2 intervention summary and recommendations (must include data chart):

I implemented the Tier 2 intervention for Alphonso and monitored his aggressive name calling daily for three weeks. I met with him as indicated in that intervention plan, but he only rarely earned his reinforcement, and seeing no real improvement, I talked with Mr. Daggley, who recommended that I request a meeting of the student support team before continuing this for four entire weeks.

The data in the accompanying chart indicate very little improvement, and I believe a more intensive intervention is necessary for Alphonso. I did note, while completing this intervention, that Alphonso seemed oblivious to how many times he was verbally aggressive, and how other students responded to that name calling and verbal aggression. It was almost as if he was surprised on days when during our conference, I indicated that he had not earned his reinforcement. I'm not sure he realizes what he is doing.

Ms. Nelson, 9/30/09

5. Tier 3 intervention plan:

At my request, the student support team met to consider Alphonso's aggressive behavior and the results of the Tier 2 intervention. Alphonso's mother, Mrs. Jacobs, was invited and attended that meeting. Others in attendance included Ms. Toulieu, the chairperson of the student support team, Mr. Daggley, myself, Ms. Thompson, lead teacher for grade four, Ms. Pope, the guidance counselor, Mr. Jefferies, a fifth-grade teacher, and Ms. Strombolli, the special education teacher. We met on 10/1/09, and at that meeting, I shared the intervention plan for the Tier 2 intervention and the performance-monitoring data, tracking Alphonso's aggressive name calling daily through three weeks of that Tier 2 intervention.

Initially, the team noted that Alphonso had received the benefit of a full range of positive behavioral supports, as noted above. These included an FBA (the ABC log), a Tier 1, classwide intervention (reinforcement through the treat bag and praising), and a targeted reinforcement created exclusively for Alphonso (the computer time option in Tier 2). Even with the benefit of these positive behavioral supports, the data do not show a reduction in name calling and verbal aggressive behavior. The team then agreed that a more intensive intervention was necessary, and we discussed a Tier 3 intervention for Alphonso.

After some discussion, Ms. Strombolli picked up on my comments about Alphonso not being aware of his name calling or perhaps not really seeing those behaviors as inappropriate. The team discussed a self-monitoring type of intervention in which Alphonso would chart his own behavior and perhaps become more aware of his name calling and verbal aggression. Ms. Strombolli mentioned an intervention called "Check In, Check Out" that included a strong self-monitoring component. That intervention has received research support, and she recommended that I review that option and implement that procedure for four weeks.

This will be much more intensive in that I will be conferencing with Alphonso throughout the day (rather than once a day, as stipulated in the Tier 2 intervention plan), and Alphonso will be charting his own behavior along with me, which should increase his awareness of his aggression. The team recommended that I emphasize the feelings of others during our debrief chats after he has demonstrated name-calling behavior. Also, the team determined that I should use that procedure only during the AM instruction period (not all day) since I had the services of a paraprofessional at that point in the day, and would be able to debrief Alphonso whenever he demonstrated aggression since I could, in most cases, turn the instruction over to the paraprofessional for three to four minutes.

I'll review two studies on that procedure, and I plan to begin this intervention on 10/5/09.

Ms. Nelson, 10/1/09

6. Observation of student in Tier 3 intervention:

I recommended the CICO intervention to Ms. Nelson for use with Alphonso, and thus I requested the option of observing in Ms. Nelson's class on a morning when Alphonso was receiving that intervention. I visited her class twice, and on the first observational visit (10/9/09), Alphonso did not demonstrate any name calling.

When I observed the class on 10/13/09, I noted that Alphonso did call another student a name, at a point when Ms. Nelson had asked the entire class a question. After listening to the other student, Alphonso said, "That's stupid!"

continued on next page →

Ms. Nelson immediately asked the paraprofessional to continue the questioning for the class, while she and Alphonso met briefly in the back of the room to discuss his name calling. I heard most of that conversation and noted that Ms. Nelson discussed how Alphonso might feel if someone indicated one of his ideas was stupid. I noted that Ms. Nelson was following the planned intervention, as described in the CICO literature.

I reviewed Alphonso's CICO cards for the last week, and I also reviewed the data chart of his aggressive name calling. Those data indicate a small decline in Alphonso's name-calling behavior, but he is still doing this on certain days.

Ms. Strombolli, 10/13/09

7.   Tier 3 intervention summary and recommendations (must include data chart):

On the evening of the monthly PTA meeting (10/22/09), Mrs. Jacobs came to the school and asked how Alphonso was doing. Ms. Nelson had great news to share and quickly rounded up Ms. Toulieu, the chairperson of the student support team, and myself. We four reviewed the data on aggressive behavior of Alphonso. Ms. Nelson has implemented the CICO intervention, and the data (presented in the accompanying chart) indicate that this intervention had all but eliminated Alphonso's aggressive behavior. While Alphonso had experienced a challenging day on the same day as the PTA meeting, overall, his behavior was much improved. Mrs. Jacobs was very happy with the positive report, and we jointly decided to continue the CICO, but fade it over time, by reducing the teacher/student conferences to only one per day.

Ms. Toulieu indicated that I should make notes on that meeting, on the RTI summary form, and she further noted that there was no need to bring that matter before the entire student support team at their meeting in January since the problem seemed largely resolved.

Ms. Strombolli, 10/22/09

Note in the first section of this RTI summary report that Ms. Nelson presented an excellent report to the subcommittee of the student support team based on Alphonso's ABC log. She indicated specifically the types and frequencies of problem behaviors demonstrated by Alphonso. She noted the types of reinforcement for positive behaviors that she used for all students in the class—this classwide reinforcement procedure should be considered a Tier 1 behavioral support intervention. She also noted her communications with Alphonso's mother, Mrs. Jacobs, and with Mr. Daggley, the school administrator.

A Tier 2 Intervention for Aggressive Behavior

As mentioned in previous chapters, the responsibility for the Tier 2 intervention under the RTI model rests with the general education teacher—this is true for both academic and behavioral interventions. Because the principal had already become involved, the principal, Ms. Nelson, and the small subcommittee of the student support team for the school discussed the need for a Tier 2 intervention for Alphonso. Although Ms. Nelson routinely provided praise and reinforcement in her class, as described on the RTI summary form, these good teaching habits were not enough to curb Alphonso's problematic behavior. Thus, Ms. Nelson developed a more involved Tier 2 intervention, as described in table 5.4.

We should note how these RTI summary forms may be adapted, as they were in this example. Even though the form did not include specific space for summarizing the meeting of the subcommittee of the student support team, that meeting and those decisions can easily be summarized on this summary form merely by creating a bit more space, as was the case in table 5.4.

While there is no requirement in most school districts to involve the student support team before a Tier 2 behavioral intervention, Ms. Nelson and Mr. Daggley chose to involve that team at this point to generate additional intervention ideas. I recommend that teachers check with their administrators—principals and/or directors of curriculum—to find out at what point the district recommends involvement of the student support team for behavioral RTI procedures. In some districts, behavioral RTI procedures differ from academically based RTI procedures, so checking with the local district administrators is recommended.

> I recommend that teachers check with their administrators to find out exactly when their local school districts recommend or require involvement of the student support team for behavioral RTI procedures.

Ms. Nelson wrote a brief behavioral intervention plan, which indicated that she would meet with Alphonso daily and discuss his behavior. Furthermore, each day that he reduced his verbal aggression instances, he earned ten minutes of computer time at the end of the day. He always enjoyed playing educational games on the computer, and Ms. Nelson felt this would be a great reinforcement for him. The plan also involved Ms. Nelson counting and charting his aggressive behavior rather than maintaining the ABC log. A description of that Tier 2 intervention is presented in table 5.4, and the data chart from the Tier 2 intervention is presented in figure 5.2 (page 134).

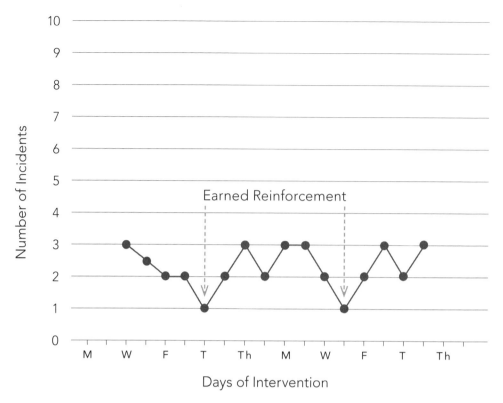

Figure 5.2 Alphonso's Tier 2 performance data: incidents of aggressive behavior.

Unfortunately, after only the first three weeks of this Tier 2 intervention, the data chart included a number of additional instances of verbal aggression by Alphonso. Thus, data show that this Tier 2 intervention, although more intensive than the reinforcement Ms. Nelson provided for all students, was not successful for Alphonso. These data from the Tier 2 intervention thus provided the basis for subsequent decision making for Alphonso, as required in the RTI process.

However, in completing the Tier 2 intervention, Ms. Nelson did note one interesting fact about Alphonso's performance. Specifically, Ms. Nelson noticed that when Alphonso committed aggression by calling other students names, he often did so with no obvious forethought. In fact, she became convinced that Alphonso was virtually unaware of both his aggression and its impact on his classmates, and she noted that on the RTI summary form. Such a total lack of awareness is, unfortunately, not uncommon among students who come from homes characterized by high levels of emotional intensity and/or verbal aggression. Ms. Nelson's insight provided the basis for the Tier 3 intervention.

One more point should be noted about the progress of this RTI procedure. In this example, Ms. Nelson requested an earlier meeting about this student than was initially stipulated in the Tier 2 intervention plan. Typically, when an intervention's duration is specified, teachers should complete that intervention. However, should a student's inappropriate behavior escalate, or remain at consistently high levels over several weeks as indicated in figure 5.2, teachers may conclude that a more intensive intervention is necessary even before the official end of the Tier 2 intervention. After only three weeks of data collection, Mr. Daggley and Ms. Nelson noted that the Tier 2 intervention was not successful. Thus, they requested an earlier meeting with the student support team.

> When the duration of an intervention is specified in an intervention plan, teachers should generally complete that intervention. However, exceptions may be made when a student's inappropriate behavior escalates or remains at consistently high levels.

A Tier 3 Intervention for Aggressive Behavior

Section 5 of table 5.4 (pages 130–131) presents a discussion of a Tier 3 behavioral intervention. The Tier 3 plan seems to be a logical extension of the Tier 2 intervention, though we should highlight several points. First, parental involvement is even more important in behavioral RTI procedures than in academic RTI procedures. While special education law mandates parental notification before assessment for special education placement, RTI legislation itself does not specifically mandate parental participation or notification in the earlier stages of the RTI process. However, as indicated previously in this text, parent involvement in intervention planning is desirable from the initial consideration of the behavioral problem throughout the RTI process. Furthermore, in behavioral RTI procedures, as indicated in the previous discussion of the wraparound philosophy, all stakeholders in the child's environment should be actively involved since this leads to comprehensive follow up and improves the chances for positive behavioral change. Furthermore, one critical aspect of the CICO process involves sharing the daily report card with the parent. Thus, in this example, it is critically important that Alphonso's mother, Mrs. Jacobs, be directly involved in selection of the intervention.

Next, note that section 5 of the RTI summary form (table 5.4, pages 130–131) essentially summarized many of the previous actions, specifically mentioning the FBA, the Tier 1 reinforcement plan, and the Tier 2 intervention. While other areas of the summary form describe all of these in detail, this meeting represents the first time the full student support team met in consideration of Alphonso's behavior, and thus some brief summary of these aspects of the positive behavior support process is appropriate.

In some cases involving behavioral RTI procedures, a teacher's informal notes may suggest an intervention plan, as was the case here. Ms. Nelson's careful consideration of Alphonso's behavioral responses during the Tier 2 intervention provided the basis for the more involved self-monitoring in Tier 3. Teachers should be encouraged to make such notes in the context of the RTI summary form; they should view that form as a working, idea-sharing, type of document that can become a repository for ideas that may be useful for the student later.

In this instance, the facilitating teacher for the Tier 3 intervention was the general education teacher, unlike many of the academic interventions presented earlier. In behavioral interventions, it is often the case that the general education teacher can conduct the intervention and continue to hold class for the other students, as she did in this example. In this case, Ms. Nelson needed only two or three minutes to conference individually with Alphonso after he committed a behavioral offense, and she managed that by having her paraprofessional continue the class for those few minutes.

Next, before Tier 3, note that a variety of persons became involved who had not previously been consulted. While the mother, Mrs. Jacobs, had been involved in the Tier 2 intervention, after that did not succeed, the entire student support team for the school was consulted. That team often contains a special education teacher, which makes sense because should the third-tier intervention not succeed, the data suggest that a child study team needs to convene and consider the student's eligibility for special education placement. At that point, the special education teacher would then be expected to plan a specialized intervention for that child, and having some prior involvement with the student would be advantageous.

Of course, this raises the question concerning the relationship between eligibility for special education in the categories of emotional disturbance/behavioral disorders on one hand and the RTI process on the other. Fairbanks et al. (2008) indicate that a team discussing a child's eligibility for special education may consider failure to alleviate a behavioral problem based on multiple interventions. Unlike assessment and eligibility for learning disabilities, there has been no specific legislation linking multitier RTI procedures to eligibility determinations for emotional disturbance and/or behavioral disorders. Nevertheless, data such as those generated by an RTI procedure could and should certainly be considered in such eligibility proceedings.

Results of the Tier 3 Intervention

As shown in figure 5.3, the Tier 3 intervention worked to curb Alphonso's verbal aggression toward others. By the end of a multiweek intervention period, his name calling and other verbal aggression were almost eliminated, and thus, there was not a need for this child to be brought before the student support team again.

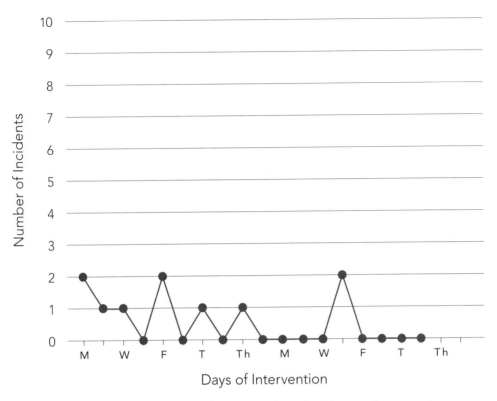

Figure 5.3 Alphonso's Tier 3 performance data: incidents of aggressive behavior.

Conclusion

All teachers should expect to implement multitier behavioral interventions in the near future for general education students with behavior problems since research has shown that these procedures work (Bender, 2007; Fairbanks et al., 2007; Spectrum K12/CASE, 2008; Sugai et al., 2008). Thus, this is the right thing to do for our students. In point of fact, most teachers are implementing these interventions currently in the form of positive behavioral supports for students previously diagnosed as behaviorally disordered. Furthermore, the RTI framework fits well with most positive behavioral support models, as described in this chapter, and general education teachers truly appreciate the help of this supportive framework for dealing with serious behavior problems.

However, too often in the past, a few teachers have merely "shuffled" their students with behavioral problems on toward special education, without seriously attempting to alleviate the disciplinary issues in the context of general education. Fortunately, those days are gone! Working under the RTI paradigm, educators nationwide are ramping up their skills in dealing with students with significant behavior problems in the classroom since these procedures work so effectively, and this will result in a better education for many students with behavioral problems. A wide variety of behavioral interventions have been shown to be effective in curbing behavior problems in the classroom, and the emphasis on RTI is now providing a vehicle for implementing those interventions for students with behavioral difficulties in general education.

Thus, RTI is a very effective, best-practice behavioral management process that easily provides a mechanism for FBAs as well as a backdrop for the multitier positive behavioral supports that have been required by law for the last decade. As teachers master and perfect these procedures, their teaching efficacy will increase drastically, which is, of course, an excellent result for all students.

Working under the RTI paradigm, educators nationwide are ramping up their skills in dealing with students with significant behavior problems in the general education classroom, and this will result in much improved education for many students with behavioral needs.

6

RTI in Middle and High Schools

While RTI is beginning to be fairly well understood at the elementary level, significant questions on RTI implementation in middle and secondary schools remain. Furthermore, it is clear from practitioners that RTI procedures are being implemented more frequently in elementary grades than in the higher grade levels, at least initially. For example, in a survey of administrators of special education (Spectrum K12/CASE, 2008), 67 percent of those administrators reported that implementation of RTI had already begun in the elementary grades, while only 27 percent indicated such implementation had begun for middle school, and 16 percent indicated their district had begun RTI implementation in high school. Some districts have policies that specifically defer RTI implementation in higher grades for a few years. As mentioned previously, West Virginia has chosen to implement RTI in a multiyear fashion, emphasizing implementation for elementary schools only in 2009, to be followed the next year by middle schools, and the following year by implementation in secondary schools.

This is not surprising in that almost all the literature to date on RTI has focused on implementation in primary and elementary general education classes (Bender & Shores, 2007), and this leaves many questions unanswered concerning RTI implementation in middle and secondary classes. While educators across the nation realize that many students in middle and secondary grades struggle in various academic subjects, few proponents of RTI have provided examples of how the RTI process might function within a secondary classroom. Thus, many questions remain on how RTI fits within middle and secondary curriculum.

While several of the previous chapters mentioned the formation of a school-based RTI task force, such a group is even more critical at the middle and secondary levels. Given the wide array of unanswered questions concerning how to implement RTI in these grade levels, having a group of faculty conduct some serious small-group discussions on RTI implementation in the school will be quite advantageous.

Some of these unanswered questions stem from the fundamental differences between middle or secondary classes and elementary classes. Focusing on those differences can shed light on some of the challenges for RTI implementation in middle and secondary schools. Identifying the specific challenges for RTI implementation in departmentalized curricula may, in turn, provide some guidance on how RTI implementation in middle and secondary schools might proceed. While it is clear that middle and secondary school faculty across the nation are "feeling their way" through the RTI process, even more so than their elementary school colleagues, this chapter provides many more questions overall than concrete answers.

First, this chapter will present a brief discussion of the difference between elementary and departmentalized middle/secondary school programming, followed by a series of questions and specific recommendations on how to implement RTI in a departmentalized program. Next, several innovative ideas on middle secondary programming will be presented that should facilitate implementation of RTI in middle and high school classes. Finally, a case study of RTI in a secondary subject area will show one example of how a departmentalized middle school can conduct response to intervention.

The Departmentalized School

In the United States, almost all school districts have implemented an educational system focused on differentiating middle and high school programs from elementary programs. For example, from grade 6 and up in most school districts, students participate in a departmentalized curriculum in which the students switch classes and teachers for different subjects throughout the school day based on the subject-area expertise of the teachers in those grade levels. Given this departmentalization of curricular content in middle and high schools, there are significant differences between elementary grade and departmentalized school programs (Nunley, 2006). Several of these differences are presented in table 6.1, and each is briefly discussed. Traditionally, the primary/elementary grades have been considered to include kindergarten through grade 5, middle schools have included teachers in grades 6 through 8, and high schools have included grades 9 through 12. While wide variations are common depending on the district, the availability of appropriate building space, and a variety of other factors, I will discuss the departmentalized school curriculum with those general grade levels in mind.

Table 6.1 Differences Between Elementary Education and Departmentalized Secondary Schools

1.	The number of students taught each day increases in departmentalized schools.
2.	The greater number of students results in teachers in departmentalized schools not getting to know their students quite as quickly, and perhaps not quite as well.
3.	Curricula changes from elementary to secondary schools.
4.	More independence and educational maturity are required of students in secondary programs.

More Students

The first difference between elementary and departmentalized instruction involves the number of students a teacher sees each day. In schools that offer departmentalized curricula, a single teacher may have anywhere from five to seven different classes of students each day, depending on the length of the instructional period at that school. With 20 to 30 students in each class, it is clear that some middle and high school teachers may deal with between 75 and 220 students per day (Nunley, 2006)!

In that context, the number of students dealt with by a single general educator in middle and secondary schools is almost overpowering, and putting the small-group and/or individualized instruction requirements of the RTI process into that mix of teaching responsibilities may make RTI seem overwhelming. Having addressed this issue in a number of workshops around the nation, with faculty in various middle and secondary subject areas, I can assure the reader that the uneasiness among secondary educators concerning RTI is both profound and quite understandable.

Less Knowledge of Individual Student Needs

The numbers hold direct implications for instruction. Most secondary general education teachers will not know or understand the individual learning styles of their pupils as well as perhaps a third-grade teacher who has twenty-two to twenty-five students all day (Nunley, 2006). Thus, teachers in higher grades may not know their students' individual strengths and weaknesses as well as they might like. In addition, teachers in departmentalized schools rarely have the time to talk with other teachers of any particular student to compare notes on effective strategies for that individual.

This is not intended as a criticism of middle and secondary teachers, but rather as a statement of the reality of teaching in departmentalized schools (Nunley, 2006). In most departmentalized schools, the number of students precludes a great deal of these interactions.

Subject-Specific Instruction

Another difference between elementary school and departmentalized grades in middle and high school is the shift in instructional focus. Primary and elementary grades tend to be heavily geared to instruction in basic skill subjects such as reading, writing, and mathematics, since those subjects serve as the basis for instruction in a wide variety of subject content areas later in school. However, this emphasis on basic skills decreases over time, and the curricular emphasis shifts a bit in middle school. In middle and high school, the curriculum is dominated by subject-specific courses (for example, science, mathematics, literature, history, health, and vocational programs), rather than a direct emphasis on basic skills such as reading, writing, or literacy. It is quite common to find middle and secondary schools that offer no single course called "Reading," though teachers are encouraged to emphasize reading skills across the curriculum. Writing courses are virtually unknown in secondary schools, and mathematics becomes specialized into a variety of diverse areas (for example, geometry, algebra, and calculus), rather than the more skill-oriented general mathematics courses that characterize elementary grade mathematics. These differences raise questions on RTI implementation that I've heard in various workshops around the nation:

▶ Should RTI procedures in middle and secondary school address problems in basic skills (for example, reading or writing), even though those students may not be taking a reading class?

▶ Will RTI procedures in middle and high school emphasize specific subject-area content?

▶ How can I do repeated assessment performance monitoring when my content changes from one instructional unit to another?

▶ How can I implement a Tier 2 intervention for a small number of students during forty-five minutes of a fifty-five-minute period?

As these questions suggest, many issues have yet to be adequately addressed. Furthermore, while teachers in middle and secondary schools are specialized in various subject-area content fields and are thus able to offer highly challenging curricular content, some teachers are less well prepared to provide instruction for students struggling in reading or basic math or writing skills. Therefore, the preceding questions result in further questions, such as the following:

▶ Who will administer a Tier 2 reading intervention for a high school student who doesn't have a reading class?

Again, this is not a criticism of middle and secondary teachers, but rather a summation of where schools stand today. Middle and secondary teachers are very well prepared in their subject areas, but have only limited courses in reading or math instruction. In fact, teacher preparation programs around the nation were founded on the assumption that students have mastered basic skills before reaching higher-level subjects, and while there have been modifications in teacher preparation for secondary teachers (for example, reading in the content area courses has been added), unfortunately, this overall assumption has not yet changed. Thus, teaching of basic skills within subject areas has not been heavily emphasized, at least not until fairly recently.

Assumption of Student Maturity

Finally, as students reach middle and secondary grade levels, the students are presumed to be capable of taking more responsibility for themselves and their work. For example, no educator would assume that kindergarten children could manage their books in a hallway locker and change classes six or seven times per day since those students do not have the level of maturity for those school expectations. However, such self-management behavior is regularly expected of students in middle and high school. Clearly, the students in those middle and secondary grades are expected to have reached a point of maturity where such self-management is the norm. This begs the next question:

▶ How do we manage an RTI for middle or secondary students who do not have the level of maturity expected of students that age?

As shown in this section, middle and secondary educators have raised many questions that have yet to be answered. In fact, federal policy does not provide much guidance on several of these questions, nor do most state websites on RTI (Berkeley et al., 2009). In the future, the answers to most of these will stem either from state departments of education or from local district policies. Every teacher should check those sources for policies on these questions. To date, any answers to these questions must be tentative, but at the very least, some possible answers can be articulated, and the advantages and/or implications of the various RTI options presented.

> The answers to many questions on RTI implementation in middle and secondary grades will either stem from state departments of education or local district policies, and every teacher is strongly encouraged to check those sources for local policy on these questions.

A Self-Report Needs Assessment

As these questions indicate, a number of serious issues are involved in implementation of RTI in middle and secondary schools. Given that RTI has been more heavily emphasized in lower grades, it's uncertain how much middle and secondary school faculty actually *know* about RTI overall, and this is where proponents of RTI procedures must start.

Earlier in this book, I provided a needs assessment that is intended to provide initial information on what teachers currently understand about the overall RTI process. While many primary and elementary faculty may have been exposed to such needs assessments previously, some middle and secondary teachers have not. As districts move into implementation of RTI across the middle and secondary grade levels, a similar needs assessment assists administrators and teachers. At a minimum, such a self-report needs assessment documents what the faculty currently knows about RTI overall and the issues of RTI implementation in the middle and secondary grades. The self-report needs assessment presented in chapter 1 has been adapted for middle and secondary grades in table 6.2 (page 144; see page 199 for a reproducible form, or visit **go.solution-tree.com/rti** to download it).

Table 6.2 Response to Intervention Self-Report Needs Assessment for Content-Area Teachers of Middle and Secondary Grades

Circle one numeral for each descriptive indicator.					
1 = I have little knowledge and want additional in-service on this.					
2 = I have some knowledge, but some additional in-service will be helpful.					
3 = I have a good understanding of this, but need to put this into practice this year.					
4 = I have complete understanding and have reached proficiency at this practice.					
N/A = Not applicable for our state, school, or district.					
General Understanding of RTI in Content Areas					
1. The pyramid of interventions used in our state and district	1	2	3	4	N/A
2. The problem-solving RTI model for our state or district	1	2	3	4	N/A
3. The tiers of intervention required by our school	1	2	3	4	N/A
4. How all teachers have joint responsibility for RTI for all students	1	2	3	4	N/A
5. The intervention timelines for each intervention tier	1	2	3	4	N/A
6. Frequency and intensity of interventions in each tier	1	2	3	4	N/A
7. How to use flexible grouping for Tiers 1 and 2	1	2	3	4	N/A
8. How RTI applies to all students	1	2	3	4	N/A
General Knowledge of Universal Screening and Progress-Monitoring Procedures					
1. The reading screening tests used in our school	1	2	3	4	N/A
2. The assessment of the five components of reading used in our school	1	2	3	4	N/A
3. The math assessments used in our school	1	2	3	4	N/A
4. Behavioral progress-monitoring techniques	1	2	3	4	N/A
5. Progress-monitoring techniques for Tiers 1 and 2	1	2	3	4	N/A
6. Data-gathering procedures for my subject for RTI	1	2	3	4	N/A
7. Progress-monitoring procedures in content areas	1	2	3	4	N/A
8. The data management system for RTI in our school	1	2	3	4	N/A
Interventions to Facilitate Student Progress					
1. Reading instructional programs used in our school	1	2	3	4	N/A
2. Instructional ideas for reading in content areas	1	2	3	4	N/A
3. Supplemental math programs for RTI used in our school	1	2	3	4	N/A
4. Behavioral interventions used in our school	1	2	3	4	N/A
5. Supplemental subject-area curricula used for RTI	1	2	3	4	N/A
6. How to differentiate instruction in subject-area classes	1	2	3	4	N/A
7. Modified assessment options used in my subject area	1	2	3	4	N/A

My Contributions and Suggestions for RTI in Our School	
1. What instructional modifications would assist struggling students in your content area, and how might those modifications be provided?	
2. How can you modify your instruction to facilitate RTI?	
3. In what RTI areas should we plan further staff development?	
4. What suggestions can you offer for making RTI work better for students in our school?	

As recommended previously, middle and secondary administrators should form an RTI task force to facilitate RTI implementation. Pulling a committee together for this type of system change typically results in increased buy-in from the faculty and can provide an effective basis for RTI implementation. That committee's first step could then be the use of this self-report needs assessment. Administrators and committee members should feel free to adapt this in any reasonable manner that assists them in obtaining the information they need for implementation.

I recommend that middle and secondary administrators begin by forming an RTI task force to facilitate RTI implementation.

Academic Content for a Middle or Secondary Grade RTI Procedure

In discussions with educators across the nation, I've seen considerable uncertainty as to what should be the academic emphasis of RTI procedures in middle and secondary grades. Some educators envision struggling students—first identified in middle school subjects or perhaps even in secondary history or science classes—undertaking Tier 2 and 3 interventions in the area of reading rather than in the subject area. However, others believe some type of RTI in the content (history or science) would be more appropriate. In fact, there are at least three distinct views on what should be the subject content for RTI procedures in middle and secondary grades:

1 RTI procedures should focus on only basic skill deficits since those have traditionally been the basis for special education referrals.

2 RTI procedures should focus on specific content-area instruction with which the student is struggling.

3 RTI procedures may be needed for either basic skills or content, depending on the student.

Basic Skills Only

Because virtually all of the newer literature on RTI has focused on deficits in either basic academic skills (reading, literacy, or math) or on behavior problems, some educators envision middle and secondary RTI procedures that focus exclusively on those areas, since they appear to be the most important threats to long-term success in learning overall. Thus, even if a student's learning problem is first noticed on written work in a seventh-grade health class, an RTI procedure emphasizing reading would be implemented, based on the assumption that inability to succeed in health might be related to an underlying reading problem.

I refer to this as the *basic skills only* position on RTI implementation in middle and secondary schools, and there are several reasons that some educators have adopted this belief or position. First, traditional placement determinations involving special education services have largely depended on a student's academic functioning in basic skills, even in the higher grades. For example, the use of a reading achievement score for a grade 9 student might help document the existence of a learning disability. Thus, there is some comfort in a policy that stipulates that RTI procedures should be undertaken only in the basic skill areas, regardless of whether the student has a course in that area. In fact, survey results from special education administrators have indicated that most RTI procedures to date have been implemented in reading, math, and behavior and not as frequently in the other subject content areas. Only 30 percent of those administrators indicated they had implemented any RTI for writing, only 26 percent indicated RTI implementation in the area of language, and only 19 percent indicated they had implemented RTI procedures in any other subject area (Spectrum K12/CASE, 2008).

Research on how to implement RTI procedures in reading and behavior is relatively plentiful, and as noted in chapter 4, research on RTI procedures in math is forthcoming. Thus, we have a body of research on how to implement RTI in these basic skill academic areas and in the behavioral area since implementation of these procedures in these specific areas is fairly well researched. However, implementation of an RTI in a secondary science course, as one example, would probably overshoot the research base that we have today. For these reasons, some educators have assumed that RTI procedures in all grades will address basic skill deficits, regardless of the student's age, course assignments, or grade placement.

However, the basic skills only policy entails a critically important limitation: it does not really provide any assistance to the student (or to the student's teacher) who is struggling in other areas, such as algebra or tenth-grade science! The proponents of RTI make clear that it is intended to be a function of the entire general education curriculum, and as such, the process simply must provide a mechanism to assist struggling students in a wide number of academic areas across the grade levels (Bender & Shores, 2007). In short, student needs, as documented by student performance data, should be the determining factor, and some students need basic skills interventions, whereas others need interventions in content areas. Thus, I think the assumption that RTI procedures should be implemented exclusively in basic skill areas is neither realistic nor consistent with the overall goals of RTI—identification of all threats to learning and making education more responsive to meet the needs of all students in every area. Still, beyond lists of educational standards in each subject area, federal guidelines and most state guidelines do not give specific guidance on what should be the content of the RTI interventions. Thus, schools and school districts will, in many cases, make these determinations themselves. I anticipate that some districts will invest all of their energy in basic skills interventions, whereas others will choose to implement RTI much more broadly. Broader implementation—in all subject areas, depending on the needs of particular students—is more consistent with the stated goals of the RTI process.

Subject-Area Content

The advantage of using RTI in all curricular areas is that it is a profoundly powerful teaching technique that offers meaningful assistance to struggling students. Administrators should encourage use of the RTI process in all academic areas as well as for behavior change across all grade levels.

> RTI is intended to be a function of the entire general education curriculum, and as such, the RTI process simply must provide a mechanism to assist struggling students in a wide number of academic areas across the grade levels. RTI should be encouraged in all academic areas as well as for behavior change across all grade levels.

Unfortunately, it is easier to state this lofty goal than to attain it, and there are many serious questions concerning how to implement RTI procedures in a subject-area class in middle or high school. For example, as we have seen, RTI is founded on universal screening and repeated assessments for progress monitoring, and neither of these is typically implemented in middle and secondary subject areas. Some states have no universal screening at all in some subject areas (for example, health, social studies, and science), and in those instances, teachers may be using various teacher-made tests or formative assessments. Initiating an RTI in those instances becomes more problematic since no statewide baseline or benchmark data exist to indicate early problems.

Next, the concept of *repeated assessment* doesn't fit very well into many middle and high school subject-area classes. Repeated assessment involves assessments on the same skill content, such as a child's word reading fluency or ability to detect matched initial phoneme sounds. Furthermore, most repeated assessment examples in the RTI literature occur over a period of eight or twelve weeks. However, many measures of academic success remain relevant for a number of weeks, or even years in the primary and elementary grades (for example, the number of words read correctly per minute or the number of correct comprehension questions completed after a reading selection), and this makes repeated assessment over a period of time possible.

In contrast, the subject content in middle and secondary classes changes with every instructional unit (for example, in middle school science, a one-week unit on invertebrates may be followed by a two-week unit on vertebrates). Thus, a *repeated* assessment and weekly monitoring across a six-week time frame for RTI is not as meaningful in many middle and secondary subject areas since the subject content changes during that period.

Of course, teachers can address this issue in several ways. For example, many middle and secondary teachers can and do implement unit tests or perhaps even weekly assessments that generate data on how well a child is doing across several units of instruction. Data from those assessments can certainly be charted and used to discuss a child's performance over time. While these should not be considered "repeated assessments" in the traditional sense, as the subject content changes from unit to unit, charted data from these types of assessments can certainly provide a basis for discussion of a child's long-term academic performance.

> Many middle and secondary teachers can and do implement unit tests, or perhaps weekly assessments, and data from those tests can certainly be charted and used to discuss a child's performance over time.

Another possibility for conducting performance monitoring in middle and secondary subject content involves *precision teaching*. This option is presented in some detail later in the chapter. At this point, suffice it to note that the subject content and repeated assessments that should be the basis for RTI procedures do remain a serious concern for many teachers in middle and secondary schools. Many do not instruct their classes in a manner that lends itself to repeated assessment for performance monitoring, and proponents of RTI should be prepared to address this question with some specific suggestions and recommendations such as those presented herein.

Basic Skills and Subject-Area Content

When discussing RTI procedures with middle and secondary educators, I tend to encourage implementation of a combination of subject-area content and basic skill content, given a standard three-tier model such as that implemented in most states: appropriate subject-area content in Tier 1 and/or Tier 2, and relevant basic skill deficits in either Tier 2 or Tier 3.

Given a standard three-tier model, I recommend emphasis on subject-area content in the first or perhaps the first and second tier of the process, and then an increased emphasis on the underlying basic skill deficit in Tier 2 or 3.

This combination allows a subject-area teacher to implement the first tiers of an RTI procedure in the classroom based on content; should those instructional interventions not be effective, the student support team at the school can then take the lead in implementing a highly focused intervention targeted toward a basic skill that the committee believes may underlie the failure to perform in the general education class. In fact, I have noted that the most common approach to RTI among middle and secondary schools seems to be implementation of a combination approach, with interventions offered in both content classes and in basic skill areas. Such RTI efforts typically stress high quality instruction in Tier 1, coupled with tutoring in the general education class when appropriate. In conjunction with that Tier 1 effort, most of these schools are likewise stressing Tier 2 and 3 interventions in basic areas such as reading and mathematics. Of course, this is merely my observation on what middle and secondary schools are actually doing, since no research on implementation of RTI specifically in middle or secondary schools is currently available. A case study that involves this combined approach is presented later in this chapter.

First, however, we'll explore interventions for Tier 1 general education classes in middle and secondary schools. While all levels of intervention are critical to the overall RTI process, the general education teacher has more direct control on the instruction offered in Tier 1, and making certain that the Tier 1 instruction is appropriate should be the first concern of every general education teacher. Again, the middle and secondary schools in which I've worked with faculty on RTI implementation have focused primarily on providing robust Tier 1 instruction, supplemented with basic skills intervention classes for Tiers 2 and 3. The next section of this chapter presents several content-rich instructional interventions that strengthen the first tier of the RTI pyramid for the middle school and secondary content areas.

Tier 1 Instructional Interventions for Middle and Secondary Schools

Whether or not middle and secondary schools choose to implement the combined content and basic skill RTI option described earlier, the Tier 1 and Tier 2 interventions conducted by general education teachers will be critical in the RTI process. In fact, Tier 1 instructional options are crucially important for a variety of reasons in this process.

While the variety of instructional options is almost endless, middle and secondary school faculty should consider several instructional innovations, including differentiating instruction, scheduling an intervention period, precision teaching, and implementing a *Learning Strategies Curriculum*. A full description of these instructional options is beyond the scope of this text, but a brief description of each will suggest ways they facilitate the RTI process in departmentalized middle and secondary schools.

Differentiated Instruction

Differentiated instruction involves presentation of curricular content in a wider variety of methods that are consistent with current understandings of student learning styles and the emerging research on brain functioning in various learning environments (Bender, 2008; Nunley, 2006). The methods that characterize a differentiated instructional model can be as varied as small-group instruction aimed at particular learning styles, focused short- or long-term group projects, or cooperative learning strategies (Bender, 2008; Slavin, Chamberlain, & Daniels, 2007). Effective differentiation can provide a strong opportunity for learning in the middle and secondary general education classroom and should be considered absolutely critical for Tier 1 instruction. In fact, various state RTI models (for example, Georgia) stipulate differentiated instruction as one of the fundamental aspects of Tier 1 instructional interventions.

By Content

Tomlinson first described differentiation as variations in the learning content, the learning process, and the learning products (Tomlinson, 1999) that are intended to accommodate the learning differences presented by students in today's classrooms. Differentiating by learning content involves consideration of the content students are expected to master. While variations in content should not result in a "watered down" curriculum that is less rich in global understandings overall, students will master varying content foci depending on their ability level, previous knowledge, and so on. Overall, however, the curriculum goals, broad conceptual understandings, and essential questions within the content should remain consistent for all students (Tomlinson & McTighe, 2006).

> Differentiation provides a strong opportunity for learning in middle and secondary general education classrooms and should be considered absolutely critical for Tier 1 instruction.

By Learning Process

Differentiating by learning process acknowledges that students learn in a variety of ways based on natural differences in learning styles. Some students excel when small-group instruction encourages social interaction, student questioning, and peer support, whereas other students learn by "doing," which may include bodily kinesthetic movement activities. While teachers in kindergarten and the lower grades frequently use movement to teach content, this type of instruction is much more rare in middle and secondary classes, even though the recent research on brain functioning suggests that movement is a critically important learning tool for all ages (Sousa, 2005).

Here's one example of how to use movement to teach secondary content in a high school biology class. The teacher introduces a unit of instruction on the *cell* and begins with an overhead of the cell wall that includes several arrows that appear to "attack" the cell, but are repelled by the cell wall. These are labeled *bacteria* since one function of the cell is to keep out bacteria. Another set of arrows that successfully puncture the cell wall are labeled *food enzymes*, since another function of the cell wall is to let in food enzymes.

After a quick discussion of the diagram, the teacher points to five students and has them "become a cell wall" by locking elbows as they stand in a circle. The teacher then chooses another student to be bacteria and has that student "attack" the cell by tickling and trying to get into the cell. The teacher tells the "cell wall" students to keep out that bacteria cell. Next, the teacher identifies another student to become the food enzyme and try to get into the cell by tickling. The teacher tells the "cell wall," "Make the food enzyme work for it, but then let in that student, just like a cell wall does."

After a few seconds of fun, the bacterium is outside the cell wall and the food enzyme is inside. The teacher then verbally rehearses with the students by asking, "What does a cell wall do with bacteria?" and the class chants, "Keeps it out!" The teacher then asks, "What does a cell wall do with food enzymes?" The class responds, "Lets it in!" The teacher repeats those questions several times, pretending not to hear the answer.

The students clearly enjoy the activity, and the teacher realizes she has a winner of a teaching idea! That teacher can use the same example daily throughout a two-week unit. The teacher varies the students in these roles from day to day and also modifies the movement activity by changing it from cell wall to cell membrane and adding a nucleus. The lesson is repeated frequently using a fun movement to illustrate its content, and this probably results in long-term retention. Teachers should plan and repeatedly use a fun, content-based movement of this nature to illustrate the "essence" of a lesson during each unit of instruction.

By Learning Product

Differentiation by learning product involves *variations in the products* that indicate mastery of knowledge (Tomlinson & McTighe, 2006). For example, a wide variety of assessments can illustrate a student's understanding of critical content in an instructional unit, and some types of assessments provide a richer opportunity for some students. Students who learn best through experiential-based instructional activities may be at a significant disadvantage when confronted by a written unit test. Most proponents recommend an array of assessment options that emphasize authentic learning experiences such as rubric-based performance tasks, product demonstrations and explanations, and portfolio-based assessment. All of these types of assessments fit easily within the RTI paradigm.

A wide number of proponents have now recommended differentiated instruction for middle and secondary grades (Bender, 2008; Gregory & Kuzmich, 2005; Nunley, 2006). In fact, the concept of differentiation is particularly applicable in middle and secondary grades since instruction in those grades has traditionally involved somewhat less variance in instructional strategies overall (Nunley, 2006). Differentiated instruction can interface with curriculum design to result in a wide variety of instructional activities for middle and secondary grades (Tomlinson & McTighe, 2006). Furthermore, differentiated instruction incorporates much of the recently developed understanding of how adolescent brains function, and thus strategies derived from this perspective typically result in broader and deeper understandings. While research on differentiation and brain compatible learning in middle and secondary grades is limited, some research has documented efficacy of these tactics in lower grades.

King and Gurian (2006), as one example, reported on a school in Colorado in which young boys were achieving considerably less well than young girls. The faculty became concerned, and over the course of a year, they made a number of curricular modifications based on the research on how brains of males function. To develop "boy-friendly" classrooms, the faculty increased experiential and kinesthetic learning opportunities, since boys benefit from those types of activities. Faculty learned to develop and more frequently employ visual representations, since male brains are somewhat more adapted to that type of learning presentation than female brains. As a result of these and other differentiated brain-friendly instructional techniques, the achievement of the males in that particular school increased by 24 percent in reading and writing in one year.

> As a result of differentiated brain-friendly instructional techniques, the reading and writing achievement of males in one school in Colorado increased by 24 percent in one year!

A full discussion of differentiated instruction and brain compatible teaching is beyond the scope of this text (see Bender, 2008; Sousa, 2009), but the acronym SHEMR (songs/ chants, humor, emotion, movement, and repetition) provides a quick summation of brain compatible instructional tactics (Bender, 2009). This is presented in table 6.3. Middle and secondary teachers should consider the use of the activities represented by SHEMR in each unit of instruction during the year. Furthermore, the students themselves in those grades can often be used to develop the teaching tactics suggested by the ideas in SHEMR. For example, in a given unit, the teacher might present ten or twelve critical points that form the basis of the unit and have the students develop a song to teach those points, or a movement to illustrate them.

Table 6.3 SHEMR: Brain-Compatible Teaching Techniques

SHEMR is an acronym that represents brain-compatible instructional activities that have been shown to be highly effective in focusing students on the essential components of the learning content and increasing retention (Bender, 2009). Use of one type of each of these activities is highly recommended in each instructional unit in every middle and secondary school subject.	
S: Songs/chants	Use of songs to summarize content, coupled with repetition of the song (or chant), is likely to focus students on critical aspects of the content and result in longer retention of the material. While this idea has been used extensively in lower grades (for example, the ABC song), it works just as well in middle and secondary grades. Songs developed by students that summarize six to eight critical concepts sung daily during a ten-day unit will help students recall that content.
H: Humor	Using humor to help students memorize factual content will increase retention since humor results in increased brain production of several neurotransmitters associated with happiness and well-being. Jokes that summarize important concepts should be told and discussed in each unit. Discuss in terms of "Why is that funny?" or "Is that funny to all characters in our unit?" Humor also creates a more positive class climate, and students that enjoy being in class will more actively participate.
E: Emotion	Emotion is highly related to learning; students will learn more readily information that has an emotional "hook." Sensory information is deemed to be important for notice by the brain, based in part on emotional import, so hooking content with an emotional story is likely to increase both attention and retention. As one example, having a family member talk about family stories of the civil rights movement can make that content much more emotionally charged for students.
M: Movement	Movement activates the brain in many ways and should be used to represent content across the grade levels. One movement should be created for each instructional unit that emphasizes the critical big ideas. While some teachers may think this a bit "juvenile" for middle or high school, the students typically love it after they have been exposed to it for a while.
R: Repetition	Repetition increases learning, and when the repetition activates multiple brain areas, as do these activities summarized by SHEMR, the repetition is even more effective. SHEMR activities should be repeated daily in the instructional unit.

Differentiation, brain compatible instruction, and the RTI process are, to a large degree, mutually supportive at the Tier 1 level. First, the RTI process is absolutely dependent on provision of effective instruction at every tier in the pyramid, but perhaps most at Tier 1. To emphasize the critical importance of effective instruction in Tier 1, many RTI models stipulate using a wide variety of instructional activities at that level specifically to address the varied needs of students. Clearly, differentiated instruction, addressing the unique needs of the various learners in the class based on their individual learning styles, is highly effective as a Tier 1 instructional model, and for that reason, middle and secondary teachers across the nation have begun to adopt this instructional approach in subject content areas.

Next, in differentiated classes, many of the concerns with RTI implementation become less troublesome. For example, in differentiated classes, it is somewhat easier to make time for the type of small-group instruction required for a Tier 2 intervention since differentiated classes tend to feature small-group instruction very frequently anyway (Bender, 2008).

Differentiation at the middle and secondary school levels, then, should be viewed as a critically important aspect of the RTI process. Teachers across the nation are ramping up their instruction to include differentiated instructional tactics and activities such as those described here. Simply put, differentiation provides the best possible basis for RTI procedures at Tier 1, and for that reason, a number of proponents have recommended differentiated instructional tactics for the middle and secondary grades (Bender, 2008; Gregory & Kuzmich, 2005; Nunley, 2006). These sources can greatly assist middle and secondary teachers in general education prepare for RTI.

> Differentiation at the middle and secondary school levels should be viewed as a critically important aspect of the RTI process, and teachers across the nation are responding by ramping up their instruction to include differentiated instructional tactics and activities.

Intervention Periods

The possibility of scheduling an intervention period during which various Tier 2 and Tier 3 instructional interventions take place was initially discussed in chapter 3, which addressed the issue of teacher time for these interventions; using a scheduled intervention period for various tiers of instruction certainly assists in that concern. However, the time issue is perhaps more of a concern in departmentalized schools in which teachers face many students daily. While some recommendations on using a specified intervention period were made earlier, particular aspects of this concept apply more directly to middle and secondary schools.

One option for using an intervention period to provide Tier 2 or Tier 3 interventions involves scheduling classes. Whereas elementary schools do not "schedule" classes on a period-by-period basis, departmentalized schools do, and that makes the intervention period an option of choice for middle and secondary programs. In fact, many middle and secondary schools are now scheduling RTI intervention periods whose duration ranges from one grading period to a semester or half year.

> Whereas elementary schools do not "schedule" classes on a period-by-period basis, departmentalized schools do, and that makes the intervention period an option of choice for middle and secondary programs.

For example, some secondary schools schedule classes on a semester basis, rather than exclusively year-long classes, and that flexibility could be applied in the RTI process. Classes such as driver's education, choir, chamber music, or fine arts classes are sometimes scheduled for only one grading period. Using those scheduled classes as a model, an intervention class could be scheduled to allow for delivery of Tier 2 and/or Tier 3 interventions. I've worked with several middle schools in which the faculty had determined to implement Tier 2 and Tier 3 interventions using an instructional intervention period.

Students in those intervention classes should, of course, receive either small-group or totally individualized instruction specifically targeted to their exact need, and for that reason, intervention classes that incorporate the use of technology-based instruction are becoming more frequent. Students may begin an intervention class on the first day of any grading period or even in the middle of a grading period. Some students need more intensive instruction for a longer period of time, and those students should merely continue in that intervention class for another grading period. In terms of instructional content, teachers in the intervention classes could offer either basic skill instruction in content area reading or math or content-based instruction in specific subject areas, depending on the teacher's training and instructional certification. Of course, those teachers should be specifically trained on performance-monitoring techniques that include weekly assessment for all students. Clearly, the intervention period—scheduled on a student-by-student basis for one or more grading periods—should be considered in departmentalized schools.

Precision Teaching

Precision teaching has been used to facilitate effective instructional interventions and repeated performance-monitoring assessments of students in middle and secondary content classes during the RTI process (Bender, 2008; Bender & Shores, 2007). Precision teaching originated in behavioral psychology several decades ago and has subsequently been applied in various areas of education (Lindsley, 1971; White, 1986).

It emphasizes accurate, repeated measurement of highly defined and measurable academic behaviors, frequent modification of instruction based on the actual data resulting from student performance, and presentation of those assessment data in charted form (Lindsley, 1990, 1992). This concept became one basis for the later concept of curriculum-based measurement, and subsequently, RTI. While implementation of the principles of precision teaching has been growing, the term *precision teaching* has not been widely used. However, many of these principles are currently embodied in curriculum-based measurement procedures that, during the last thirty years, have been widely studied, and the research has shown these methods to be effective (Deno, 2003). For that reason, many curricula published today employ the concept of daily performance monitoring for academic behaviors and thus are rooted in precision teaching. This includes several curricula discussed in this book, such as the *Learning Strategies Curriculum* and *Read Naturally*.

Case Study: A Precision-Teaching Tier 1 Intervention

Here is an example of how to apply precision teaching in a Tier 1 RTI procedure in a high school classroom. Ms. Dillsworth noted in her tenth-grade U.S. history class that Enrico was having consistent difficulty with vocabulary terms from one unit to the next. While he had never been a stellar student, he had also never failed a grade, and a quick review of his previous grades indicated only infrequent failures in various courses. Ms. Dillsworth was unsure if Enrico merely needed more intensive instructional assistance on vocabulary or if he had some type of underlying learning difficulty or perhaps a learning disability in decoding that could account for his problems learning new vocabulary. She believed that he might have some difficulty attacking and decoding multisyllabic terms, which constituted the majority of the vocabulary terms in each unit. She decided to implement a precision-teaching project in her tenth-grade history class to see how Enrico responded to more intensive instruction on vocabulary.

As a first step, Ms. Dillsworth selected an instructional method to provide more intensive vocabulary instruction for the entire class; she chose to use graphic organizers to emphasize vocabulary. Graphic organizers provide an excellent way to present not only factual material but also relationships and broad concepts (Bulgren, Deshler, & Lenz, 2007; Lovitt & Horton, 1994), and can highlight and emphasize vocabulary terms representing these facts and concepts. She found that she could depict all of the fifteen vocabulary terms on only two graphic organizers for her next unit of instruction, and after providing these to the class, she required students to complete those organizers as class progressed each day. When a vocabulary term came up in class activities such as class discussion, video, or role-play, she reminded the class to look at their two graphic organizers, find that term, and note the pronunciation and the definition. She then rediscussed the term, its definition, and the broader concept it represented. Sometimes she would call on class members to lead that brief discussion. Thus, she was confident that she was presenting more intensive work on specific vocabulary terms and the underlying concepts than she had previously.

Next, Ms. Dillsworth had to develop a daily academic measure that was directly tied to the understanding of these vocabulary terms. Because every unit involved twelve to fifteen new vocabulary terms, she merely developed a fill-in-the-blank sheet that included the terms and their definitions for a unit on the Federalist period in U.S. history. In her class, she was not so much concerned with exact spelling of the terms, but students did need to know their pronunciation and definitions (for example, *federalism*, *constitution*, *presidency*, *national bank*, *bill of rights*, and *reserved powers*). On that worksheet, she wrote the definitions and had the students fill in the blanks with the appropriate terms.

To get a sense of Enrico's daily performance, Ms. Dillsworth decided to use that same fill-in-the-blank sheet every day during the twelve-day instructional unit. After some consideration, she reasoned that such an activity would be beneficial for the entire class. First, she built the unit around those vocabulary terms and the concepts they represented; thus, that content was the "essence" of the instructional unit and should be stressed frequently. Next, on the first day of the unit, even the brightest students only got four or five of those terms correct since the other terms had not been introduced yet. Thus, she gave the worksheet to the class at the end of the period on the first day and told them,

> "Spend the last ten minutes today answering these questions. In each case, everyone in the class should say the term out loud (using a whisper!) and then fill in the blank. I don't expect you to get them all correct since we haven't covered some of the terms, but you'll have another chance tomorrow!"

Of course, some students got more correct than others, but she merely collected the papers from the class and noted how many Enrico and the other students had gotten correct. She created a daily performance chart to show his progress and also charted the progress of one of the "average" students in the class for comparison purposes.

Ms. Dillsworth anticipated that some students would quickly "top out" on the worksheet—that they would be achieving more than 90 percent within the first week, since they would have read the appropriate chapter by then and should have picked up most of the terms. Once any student hit a score of 100 for two consecutive days, that student did not have to complete the vocabulary worksheet any longer. She provided an alternative assignment for the last ten minutes of class for that group of students. However, most of the class continued to complete that worksheet daily, and for those students, the repetition of those terms, their definitions, and the concepts they represented was very effective instruction.

By the end of the twelve-day instructional unit, Ms. Dillsworth had generated the following information. First, most of her class did learn almost all of the vocabulary terms over a period of seven or eight days. By the end of the instructional unit, only six students were still completing the vocabulary sheet. These conclusions demonstrated for Ms. Dillsworth that her newly devised instructional method using graphic organizers and a daily performance-monitoring worksheet was helping many class members learn the vocabulary. Moreover, Ms. Dillsworth was able to collect data on how Enrico responded to this more intensive level of vocabulary instruction, as presented in figure 6.1.

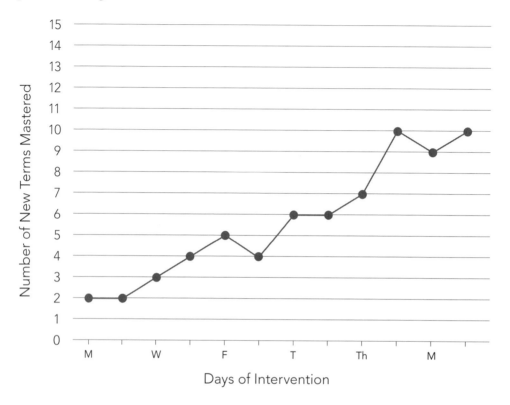

Figure 6.1 Enrico's precision-teaching Tier 1 performance data: mastery of vocabulary.

In this example, the data indicated that with more intensive instruction, Enrico could master content vocabulary, though it took him a bit longer than others. These data indicate that he had not mastered all of the important vocabulary terms by the end of the instructional unit, and thus, there is a serious question as to his capability for learning new vocabulary in secondary content area classes.

Educators should consider several points, given these data. First, while the data show Enrico can learn, they also suggest that he will not keep up with his peers in learning new vocabulary since he did not master all of the specific vocabulary during this unit. Thus, the data are open to interpretation; in short, do they suggest the possibility of a learning disability or not? When Ms. Dillsworth presented these data to the student support team, that team could make a number of recommendations, such as:

1   That Ms. Dillsworth continue this level of intensive instruction on vocabulary in the next unit

2   That she try another instructional approach that may be more effective than the use of graphic organizers, while continuing to monitor Enrico's performance daily

3   That Enrico's other teachers check his mastery of vocabulary in their classes

4   That Enrico receive increased support in the general education class for vocabulary work, perhaps using an inclusion (that is, special education) teacher once or twice per week to work with him specifically on vocabulary

5   That the school psychologist or speech pathologist consider working with Enrico to conduct a Tier 2 instructional intervention, or perhaps even determine if an underlying ability deficit exists in phonological understanding that suggests a learning disability

Of course, the last possibility brings up several additional questions. While Ms. Dillsworth considered this brief precision-teaching intervention to be a Tier 1 intervention when she began, it might also be considered a Tier 2 intervention since it involved (1) increased intensity of vocabulary instruction and (2) increased performance monitoring directly targeted at Enrico. Furthermore, while this was a relatively brief intervention (lasting just more than two weeks), it produced considerable data on how Enrico responds to instruction. With twelve data points in this twelve-day intervention project (fig. 6.1), the teacher has more quality data than she could collect through repeated assessment every other week for a twelve-week intervention. More data points allow for a more refined interpretation of how Enrico responded to instruction. While I do not recommend basing long-term eligibility decisions on only twelve days of intervention data, clearly, such data can serve as one intervention tier and thus can be used as one basis for such a determination, when coupled with data from another intervention.

> While I do not recommend basing long-term eligibility decisions on only twelve days of intervention data, clearly such data can serve as one basis for educational decisions, when combined with data from another intervention and considered by the eligibility team.

In summary, research has documented the technical adequacy of this type of progress monitoring as well as the efficiency of precision teaching in middle and secondary classroom settings (Lindsley, 1992; Deno, 2003; D. Fuchs & Fuchs, 2005; White, 1986). Furthermore, I recently had the opportunity to directly observe the exact precision-teaching intervention described here in a high school social studies class, and the students in that class responded quite positively to that learning experience. For purposes of RTI implementation, precision teaching, as embodied in the current emphasis on curriculum-based measurement, is an excellent option for appropriately monitoring a student's response to interventions in middle and secondary subject content classes (Bender & Shores, 2007)—not to mention the fact that this is an excellent instructional technique for all students in the general education class.

The Learning Strategies Curriculum

When considering the types of curricular content that will serve as the basis for RTI procedures, one option is implementation of cognitive strategy instruction. *Cognitive strategy instruction* is designed to provide students with the cognitive steps needed to complete various types of academic tasks. The literature uses various terms to represent this instructional approach, including *metacognitive instruction, learning strategies*, and *cognitive instruction*, and research on cognitive strategy instruction has shown the efficacy of this instructional approach (Deshler, 2006; Lenz, 2006; Montague, 2008).

One middle and secondary curriculum that embodies this instructional approach is the *Learning Strategies Curriculum,* which was originally developed by Don Deshler and his colleagues at the University of Kansas (Bulgren et al., 2007; Clark, Deshler, Schumaker, Alley, & Warner, 1984; Deshler, 2006; Deshler et al., 2001; Lenz, 2006). This curriculum was developed to assist struggling students in general education classes in the secondary grades and has also been implemented with middle school students with considerable success (Deshler, 2006).

In consideration of the types of skills struggling students need to have in order to succeed in subject content classes, a variety of skills were identified and then a series of instructional activities were developed as structured "learning strategies." These skills included a variety of tasks that students needed in many middle and secondary subject-area courses, including the following:

- ▶ Comprehending subject matter
- ▶ Checking written paragraphs for errors
- ▶ Writing research papers and themes
- ▶ Self-questioning during a reading selection
- ▶ Word identification/word attack skills
- ▶ Test-taking skills
- ▶ Searching for answers in text material
- ▶ Interpreting pictures in text
- ▶ Using visual imagery to improve comprehension

As this list indicates, these skills are not related to any particular content area, yet are essential in many if not all middle and secondary content area classes. Mastery of strategies for these tasks does result in improvement in subject-area classes for struggling learners (Clark et al., 1984; Deshler et al., 2001; Lenz, 2006). Furthermore, learning these strategies affects all subsequent courses a student takes; once a student learns the skills associated with checking and editing a paragraph he or she has written, or word decoding for multisyllabic vocabulary terms, that strategy is applicable throughout the student's academic life. The universal application of the strategies makes this curriculum very appropriate for implementation within an RTI process.

The curriculum is based on identifying specific academic tasks that facilitate learning in a variety of different activities such as those in the preceding list, and then designing a specific strategy that helps students plan and complete the task (Deshler, 2006). These strategies are typically represented by an acronym. For example, self-checking one's written paragraphs is required for success in many subject areas in middle and secondary school, and teaching that specific skill can result in higher student achievement in almost any school subject. The learning strategy COPS facilitates this task (Clark et al., 1984) by reminding students of the steps they must complete to check their work:

- ▶ Capitalization—Check first word in each sentence/proper nouns.

- ▶ Overall appearance—Are erasures clean? Is paragraph neat?

- ▶ Punctuation—Check all punctuation for each sentence and quotes.

- ▶ Spelling—Check spelling of vocabulary and unknown words.

Proponents of the *Learning Strategies Curriculum* developed an instructional procedure involving multiple instructional steps, lasting from pretest and initial student buy-in through generalization. Students practice this (or any other) particular learning strategy daily, over an extended period ranging from twenty-five to forty-five days (see Bender, 2008, pp. 94–105, for an extended description of these steps). Each day, students are given an assignment and instructed to use the COPS strategy to check their work. In fact, most of the strategies in this curriculum result in a daily assessment that could serve as a daily performance-monitoring measure for the RTI process.

> The *Learning Strategies Curriculum* results in a daily assessment that could serve as a daily performance-monitoring measure for the RTI process.

Many learning strategies have emerged during the years, and while many of these have their roots in the work cited earlier, others have been developed by other researchers. For example, use of graphic organizers (Horton, Lovitt, & Bergerud, 1990; Lovitt & Horton, 1994) helps cognitively focus the student's attention in secondary content areas. These organizers have been shown to be quite effective in assisting struggling students in history and science in both the middle and secondary grade classes. Table 6.4 (page 162) presents several research-proven learning strategies that can assist students in middle and secondary grades.

These strategies are adapted from a variety of sources in the literature (Bender, 2008; Clark et al., 1984; Deshler, 2006; Deshler et al., 2001; Lenz, 2006). Training on implementation of the *Learning Strategies Curriculum* is recommended and is currently available through the Learning Strategies Institute at the University of Kansas.

Table 6.4 Several Common Learning Strategies

RAP *(a reading comprehension strategy)*	**AIDE** *(a strategy for picture interpretation in a subject-area text)*
R: Read the paragraph.	A: Look for *action* in the picture.
A: Ask questions about content.	I: Guess the main *idea*.
P: Paraphrase the content.	D: Describe picture *details*.
	E: Read the *explanation*.
RIDER *(a visual imagery strategy for paragraph comprehension)*	**SCORE A** *(a strategy for writing a research paper)*
R: Read the first or next sentence.	S: Select a subject.
I: Imagine a picture of it in your mind.	C: Create categories.
D: Describe how the new image differs from the previous image.	O: Obtain resources and information.
E: Evaluate to see that the image contains everything.	R: Read and take notes.
R: Repeat as you read the next sentence.	E: Evenly organize the information.
	A: Apply the process writing steps—
	• Planning
	• Drafting
	• Revising

Content Enhancement Routines

More recently, proponents of learning strategies instruction have recommended the use of *content enhancement routines* (CERs) to facilitate higher-order thinking among secondary students (Bulgren et al., 2007). CERs are graphic organizers that assist both the teacher and the student in planning the curriculum and instructional activities, and in developing a teacher/pupil partnership for learning. CERs emphasize the important concepts or "big ideas" in an instructional unit and focus on using factual material to address critical questions and make meaningful connections between content. The CERs are also intended to facilitate higher-order thinking skills such as categorizing, comparing/contrasting, seeking cause/effect relationships, and explaining the big ideas to others.

The *Learning Strategies Curriculum*, coupled with the plethora of additional cognitive strategies, can serve as a basis for the RTI process for middle and secondary students struggling with work in the general education classroom. In fact, use of these cognitive strategies addresses several of the questions posed earlier relative to what should be the academic basis for the RTI process and how to frequently monitor performance.

For that reason, one middle school in southeastern Arkansas chose to adopt this curriculum specifically in support of their RTI effort, and one may well anticipate that other schools across the nation will do the same. In that school, the faculty felt that some students who were struggling in various content areas were not having difficulty because of reading or comprehension problems in the specific subject areas, but rather were experiencing problems as a result of the fact that they did not have access to various cognitive strategies that facilitate successful learning in middle school classes. For those students, the *Learning Strategies Curriculum* seemed a perfect fit as a Tier 2 intervention in the RTI process.

For middle and secondary schools that are struggling with questions on how to implement RTI, what should be the academic focus of the RTI process, and most importantly, how the school can best benefit struggling students, I strongly recommend consideration of the *Learning Strategies Curriculum* as one possible Tier 1 or Tier 2 intervention. Research has shown it to be effective in general education, and this will result in increased student success in content areas.

However, one caution is in order. Like every curriculum, the *Learning Strategies Curriculum* is most effective when implemented with fidelity (that is, when used as the authors intended). For that reason, training for this curriculum is required in order to obtain the curriculum itself, and that training is available through the Learning Strategies Institute associated with the University of Kansas.

> I recommend consideration of the learning strategies instructional model as one possible Tier 2 intervention, since research has shown it to be effective, resulting in increased student success in subject content areas.

Case Study: A Secondary Content-Based RTI Procedure

While teaching health for seventh-grade students, Mr. Travis noticed that several students in his class were having difficulty in writing clean, coherent paragraphs, and he wanted to find an instructional technique that would assist those students with that skill. In particular, he was particularly concerned with Alex's written work, which was often subpar and seemed to indicate a lack of ability to formulate a coherent paragraph and to check his work for overall neatness and acceptability before handing in the assignment.

A Seventh-Grade Tier 1 Intervention in Writing Skill

Mr. Travis had previously received training in the *Learning Strategies Curriculum*, and he chose to implement a learning strategy focused on effective writing and self-editing.

To accomplish that instruction during a fifty-five-minute health class that met fourth period each day, he instituted a "health journal" assignment. All students in the class were required to write a journal entry of at least seventy-five words, three times each week in their health journal. The twenty-four students in that class were given fifteen minutes at the end of the period every Monday, Wednesday, and Friday to write and check their journal entry. The "writing checks" were completed by having students exchange papers and check each other's journal entries by circling errors. Then students recopied their work, correcting the errors. While the actual notebook journal included the original draft of each entry, students had to show Mr. Travis that either the revised paragraph or the original journal entry was error free. Students quickly realized the benefit of using the COPS self-checking strategy, before having their work checked by others, since that usually meant that they would not be required to rewrite or recopy their journal entries to produce a clean edited copy.

To make this assignment relevant, Mr. Travis indicated that students were expected to show insight into bodily systems studied in the health class in their journal entry, and also to incorporate a news story related to the topic of the journal entry. Mr. Travis suggested, "Whenever possible, you should journal about comparisons between health topics we are studying now or have previously studied and daily headlines or news stories on the Internet regarding health issues."

This assignment therefore encouraged the higher-order thinking skills such as comparing/contrasting and seeking connections based on the big ideas in the health class. Furthermore, many news organizations have Internet pages specifically dedicated to that topic, so Mr. Travis considered such a requirement very appropriate. While this type of assignment may be more beneficial in health, science, or the social sciences than in drama or art, the main point is that teachers can easily incorporate various learning strategies into ongoing lessons. In fact, most strategies within the *Learning Strategies Curriculum* can be easily implemented in large general education classes and thus can serve as one component of the general education Tier 1 instruction. Clearly, this curriculum should not be relegated exclusively to Tier 2 or Tier 3 interventions within the broader RTI process.

> Many strategies within the *Learning Strategies Curriculum* can be easily implemented in large general education classes, and thus can serve as one component of the general education Tier 1 instruction.

As a performance-monitoring check, Mr. Travis counted the exact number of errors in capitalization, overall appearance, punctuation, and spelling for each paragraph during a five-week period for the targeted students. While all students exchanged their work and checked each other's work, Mr. Travis himself collected these data for three target students and produced a chart based on those data for each student. As the data in figure 6.2 indicate, the intensity of this intervention did result in reducing

Alex's errors somewhat during those five weeks, but Alex's errors in written work were not eliminated. Because of his continuing concern, Mr. Travis shared these data with the student support team in his building and requested assistance.

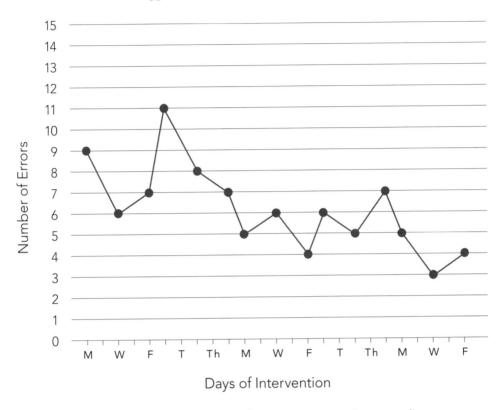

Figure 6.2 Alex's Tier 1 performance data: errors on written work.

Data-Based Decision Making and the Tier 2 Intervention

After the student support team examined the data chart and looked over a couple initial drafts of Alex's journal entries—drafts that included his errors before error correction involving the application of COPS—the team determined that a more intensive tier of instruction specifically focused on writing skills was necessary for Alex. The team encouraged Mr. Travis to continue his work on paragraphs by continuing the journal-based instruction three times each week. In addition, they decided to place Alex in a literacy intervention class, focused on reading and writing skills, that was scheduled to begin within two weeks at the beginning of the next grading period.

A literacy coach at the school, Ms. Appling, was leading instruction in that class and was included on the student support team for this school. She indicated that she would be able to focus all of Alex's work on his writing, emphasizing elimination of errors and improvement of overall paragraph structure. Ms. Appling would emphasize a clear, concise topic sentence and supporting details that add to that topic sentence. Thus, Alex would receive daily writing instruction with Ms. Appling, and she would grade one paragraph written by Alex each day. She would use those daily grades for monitoring Alex's performance. As Alex participated in the literacy intervention class, Ms. Appling collected his daily scores on his written paragraphs and graphed those data for the next five weeks (fig. 6.3). She also graphed the ongoing intervention data from Mr. Travis, as shown in figure 6.4.

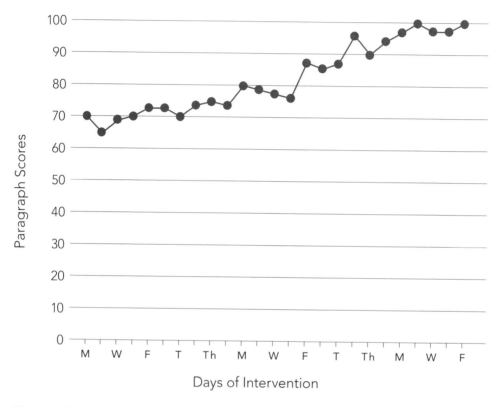

Figure 6.3 Alex's Tier 2 performance data: daily grades on paragraph formation.

This combination of interventions—the COPS editing strategy in Mr. Travis' class and the daily intensive instruction in paragraph structure with Ms. Appling—seemed to work for Alex. As the data indicate, his written work improved nicely. In this case, a third intervention tier was not required since this intensive intervention worked to alleviate Alex's writing problems. Furthermore, at the end of that six-week grading period, Ms. Appling recommended that Alex not be required to continue in the literacy intervention class since his problems seemed to have been alleviated. The student support team accepted that recommendation but did suggest that Mr. Travis continue his work on helping Alex in paragraph writing.

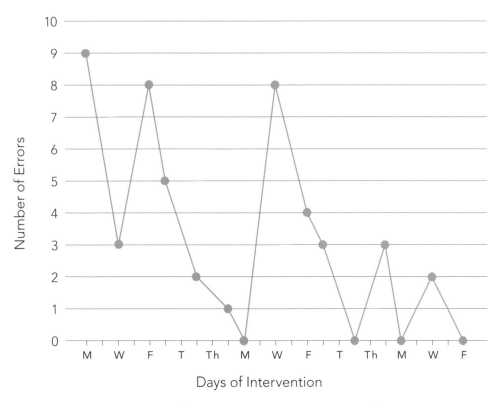

Figure 6.4 Alex's Tier 2 performance data: errors on journal assignments.

In this instance, the advantage of a scheduled intervention period in a departmental-ized school is clear. As shown, when problems cannot be alleviated with additional intensive instruction offered in the general education class, the Tier 1 instruction can be supplemented by general education intervention programs such as the literacy intervention period described here. For many middle and secondary schools, scheduling in an intervention period is one option for providing Tier 2 and Tier 3 interventions.

Having a qualified literacy coach conduct those interventions can be quite advantageous in several ways. Clearly, the students will receive a high-quality inter-vention, and in addition to directly teaching students in specific interventions, the literacy coach could use those intervention periods as demonstration teaching time for all general educators in the school by inviting them to come observe the vari-ous interventions. Then, in some situations, those teachers may continue particular interventions in their own classes.

Conclusion

As indicated throughout this chapter, guidelines for implementation of RTI pro-cedures in middle and secondary schools are considerably less developed than for primary and elementary grades. While some states have chosen to implement RTI in middle and secondary grades immediately, other states have chosen to emphasize primary and elementary grade implementation first, and implement RTI later for middle and secondary schools. While no research data is available on how middle and secondary schools are implementing RTI, the schools I have worked with use a combination of a robust array of instructional procedures in Tier 1, coupled with targeted interventions when possible (perhaps using the various curricula described earlier), and followed by basic skill interventions for Tier 2 and 3 requirements.

With that stated, the RTI process is such a powerful process for assisting students who are struggling in their school work, it simply must become an option for teachers and students at all grade levels. All teachers, regardless of grade level, will be involved in RTI at some point in the near future. This chapter has provided some guidance, or at least some suggestions, for how to implement this process in departmentalized schools. In addition, all educators should turn to their state department of education website for additional guidance, suggestions, and policy requirements.

7

Speech Language Pathologists, Psychologists, and Special Educators: Changing Roles in RTI

As RTI is implemented across the nation, many educators and support personnel such as speech language pathologists (SLPs), school psychologists, and special education teachers will find that their role is changing somewhat (Cummings et al., 2008; Gerber & Klein, 2004). Because of the increased expectations for intensive interventions specifically targeted toward particular deficits, these persons may be expected to become involved in more direct provision of services for students in need, particularly in support of interventions at the Tier 2 and Tier 3 levels. This will vary widely from state to state and district to district, but it is certain that the implementation of RTI will entail shifting responsibilities for many support persons in education, as it will for general education teachers. Therefore, some consideration of these changing roles is certainly warranted in the implementation process, and thoughtful reflection by school faculty can often provide some ideas for how various educators and support personnel can accomplish the various tasks demanded by full implementation of RTI. Again, I recommend that a school-based RTI task force lead the discussions to build consensus on what these changing roles entail.

> As RTI is implemented, many SLPs, psychologists, and special education teachers will find that their role is changing.

SLPs, for example, have long provided direct services to students who struggled with articulation disorders, speech production deficits, phonological manipulation deficits, speech fluency, and overall speech communication skills. Furthermore, research has documented that many of these skills and abilities are directly related to success in early reading (Bishop & Adams, 1990; Gerber & Klein, 2004; Gillon, 2005; Puranik, Petscher, Otaiba, Catts, & Lonigan, 2008; Roth, Troia, Worthington, & Handy, 2006). For this reason, many educators are considering the types of roles that SLPs play in the overall RTI process for both children with specifically diagnosed speech/language needs as well as for students in general education.

Like SLPs, psychologists have traditionally provided some indirect and direct service to students as well as supported general education and special education teachers in a variety of assessment tasks. Typical services include sharing instructional ideas and tactics to assist students, providing and monitoring behavioral improvement plans for students with behavioral challenges, assisting in assessment for developing educational or behavioral plans, and giving assessments for documenting eligibility for special education services. Clearly, several of these roles will change as a result of the implementation of RTI.

For example, in some states, an IQ assessment will no longer be required for students suspected of having a learning disability since it will not be necessary to use an IQ score for a discrepancy calculation (Berkeley et al., 2009). However, in most states, such assessments will continue to be required. Thus, for some psychologists, that aspect of the role may not change substantially, whereas it will for others. In some districts, psychologists play an increasingly large role in implementation of behavior improvement plans and behavior improvement interventions, but that is not the case for all school districts. However, RTI will impact those roles among psychologists, and it will be advantageous for school district personnel to discuss what types of roles school psychologists have in RTI implementation.

Finally, the role of many if not most special educators will change as a result of RTI implementation (Cummings et al., 2008). Of course, the role of this group of educators has been modified many times within recent memory, from teachers in resource or self-contained special education classes to consultants, and further, to inclusive collaborating educators. Given the wide variations from district to district in RTI implementation (Kame'enui, 2007), these roles will certainly be changing again.

This chapter provides an initial discussion of these changing roles. As noted throughout this text, the federal government and most state governments have not provided ironclad stipulations on how implementation of RTI should proceed, so states and local school districts will probably make many of the final decisions on these changing roles. Furthermore, given this lack of solid information, much of this chapter's discussion should be considered quite tentative. However, several considerations can be used as a basis for these discussions. First, some discussion of the types and functions of various interventions within an RTI process is necessary. Next, we consider the changing roles for these educators, based on discussion of their current tasks. Then, an exploration of the types of scientifically validated curricular interventions that might be implemented within an RTI paradigm can shed some light on how various professionals can become more involved in the RTI process. Finally, consideration of the extent of, and types of, intensive interventions that may be required to fully implement RTI can shed light on these potentially changing roles.

> One way to consider what these changing roles involve is to examine the current tasks undertaken by these professionals.

What Functions Can Various RTI Procedures Serve?

One point that should be discussed at the state and school district levels involves the distinction between RTI as a highly effective educational process implemented for all struggling students and RTI as a mechanism to assist in determining eligibility for learning disability services. As stated repeatedly throughout this book, RTI is first and foremost a multitiered intervention process that should be implemented to assist all students struggling in any area of their educational endeavors (D. Fuchs & Deshler, 2007; East, 2006). This includes reading problems, difficulty mastering fractions, problems in learning secondary science vocabulary, problems in behavior, or any other academic or behavioral issue that presents a threat to a child's learning and overall development.

In view of that global general education focus of RTI, it is apparent that the field of education is undergoing a fundamental paradigm shift regarding delivery of effective instruction for all students (Berkeley et al., 2009; East, 2006). Within that broader educational restructuring, the implementation of RTI to assist in documenting learning disabilities is a separate issue altogether (East, 2006), and educators can benefit from a discussion of what types of instructional interventions fit within the broader RTI paradigm, but *not* facilitate decisions regarding educational placement.

In fact, not every RTI procedure provides a solid basis for eligibility determinations for students suspected of having a learning disability since some RTI procedures address educational or maturational problems that have not traditionally been considered symptoms or characteristics of a learning disability. Therefore, it is possible to implement RTI for some educational problems or threats to a child's development that do not affect the question of eligibility for learning disabilities. As one example, when an RTI process is implemented to address acting-out behaviors in the classroom, should a failure to respond to that intervention be a consideration in determination of a learning disability? Perhaps more pertinent to the historical bases of learning disabilities, would a failure to respond to an intervention aimed at curbing off-task or inattentive behaviors be relevant to an eligibility decision for learning disabilities services, given the historical emphasis on attention problems among students with learning disabilities? These questions should be discussed on a district-by-district level and also by individual school faculty working with the school-based RTI task force, while implementation of RTI is ongoing.

> Not every RTI procedure provides a solid basis for eligibility determinations since some RTI procedures address problems that have not been considered as components of a learning disability.

In the context of speech and language problems, it is also quite possible that some RTI procedures will be implemented that address speech or language problems that are unrelated or somewhat less related to a potential learning disability. For example, articulation disorders may be somewhat less related to specific reading disabilities than phonemic manipulation skills such as production of matching initial consonant sounds or final consonant sounds. That begs the question, should interventions addressing articulation disorders be considered appropriate interventions within an RTI process, in the context of eligibility decisions? This question is particularly pertinent, given the relationship to language functioning and learning disabilities, as we consider what role an SLP plays in the overall RTI process in a given school.

Of course, different states and districts make different choices regarding the types of RTI content tasks that are included in an eligibility determination, but having some discussion regarding that question is important for every school district. My recommendation on that question is that any threat to learning that is related to the types of academic delays that have historically been associated with a learning disability should be considered within the context of a discussion of eligibility for learning disabilities. Thus, given that a wide array of speech and language problems are related to later reading or literacy problems (Puranik et al., 2008), most of the interventions undertaken by SLPs should be considered in the RTI process, including eligibility discussions that arise from that process.

With that stated, many types of inattentive behavior are related to the historical emphasis on inattention among students with learning disabilities, and some districts opt to include discussions of behavioral interventions for inattention in the eligibility discussion for learning disabilities. Thus, one question that may arise as districts move into RTI is, should we use RTI procedures aimed at inappropriate behaviors in eligibility determinations?

As stated in chapter 4, the powerful RTI process should certainly be implemented to curb inappropriate behavior. However, I do not recommend using any RTI process involving exclusively behavioral interventions in learning disability determination. While behavioral issues have traditionally been a concern among students with learning disabilities, the primary diagnostic emphases have historically always been academic in nature, and for that reason, I suggest that districts consider primarily interventions that are academic in focus in the RTI process for eligibility decisions.

> Any threat to learning that is related to the types of academic delays that have historically been associated with a learning disability should be considered within the context of a discussion of eligibility for learning disabilities.

The Role of the Speech and Language Pathologist in RTI

When considering the implications of RTI implementation for SLPs, one quickly notes that SLPs have traditionally provided a great deal of direct services for students with speech problems and/or language delays, and based on those services, a few questions help frame the discussion of these changing roles. Considerations of these questions guide the school-based RTI task force and the faculty regarding the role of these educators in RTI implementation:

1 Among the types of problems that have traditionally been the purview of SLPs, which problems may lead to subsequent difficulty in reading and/or language?

2 Next, is it appropriate that an SLP directly intervene to alleviate those speech-based literacy problems, and if so, when and under what conditions?

3 Next, are scientifically validated curricula available that facilitate the development of speech-language skills and, in turn, result in academic enhancements in early literacy?

4 Finally, can performance-monitoring data generated from this type of instructional service be used to document the existence of a learning disability?

The Responsibilities of the SLP

In answer to the first question, SLPs have historically provided services to students for many aspects of speech and language that directly impact reading. Reading is, to a large extent, dependent on effective speech and basic language development (Puranik et al., 2008; Roth et al., 2006), and problem areas such as phonemic awareness and manipulation, letter sound and production, and other speech or language skills have been addressed by SLPs for many years.

Furthermore, it is certainly appropriate for a speech language pathologist, in his or her work with particular students, to intervene in those problem areas, and perhaps other areas as well. In fact, articulation disorders have traditionally been one area that SLPs address that special education teachers do not typically address, and as such, it provides a good basis for this discussion. *Articulation* refers to the actual physical production of speech sounds. It is a complex process involving appropriate placement of the tongue, teeth, palate, and proper use of many different muscles in the formation of various phonemes. Various regions within the brain direct this complex process, including various speech areas such as Broca's area and Wernicke's area as well as the muscle groups that help formulate speech sounds.

Articulation impacts overall language development since individual students with severe speech/articulation disorders often manifest ongoing language development problems that negatively affect their reading (Puranik et al., 2008). Thus, even though articulation problems may not affect reading as directly as, say, phonological skills would, articulation disorders are still a very important area of concern.

The widespread impact of articulation problems on reading suggests that intervention efforts to correct articulation efforts should be managed within an RTI paradigm, involving multitier increasingly intensive instruction. Furthermore, if districts choose to proceed in accordance with the preceding recommendations, such interventions could and should be considered appropriate in the context of an RTI process to determine eligibility for learning disabilities.

However, educators should also consider this issue in terms of the guidelines for provision of services in speech/language. In short, RTI procedures can now serve a diagnostic function in the area of learning disabilities, and while RTI has not been described as a diagnostic tool in determining eligibility for speech/language difficulties, performance data from these same interventions may certainly be discussed in eligibility determinations for students with speech problems, as can any work samples and/or intervention data. Educators within the special education district office benefit from a discussion of what types of interventions would be appropriate in either eligibility determination.

In most school districts, even if a child's articulation errors fall outside the range of the developmental norms, he or she may not be eligible to receive speech/language services, unless a negative impact of those articulation disorders on academic success is documented. Thus, provision of services for speech and language development involves the determination that the student's errors are affecting his or her access to the curriculum and/or academic performance in the classroom. Even if teachers believe that a child might benefit from speech services, before receiving those services through the school, a determination needs to be made that the articulation problem negatively impacts academic success in some area. This is similar to the eligibility issues in the area of learning disabilities, whereby documentation of the educational impact of a learning disability is necessary before initiating services. From this perspective, then, an intervention in an RTI process serves to help determine eligibility for either exceptionality. Thus, little guidance is provided here concerning which speech language interventions to consider in eligibility determinations for learning disability. On this question, the school-based RTI task force must depend on the collective judgment of the educational professionals on the team in deciding which interventions they will consider in the eligibility determination. Of course, in various districts or states, some guidelines may be or may become available on this question over the next months or years.

The fundamental concern must always be the best intervention option for the student. In short, are the student's interests best served with a designation of speech/language disorder or learning disability, or no diagnosis at all? Because the presenting symptoms and underlying causes of learning disabilities and certain speech/language disabilities overlap to some degree, there will always be some judgment on the part of the eligibility team involved in answering that question for any given student. Proponents of RTI emphatically state that the fundamental reason for RTI is alleviating problems that cause students to struggle academically in school, and that RTI is undertaken for all students (Boyer, 2008; L. S. Fuchs & Fuchs, 2007; Spectrum K12/CASE, 2008). In that view, it is quite likely that teachers and SLPs, working as a team, will implement an RTI process to alleviate early reading problems that are rooted in phonemic manipulation problems or even articulation problems, even if neither suspects that a learning disability or a significant speech/language problem exists. Furthermore, it is also quite possible to implement an RTI procedure focused on articulation difficulties as a *component* of the eligibility process for students suspected of having a learning disability.

Again, many of these questions will probably be determined at state or local school district levels, so SLPs, psychologists, and teachers should consult the director of special education and local and state policies concerning what types of intervention data are appropriate for consideration when a learning disability is suspected. While states have provided such guidelines only rarely, some local school districts have, and educators should search diligently for those local policies and guidelines.

Curricular/Instructional Ideas for Speech/Language-Based RTI Procedures

Many curricula and instructional strategies are available that address various speech and language skills that affect early reading, and any such curricula may be implemented as an intervention within the RTI process. This text cannot present these curricula generally, but it will describe several instructional ideas and curricula. These address many of the speech/language-based skills associated with early reading, and the discussion here is merely an example of the types of curricula and instructional ideas that SLPs might use in the context of an RTI procedure leading to a diagnosis of a learning disability.

The Speech-Language Approach

Gerber and Klein are two speech pathologists who developed the *Speech-Language Approach* as an intervention approach aimed at enhancing students' understanding of and production of speech sounds to improve early reading skills (Gerber & Klein, 2004). Of course, phonemic awareness and phonemic manipulation skills are highly related to early reading, and the program emphasizes a wide variety of phonemic skills. Stage 1 in the program is devoted to training on consonant-sound perception and discrimination. This stage involves six stages of instruction, as described in table 7.1.

Table 7.1 The Speech-Language Approach

Stage I: Phonemic Awareness and Consonant-Sound Perception
1. A sound is introduced using a picture sound symbol. For example, a clock is shown to illustrate the *T* sound (as in "tick-tock"), and a picture of a snake for the *S* sound (the hissing snakes make). The teacher presents each sound with a story to help illustrate the sound.
2. This step requires the student to touch the picture of the *B* sound symbol when he or she hears an isolated consonant sound in a series of individual consonant sounds. The teacher presents some instances of the *B* sound and some instances of other sounds.
3. This is a more complex step requiring the student to touch the picture for the sound when the student hears the sound embedded within a series of consonant/vowel (CV) nonsense syllables. The teacher presents some examples of the target consonant and some nonexamples.
4. This step requires the child to touch the symbol when he or she hears the sound in easy, single syllable, CVC pattern words. Again, the teacher presents both target sounds and nontarget sounds.
5. This step requires the child to touch the symbol when he or she hears the sound in more difficult words.
6. While Steps 1 through 5 merely involve examples or nonexamples of the target sound, Step 6 involves matching the correct sound/symbol with one of four sound/symbol pictures.
Stage II. Matching Letters to Sounds
1. The teacher introduces letters on separate cards, and the student pairs those letters to the corresponding picture/sound symbols.
2. This involves a more advanced matching procedure in which the teacher places multiple letter cards and sound/symbol cards on a table for the student to pair together correctly.
3. This involves presenting the child with four sound/symbol cards and having the child select the picture for the sound the teacher says. In this case, the teacher presents a word with the same sound, but not a word represented by the picture.
4. In this step, the activity is the same as in Step 3, but rather than using the sound/symbol/picture cards, the teacher presents four letter cards and requires the student to match the letter to the first sound of the word presented by the teacher.

In presenting the sounds associated with sixteen consonants, picture/sound symbols for each consonant sound are used. For example, a clock is shown for the picture/sound symbol to illustrate the *T* sound, as in the "tick-tock" sound a clock makes. A picture of a snake is paired with the *S* sound, based on the hissing snakes make.

Note that in most instances, the picture/sound symbols do not present a picture that "begins" with the sound illustrated (a common technique in later phonics and reading programs), but rather a *functional representation* of the sound.

Also, each picture/sound symbol is presented with a story to help illustrate the sound. For example, a picture of a bubble is used for the *B* sound, and the story involves "Betty, who helped her mother make beds, and liked to blow through her straw" (thus making a "bubble" sound). When using the story, the teacher actually blows into a liquid through the straw to illustrate bubbles. This pairing of sounds, symbols, and memorable interesting stories is a strength of this curriculum, and is likely to result in increased attention on the part of the young child.

Note in table 7.1 that the steps in Stage I involve no instruction on letters at all, but rather emphasize recognition of phonemes based exclusively on pictures and speech. Thus, these skills are a precursor to phonics since they do not depend on recognition of letter/sound pairs.

In contrast, Stage II in the *Speech-Language Approach* involves matching sounds to letters (Gerber & Klein, 2004), and the four steps involved in this stage are likewise presented in table 7.1. The picture/sound symbols are still used, but are discontinued as students grow in their understanding, leaving an emphasis on the sound/letter relationship. Thus, the steps in Stage II address letter/sound relationships directly.

Anecdotal evidence using this approach seems to suggest that this instructional procedure will result in enhanced reading skills among students who are struggling in reading during the first and second grades. Gerber and Klein's (2004) data from a noncontrolled study indicate that this instructional approach resulted in basic levels of proficiency in only five months of instruction for many struggling students, including students with lower IQs. Positive results were noted in a wide variety of speech/language skills, including rhyming, beginning sounds, beginning onsets and rhymes, phonemic segmentation, phonemic blending, and letter naming.

Clearly, the *Speech-Language Approach* is a curriculum that could become very useful in RTI procedures for struggling readers. Furthermore, this type of instruction on phoneme recognition and discrimination, as well as production of speech sounds, is well within the purview of SLPs. Thus, this is the type of RTI intervention that not only lends itself to effective instructional support as a Tier 3 intervention but also produces results that could appropriately be considered in any subsequent eligibility decisions. In fact, for many speech/language pathologists, this type of instruction is part of their responsibilities already and represents no dramatic change of roles. Furthermore, this curriculum lends itself to either daily or weekly performance monitoring, as a student's performance is checked through the daily instructional tasks. Again, the ease of performance monitoring in this type of activity makes this intervention well suited to the RTI process.

The Lindamood-Bell Programs

Nanci Bell, Pat Lindamood, and Phyllis Lindamood authored a series of curricular programs designed to help students develop the sensory-cognitive processes for speech, language, and literacy skills. These phonemic-based literacy programs are well researched and quite comprehensive (see www.lindamoodbell.com). The goal of the programs is to develop the processes that underlie reading, spelling, and language comprehension. Various programs have been designed for use with many struggling students, including those with speech problems, severe learning disabilities, and even for those who are academically gifted.

The *Lindamood-Bell Programs* can be used with individuals ages five through adulthood. A strength of the *Lindamood-Bell Programs* is that they provide ways to assess specific speech, reading, and phonemic-based difficulties, and then provide solutions tailored toward the needs of the specific student in the specific deficit area. There are several programs in a variety of areas and each involves phonemic-based instruction. The program that most closely addresses basic articulation is the *LiPS Program*.

The *Lindamood Phoneme Sequencing (LiPS) Program* is designed for students having difficulty with decoding, spelling, and speech or who lack phonemic awareness or the ability to judge sounds within words. This program presents various instructional procedures to develop the ability to identify and sequence individual sounds and the order of those sounds within words. Letters are categorized into groups with kid-friendly names for each group (for example, some are identified as *lip poppers*, such as the /p/ sound). The instructional activities focus on the use of the lips, tongue, and mouth in pronouncing the various sounds, and this results in phonemic awareness and correct production of these sounds, as students become aware of how to produce the target sounds. Self-correction of speech sounds is also emphasized. Components of the program include the following:

▶ A teacher's manual

▶ A classroom kit (all materials needed to implement the program)

▶ A clinical kit (smaller version of classroom kit)

▶ A practice CD-ROM

In addition to the products available from this company, extensive workshops are also offered to assist teachers in making the most of these curricular programs. Workshops can be taken at selected locations or onsite at individual schools.

The PASS Curriculum

Another curriculum that has been discussed in the literature as addressing speech/language concerns is the *PASS Curriculum* (Roth, Troia, Worthington, & Dow, 2002). PASS stands for *Promoting Awareness of Sounds in Speech*, and this curriculum is aimed squarely at early phonemic awareness and early speech skills. It includes detailed lessons tied to specific learning objectives that will facilitate performance monitoring throughout the curriculum. Three independent training modules have been developed, including modules on rhyming, sound blending, and sound segmentation capabilities. Both the rhyming module and the sound blending modules have received research support to date (Roth et al., 2002; Roth et al., 2006). Given these emphases, both special education teachers and SLPs find this curriculum useful for many struggling students, and it could become the basis for an RTI to determine eligibility for learning disabilities.

Again, these curricula are presented merely to indicate the types of instruction that have traditionally been the purview of SLPs, but which also lend themselves to an RTI procedure that results in an eligibility decision. In each curriculum presented here, performance monitoring can easily be accomplished by merely charting the results of the daily instruction, or charting results each week, as desired by the student support team. Furthermore, using any of these curricula or similar curricula, SLPs might very well find themselves conducting a Tier 2 or Tier 3 intervention that would be very appropriate for consideration in an eligibility determination for learning disabilities.

Case Study: Phonemic Substitution

In this scenario, Tanisha is a first-grade student who demonstrated various substitution errors on initial consonant sounds. She frequently said "*t*" for "*k*" and "*d*" for "*g*," which are fairly common substitution errors among younger students. However, these types of errors usually decrease considerably in grade 1, but in this instance, they did not. In addition, Tanisha had difficulty producing *s*-blends, and will frequently omit the "*s*" sound altogether (for example, saying "poon" for "spoon" and "mile" for "smile"). Ms. Stubbs, her teacher, had noted these errors involving both substitution and omission.

Ms. Stubbs used the *DIBELS* assessment described previously (Good & Kaminski, 2002) as a universal screening assessment with each child in her class. That assessment involves measures of initial sound fluency (a phonemic assessment) and letter naming fluency (a letter recognition assessment) (Hall, 2006; Langdon, 2004). Tanisha's results showed some difficulty in initial phonemic recognition that could negatively affect her reading. Specifically, when Tanisha was shown a picture of a common item and told the word for that item (for example, *tree*), she could not identify another picture on the page that began with that same initial consonant sound (a "*t*" sound). Note that this exercise was not dependent on her recognition of letters, but rather was a measure of her phonemic ability—the ability to recognize and match the same initial phoneme or initial sound in a word.

However, Ms. Stubbs was not certain if the problem involved merely phonemic awareness of various sounds or an inability to articulate letter sounds, and either could be the root of a significant subsequent reading problem. Furthermore, Tanisha's weekly grade on word recognition showed that Tanisha was falling further behind the other first-grade students, even with Ms. Stubbs providing some informal additional assistance once a week or so. Ms. Stubbs decided to talk with Ms. Booth, the SLP in the school, about these problems, since she needed guidance for how to teach Tanisha.

Ms. Stubbs presented a series of five weekly word recognition assessments to Ms. Booth and described her previous efforts with Tanisha in the general education classroom. After some discussion, Ms. Booth confirmed that the weekly scores for Tanisha's word recognition ability on a first-grade word list did indeed indicate that there was some type of problem. Ms. Booth and Ms. Stubbs then jointly completed a request for referral form, as required in that school district to request assistance from the SLPs.

Most school districts require some type of form to document the request for assistance, and a sample of such a form is presented in table 7.2 (see page 201 for a reproducible form, or visit **go.solution-tree.com/rti** to download it). Note that this form includes several questions on the types of instructional modifications that the general education teacher has used during the first instructional tier. Such documentation of the Tier 1 instructional tactics is critical and can provide guidance for selection of subsequent interventions.

Table 7.2 Student Referral Form for Speech-Language Problems

Student name:	Primary language:
Address:	Phone:
Referring teacher(s):	Referral date:
Parent/guardian:	
Date of birth:	Grade:
Retained (Yes/No) and year:	
Was the parent notified of this referral?	
Reason for referral (primary concern): ____ Articulation (speech is not understandable or certain sounds are not clear/correct; student shows omissions or substitutions of letters/sounds, distorts sounds, or adds letters or sounds to words) ____ Language (lack of understanding and/or expression, excessive grammatical errors, and vocabulary problems) ____ Fluency (stuttering, noticeable repetitions, and hesitations) ____ Voice (unclear, hoarse, strained, or abnormal pitch) ____ Other	
Please describe the specific concerns prompting this referral and the severity and the frequency of the problems you have noticed. _____ _____	

Does this student communicate effectively with other students and/or teachers? Yes/No

Please explain.

Does this problem interfere with the student's emotional, social, intellectual, or educational performance? Yes/No

Please explain.

How does this problem affect this student's learning?

What support programs are currently provided to this student? (EIP, ELL, RD, Gifted, and so on)

In what setting or situation does the problem occur?

Are there any attendance concerns with the student? (Please include absences, early check-outs, and/or tardies.)

Have you noted a particular learning style for this student?

____ Auditory ____ Visual ____ Kinesthetic ____ None noted

Does this student have learning impediments that affect his or her learning style or ability to access academic information?

____ Auditory Processing ____ Visual Processing ____ Sensory Integration ____ Other

Has hearing and vision been screened within the past six months? Yes/No

Date hearing and vision was completed: ____ Please attach results.

Explain how you have adjusted your instruction to assist this student.

What were the results of those adjustments?

continued on next page →

What are the best days/times for someone to observe the student in your class?

Please attach any additional pertinent information that you feel may be helpful in understanding how this student is struggling.

Next, Ms. Booth sat down with Tanisha, and completed a quick informal assessment of Tanisha's phonemic detection skill. She presented twenty pictures of common household items to Tanisha and asked her to name them. A number of them began with the initial consonants that Tanisha substituted for each other, while others began with an "*s*" sound. In fact, out of the twenty items presented, Tanisha demonstrated four substitution errors, and three errors with the *s* sound. In Ms. Booth's opinion, that many errors was unusually high for a student Tanisha's age.

Based on that data and her conversation with Tanisha, she determined that Ms. Stubbs was correct, and that an articulation disorder may exist, which could impede Tanisha's capability in detection and production of phonemes. Thus, Ms. Booth and Ms. Stubbs decided to initiate a Tier 2 intervention directed at these specific problems. Note that at this point, neither Ms. Stubbs nor Ms. Booth suspected a learning disability—rather, they decided to implement a Tier 2 intervention in the RTI process to remediate the articulation and phonemic difficulties noted.

Tanisha's Tier 2 Intervention

After both Ms. Booth and Ms. Stubbs decided that some type of intervention was necessary, Ms. Booth took the lead and determined to deal initially with detection and subsequently with production of the consonant sounds. She used certain materials from the *Speech-Language Approach* described previously, and she also devised several additional instructional tasks. She determined that Tanisha should receive intervention daily for at least fifteen minutes each time, over a three- to four-week period. She then wrote up a brief description of the planned intervention. Ms. Booth and Ms. Stubbs decided that they would share the responsibility of providing that intervention. Because Ms. Booth had used the *Speech-Language Approach* before, she would take the lead for the first week, and Ms. Stubbs would observe how the intervention was done, while preparing to take charge of that intervention in subsequent weeks.

Initially, to make sure that Tanisha was distinguishing between the letter sounds correctly, Ms. Booth paired the letters together that were frequently substituted ("*t*" for "*k*" and "*d*" for "*g*") and used the sound/symbol pictures from the curriculum. In one instructional activity, Ms. Booth placed a "*t*" and a "*k*" on one side of the table and "*d*" and "*g*" on the other. She then used various objects that began with those sounds in a "classification" activity. Ms. Booth said the name of the object and explained to Tanisha that she would help her tell where each object went by pointing to the letter that began the word. The intention of this activity was to take the pressure of sound production off of Tanisha, and instead, to simply make sure that she could differentiate the sounds by listening to them. As Ms. Booth presented an object, she would say the word and hand the object to Tanisha, who was expected to point to the correct sound/symbol picture and then place the object next to it.

If Tanisha correctly placed the item, Ms. Booth praised her for it. If she appeared to make an error, Ms. Booth said, "Let's think about that one again. Listen carefully while I say the name." Tanisha was then allowed to replace the object. After perhaps ten minutes of such instruction, Ms. Booth assessed Tanisha's progress by presenting ten trials of the same activity without any verbal correction or feedback. These she scored as either correct or incorrect, and she and Ms. Stubbs determined to chart those data for each instructional period during the intervention for the next several weeks.

Ms. Stubbs watched Ms. Booth conduct the intervention on the first two days, and on subsequent days, Ms. Stubbs conducted the intervention and charted the data. In fact, in most states, the Tier 1 and Tier 2 interventions are the responsibility of the general education teacher, but of course, the SLP can assist with demonstration teaching, consulting, or even conduct the intervention directly, as in this example. After almost four weeks, Ms. Stubbs wrote a brief report and presented the charted data to Ms. Booth. Figure 7.1 presents those data.

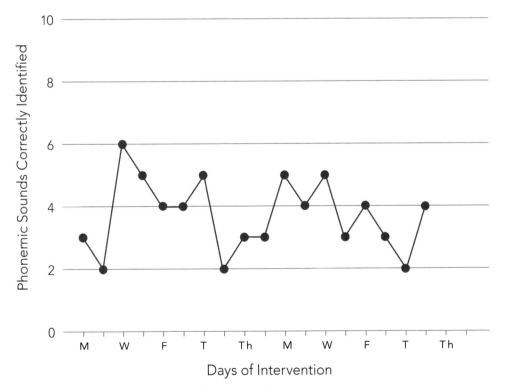

Figure 7.1 Tanisha's Tier 2 performance data: phoneme recognition.

As these data show, Tanisha failed to master these activities in the three-and-a-half week Tier 2 intervention. These data indicated either that she could not detect those sound differences or that she required a more intensive intervention to alleviate this difficulty. Ms. Booth and Ms. Stubbs could still not determine if Tanisha's substitution errors were errors in detection of sounds or errors in production of those sounds, but the data did indicate that a more intensive Tier 3 intervention was necessary.

Tanisha's Tier 3 Intervention

As noted previously, when a Tier 3 intervention is required, most school districts are providing fairly extensive support for the general education teacher since the time requirements of the general education teacher typically preclude intervening at this level. In many cases, the third tier of the intervention is typically undertaken by someone other than the general education teacher, under the guidance of the student support team. In this example, Ms. Booth and Ms. Stubbs requested a meeting of the student support team to determine what Tier 3 intervention is appropriate for Tanisha, and how to manage such an intervention.

In this particular school, Ms. Booth conducted a number of instructional interventions each day with various groups of students that addressed a variety of speech and language problems. In consideration of the various roles that SLPs might play in the implementation of RTI, many districts have indicated that the SLP should conduct the speech or language-related Tier 3 interventions within a given school.

In this example, Ms. Booth believed that Tanisha's problems could be alleviated by systematic participation in an articulation and phonemic recognition group that she met with for forty-five minutes of instruction daily. When she suggested this as a Tier 3 intervention option for Tanisha, the team decided to recommend that intervention for six weeks and then reconsider Tanisha's progress. For that intervention, Ms. Booth used a scientifically validated curriculum—the *Lindamood-Bell LiPS Program*. This curriculum addressed articulation problems by systematically teaching students lip/tongue placement in production of various letters. While that curriculum has various assessments included within the instruction, the student support team decided to recommend that Ms. Booth continue to implement the ten trial assessments every day during the Tier 3 intervention to maintain a consistent assessment for both Tier 2 and Tier 3 interventions. They also requested that Ms. Stubbs continue the *DIBELS* assessment every two weeks.

In this example, Tanisha began to demonstrate significant progress in the first four weeks of the Tier 3 intervention, and the student support team recommended that Tanisha continue in that intervention group with Ms. Booth for the next two weeks and also for the next six-week grading period. Furthermore, Tanisha's initial results, presented in figure 7.2, indicated that she had an excellent opportunity to catch up with her peers by the end of the first-grade year.

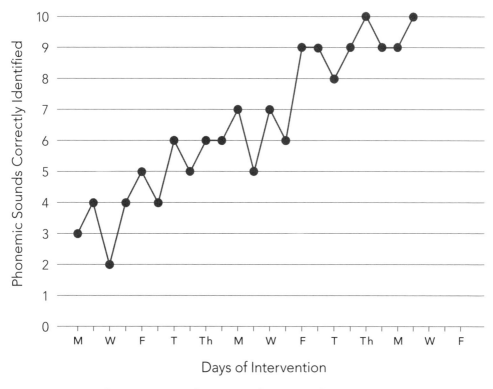

Figure 7.2 Tanisha's Tier 3 performance data: initial consonant recognition.

RTI Considerations in This Example

While it is much too soon to tell what type of role SLPs will ultimately play in RTI, the preceding example included several distinct possibilities. For example, while the general education teacher undertook the Tier 1 interventions, when Ms. Stubbs became concerned that the slow progress in reading might be related to an articulation or phonemic recognition problem, she sought the assistance of the SLP from the school. Thus, SLPs may participate in a consulting role. Furthermore, in the preceding Tier 2 intervention, the SLP took on a more direct service provision role that also involved some demonstration teaching for the general education teacher. Finally, during the third intervention tier, Ms. Booth took direct service delivery responsibility for Tanisha's work, and in this example, that direct service provision extended throughout the entire school year. Thus, the role of the SLP in Tier 3 intervention can be quite extensive, as it was in this example, even though Tanisha was never considered for any type of special education or speech/language placement. In short, the possible roles for SLPs in the RTI process range across this entire spectrum, as indeed they do today.

SLPs and Self-Advocacy

Clearly, SLPs can and should conduct many Tier 2 and Tier 3 interventions for struggling students under RTI. However, given the high level of expertise these professionals bring to the table, care should be taken that such speech/language expertise is not wasted on intervention responsibilities unrelated to that expertise. For example, while I would endorse a school-initiated plan that recommended that the SLP conduct most Tier 3 reading and literacy interventions in kindergarten and perhaps other early grade levels, I would not make that an absolute requirement in any particular school. In point of fact, some Tier 3 interventions (for example, math interventions, interventions for high-level writing skills) do not take advantage of the expertise of the SLP in the same way as phonemically based early literacy interventions would. Thus, use of the SLP in those situations would represent something of a wasted resource, and should be avoided.

Still, several things are clear. First, as RTI implementation proceeds, there will be increased need for Tier 2 and Tier 3 intervention options, and various support personnel will probably provide many of those interventions, particularly at the Tier 3 level. SLPs are going to see that aspect of their role increased somewhat for consultations in general education and in provision of intervention for students.

Finally, with the relative lack of guidance on RTI implementation from the states and the federal government, much of the decision making on these questions is left to school districts, and this clearly presents many educators with an opportunity. I recommend that speech and language pathologists take an active role in helping to delineate exactly what their responsibilities in RTI are. Furthermore, I would urge these personnel to see RTI as an opportunity for significant role redefinition, and that opportunity comes only rarely in education. This could become an opportunity for SLPs to enhance the direct service provision aspect of their duties. In schools that designate a school-based RTI task force, the SLP should certainly serve on that group, and use that opportunity as a chance to redefine his or her role, as appropriate within the context of the individual school.

Speech and language pathologists should actively articulate exactly what their responsibilities in RTI are. These personnel should see RTI implementation as an opportunity for significant role redefinition.

The Role of School Psychologists in RTI

Having discussed the role of the SLPs at some length, the discussion of the potentially changing role of school psychologists will be much briefer. Like the SLPs, school psychologists have long played an important role in schools, ranging from assessment and instructional support for general education teachers to direct service provision for some students with significant problems. In particular, school psychologists have traditionally assessed with behavior modification projects and/or with some counseling in the schools. However, such direct services by psychologists have, overall, been somewhat more limited than speech pathologists in the past. Still, many of the issues raised in the preceding discussion of the roles of SLPs also apply here.

School psychologists have always assisted educators through consultation on both behavioral and academic interventions as well as completing many assessment responsibilities, particularly for assessment of intellectual functioning. While some states have eliminated the requirement for IQ assessment in the eligibility process for learning disabilities (Berkeley et al., 2009), those states are fairly rare. In most districts in which I have consulted, psychologists will still be expected to administer the IQ assessments to try to tease out information about deficits in the child's intellectual functioning that can then be shared to assist teachers in educational programming for the child.

Where psychologists have provided direct services to students, those have been undertaken, more frequently, in the behavioral and/or counseling area than in direct academic instruction, and this is, at least in part, the result of teachers' comfort levels with certain situations. While virtually every experienced teacher feels quite comfortable in most instructional roles at their particular grade level, should a child demonstrate increasing physical aggression or threaten suicide, the school psychologist will be called immediately to assist. Thus, there is some reason to believe that implementation of the RTI process may result in increased responsibilities in those areas, and in particular, in the area of behavioral support programming.

Finally, as is the case with SLPs, the changes in service provision that RTI will entail provide an opportunity for school psychologists to consider redefinition of roles and to advocate for opportunities to more directly serve children, as appropriate within the context of the school and school district. Certainly, presenting a well-delineated, articulate case for role changes will assist the school-based RTI task force in considering what intervention roles are appropriate for school psychologists, given the expertise such persons bring to the school.

The Ever-Changing Role of Special Educators

According to the National Association of State Directors of Special Education (East, 2006), RTI represents a fundamental paradigm shift in both general and special education, and perhaps more than any other support professionals, special education teachers will see their roles modified within the context of RTI (Cummings et al., 2008). For example, in traditional models of special education service provision, special education personnel became involved in assessment when a student was referred because of a suspected disability, whereas under RTI, Cummings and her coworkers (2008) suggest that special educators may be involved in universal screening efforts. Furthermore, the intervention role for special educators used to begin after a child was declared eligible for special education services, whereas under RTI, service delivery by special education personnel may take place much earlier before the actual documentation of a disability (Cummings et al., 2008).

One indicator of these changes involves financing for special education. Based on recent changes in legislation, a school district may now choose to spend up to 15 percent of the federal special education funds they receive to provide assessment and/or prereferral instructional services for students who have not been identified as manifesting special needs. While there are stipulations on use of these funds, this change in the legislation does indicate a possible change in role for special education personnel.

As special education teachers become involved in school-based RTI task force teams, they may find their role changes considerably. For example, like the preceding discussions of the roles of SLPs and school psychologists, special education teachers may very well find themselves conducting interventions at the Tier 2 or Tier 3 level, and those interventions will involve some students who have not been identified as having a disability. In fact, in a recent survey of special education directors, nationwide, 52 percent of the respondents indicated that in their district, the Tier 3 interventions included both special and general education students (Spectrum K12/CASE, 2008). Should special education teachers be tapped to conduct those interventions—a highly likely scenario—they will find themselves teaching students without special needs, but who nevertheless are struggling in various academic tasks.

Implementation of the RTI process, therefore, is likely to provide an opportunity for special educators to become involved in the education of many students without special needs, and in my opinion, many special educators will welcome that opportunity. In fact, almost all special educators, including this author, have had the experience of teaching children with documented disabilities and yet have wondered about the accuracy of those diagnoses. In many cases, special educators suspect that with some provision for more instructional support—just a bit more instructional time on a particular problem area—many students who have been identified with learning disabilities could have, with relative ease, continued to thrive in the general education class. Under the RTI process, special educators will now have the opportunity to seek out those students in advance of a long-involved eligibility proceeding and intervene to assist those students independent of a special education diagnosis. Personally, I would have welcomed that opportunity, and I feel I could have made positive differences in the lives of certain students in that context.

As in the previous discussions, decisions on the roles of special educators will ultimately be made at a district-by-district or school-by-school level, and self-advocacy is again recommended. Moreover, in many cases, special education persons are taking a leadership role in RTI implementation (Spectrum K12/CASE, 2008) since many of the skills required for RTI (individual curriculum-based measurement for progress monitoring, individualized tutoring) have been skills that special education teachers have mastered and used previously. While such leadership can benefit schools, care should be taken that RTI efforts are not interpreted as "just another special education idea" by general education faculty since that would ultimately doom the RTI effort as an instructional support effort for all students. Still, educators will always use the skills and capabilities available, and special education teachers do have and should use many of the skills that can facilitate effective RTI efforts.

> Many of the skills required for RTI have been strengths of special education teachers, but care should be taken that RTI efforts are not interpreted as "just another special education idea" that will doom the overall RTI effort.

Conclusion

The role of many professionals is likely to change as a result of the RTI initiative across the nation, and concerned professionals should step up and make themselves heard in those discussions. In this text, I've recommended the school-based RTI task force, and many schools have designated such a group. However, regardless of the planning mechanism, the professionals whose roles change as a result of RTI should certainly participate actively in those ongoing discussions. Only through such active participation can we achieve the ultimate goal of RTI—implementation of the best, most effective instructional support system for all students in history. This is a goal worthy of our time, efforts, and talents, not to mention a goal that should direct our instructional efforts in the 21st century classroom!

Appendix A

Reproducibles

Response to Intervention Self-Report Needs-Assessment for Teachers of Elementary Grades

Circle one numeral for each descriptive indicator.

1 = I have little knowledge and want additional in-service on this.

2 = I have some knowledge, but some additional in-service will be helpful.

3 = I have a good understanding of this, but need to put this into practice this year.

4 = I have complete understanding and have reached proficiency at this practice.

N/A = Not applicable for our state, school, or district.

General Understanding of RTI

1.	The pyramid of interventions in our state and district	1	2	3	4	N/A
2.	The problem-solving model for our state or district	1	2	3	4	N/A
3.	The tiers of intervention in our school	1	2	3	4	N/A
4.	The intervention timelines for each intervention tier	1	2	3	4	N/A
5.	How RTI applies to all students	1	2	3	4	N/A

General Knowledge of Universal Screening and Progress-Monitoring Procedures

1.	The reading screening tests used in our school	1	2	3	4	N/A
2.	The assessments of the five components of reading used in our school	1	2	3	4	N/A
3.	The math assessments used in our school	1	2	3	4	N/A
4.	Progress-monitoring procedures during interventions	1	2	3	4	N/A
5.	Data-gathering procedures (weekly or daily) for RTI	1	2	3	4	N/A
6.	Progress-monitoring procedures in content areas	1	2	3	4	N/A
7.	The benchmark scores in reading and math	1	2	3	4	N/A
8.	The data management system for RTI used in our school	1	2	3	4	N/A

Knowledge of Interventions to Facilitate Student Progress

1.	The reading instructional programs used in our school	1	2	3	4	N/A
2.	The supplemental math programs for RTI used in our school	1	2	3	4	N/A
3.	Behavioral programs to foster positive behavior	1	2	2	2	N/A
4.	Frequency and intensity of interventions	1	2	3	4	N/A
5.	How to use flexible grouping for Tiers 1, 2, and 3	1	2	3	4	N/A
6.	How to use creative staffing to make time for interventions	1	2	3	4	N/A

Knowledge of Literature on the Effectiveness of RTI					
1. Effectiveness of RTI in reading	1	2	3	4	N/A
2. Effectiveness of RTI in math	1	2	3	4	N/A
3. Effectiveness of RTI for struggling students	1	2	3	4	N/A
4. Effectiveness of RTI for English language learners	1	2	3	4	N/A
5. Impact of RTI on adequate yearly progress	1	2	3	4	N/A

My Contributions and Suggestions for RTI in Our School

1. In what instructional intervention areas can you share suggestions for other teachers?

2. In what RTI areas should we plan further staff development?

3. What suggestions can you offer for making RTI work better for students in our school?

2 of 2

Response to Intervention Documentation Form

Student:	Age:	Date:
Initiating teacher:	School:	Grade:

1. Statement of student difficulty and summary of Tier 1 instruction (add supporting evidence and/or progress-monitoring data chart, if available):

2. Tier 2 supplemental intervention plan:

3. Observation of student in Tier 2 intervention:

Beyond the RTI Pyramid © 2009 Solution Tree • solution-tree.com
Visit **go.solution-tree.com/rti** to download this page.

4. Tier 2 intervention summary and recommendations (must include data chart):

5. Tier 3 intervention plan:

6. Observation of student in Tier 3 intervention:

7. Tier 3 intervention summary and recommendations (must include data chart):

Response to Intervention Planning Grid

	Person Who Implements	Pupil-Teacher Ratio	Curriculum	Intervention Time and Duration	Frequency of Performance Monitoring	Treatment Fidelity Observation	Notifications
Refer for Special Education							
Tier 3 More Intensive Interventions							
Tier 2 Targeted Supplemental Interventions							
Tier 1 General Education							

A Sample School Response to Intervention Inventory

Hard Copy Supplemental Curricula Interventions
List all *supplemental* curricula that are "hard copy" (that is, not primarily computerized curricula, for example, various "curricula in a box"). Note the grade range and the areas or subjects for each. Include curricula used by every teacher within the school, including curricula used by particular teachers within specialized programs. Note who is using these and for what group? Also remember to consider any curricula that are unused in the media center or storage areas in the building.

Computerized Supplemental Curricula Interventions
List all *supplemental* curricula software (for example, *Read Naturally, Academy of READING*). Note the grade range and the areas or subjects for each. Include curricula used by every teacher within the school, including curricula used by particular teachers within specialized programs. Note who is using these and for which students.

1 of 2

Hard Copy Assessments for Universal Screening

List all individual assessments that are appropriate for universal screening or repeated assessment for performance monitoring (for example, *Dynamic Indicators of Basic Early Literacy Skills*). Note the grade range and the areas or subjects for each. Include curricula used by every teacher within the school, including curricula used by particular teachers within specialized programs. Note who is using these and for which students.

Curricula Recommended for Specific Tiers

Are there reasons for recommending particular curricula for specific tiers? For example, a limited site license for a certain computerized curriculum may suggest use of that curriculum only as a Tier 3 intervention. Explain.

Specialized Training

Have teachers received specialized training for particular supplemental curricula (for example, learning strategies training for the *Learning Strategies Curriculum* or training in *Fast ForWord*)? Can or will these teachers be responsible for certain tiers of interventions or prepare other teachers for such intervention? Can other teachers receive such training, as necessary?

Response to Intervention Self-Report Needs Assessment for Content-Area Teachers of Middle and Secondary Grades

Circle one numeral for each descriptive indicator.					
1 = I have little knowledge and want additional in-service on this.					
2 = I have some knowledge, but some additional in-service will be helpful.					
3 = I have a good understanding of this, but need to put this into practice this year.					
4 = I have complete understanding and have reached proficiency at this practice.					
N/A = Not applicable for our state, school, or district.					

General Understanding of RTI in Content Areas

1. The pyramid of interventions used in our state and district	1	2	3	4	N/A
2. The problem-solving RTI model for our state or district	1	2	3	4	N/A
3. The tiers of intervention required by our school	1	2	3	4	N/A
4. How all teachers have joint responsibility for RTI for all students	1	2	3	4	N/A
5. The intervention timelines for each intervention tier	1	2	3	4	N/A
6. Frequency and intensity of interventions in each tier	1	2	3	4	N/A
7. How to use flexible grouping for Tiers 1 and 2	1	2	3	4	N/A
8. How RTI applies to all students	1	2	3	4	N/A

General Knowledge of Universal Screening and Progress-Monitoring Procedures

1. The reading screening tests used in our school	1	2	3	4	N/A
2. The assessment of the five components of reading used in our school	1	2	3	4	N/A
3. The math assessments used in our school	1	2	3	4	N/A
4. Behavioral progress-monitoring techniques	1	2	3	4	N/A
5. Progress-monitoring techniques for Tiers 1 and 2	1	2	3	4	N/A
6. Data-gathering procedures for my subject for RTI	1	2	3	4	N/A
7. Progress-monitoring procedures in content areas	1	2	3	4	N/A
8. The data management system for RTI in our school	1	2	3	4	N/A

Interventions to Facilitate Student Progress

1. Reading instructional programs used in our school	1	2	3	4	N/A
2. Instructional ideas for reading in content areas	1	2	3	4	N/A
3. Supplemental math programs for RTI used in our school	1	2	3	4	N/A
4. Behavioral interventions used in our school	1	2	3	4	N/A
5. Supplemental subject-area curricula used for RTI	1	2	3	4	N/A
6. How to differentiate instruction in subject-area classes	1	2	3	4	N/A

1 of 2

Beyond the RTI Pyramid © 2009 Solution Tree • solution-tree.com
Visit **go.solution-tree.com/rti** to download this page.

7. Modified assessment options used in my subject area	1	2	3	4	N/A

My Contributions and Suggestions for RTI in Our School

1. What instructional modifications would assist struggling students in your content area, and how might those modifications be provided?

2. How can you modify your instruction to facilitate RTI?

3. In what RTI areas should we plan further staff development?

4. What suggestions can you offer for making RTI work better for students in our school?

Student Referral Form for Speech-Language Problems

Student:	Primary language:
Address:	Phone:
Referring teacher(s):	Referral date:
Parent/guardian:	
Date of birth:	Grade:

Retained (Yes/No) and year:

Was the parent notified of this referral?

Reason for referral (primary concern):

_____ Articulation (speech is not understandable or certain sounds are not clear/correct; student shows omissions or substitutions of letters/sounds, distorts sounds, or adds letters or sounds to words)

_____ Language (lack of understanding and/or expression, excessive grammatical errors, and vocabulary problems)

_____ Fluency (stuttering, noticeable repetitions, and hesitations)

_____ Voice (unclear, hoarse, strained, or abnormal pitch)

_____ Other

Please describe the specific concerns prompting this referral and the severity and the frequency of the problems you have noticed.

_____

_____

Does this student communicate effectively with other students and/or teachers? Yes/No

Please explain.

_____

_____

Does this problem interfere with the student's emotional, social, intellectual, or educational performance? Yes/No

Please explain.

_____

_____

How does this problem affect this student's learning?

_____

_____

1 of 2

What support programs are currently provided to this student? (EIP, ELL, RD, Gifted, and so on)

In what setting or situation does the problem occur?

Are there any attendance concerns with the student? (Please include absences, early check-outs, and/or tardies.)

Have you noted a particular learning style for this student?

_____ Auditory _____ Visual _____ Kinesthetic _____ None noted

Does this student have learning impediments that affect his or her learning style or ability to access academic information?

_____ Auditory Processing _____ Visual Processing _____ Sensory Integration _____ Other

Has hearing and vision been screened within the past six months? Yes/No

Date hearing and vision was completed: _____ Please attach results.

Explain how you have adjusted your instruction to assist this student.

What were the results of those adjustments?

What are the best days/times for someone to observe the student in your class?

Please attach any additional pertinent information that you feel may be helpful in understanding how this student is struggling.

Appendix B

Web-Based Resources to Support RTI Implementation

The Florida Center for Reading Research

www.fcrr.org

This site provides free lesson structures for differentiated reading instruction and information on core reading activities, student center reading activities for grades K–5, interventions for struggling readers, and reading assessment at the elementary, middle, and high school levels. The site also provides information targeted to parents, teachers, administrators, literacy coaches, and researchers.

IES What Works Clearinghouse

http://ies.ed.gov/ncee/wwc/publications

This is a clearinghouse sponsored by the U.S. government that describes various research-based instructional curricula in reading and math. Unlike some of the websites dedicated to reporting only on scientifically supported reading curricula, this clearinghouse likewise reports on new mathematics curricula. While rigorous research standards prevent this site from reporting on some curricula, if such a decision is made, this site will clearly state the rationale and describe the curriculum.

Kansas Institute for Positive Behavior Support

www.kipbs.org

This website was developed by the University of Kansas in 2001 to assist educators and others concerned with behavioral problems in children and youth to move forward in developing an integrated, effective plan for behavioral change, based on involvement of all stakeholders in the student's life. The site explores wraparound planning, with a strong emphasis on person-centered planning, as well as various models for team-based decision making.

National Association of State Directors of Special Education

www.nasdse.org

This site presents a number of items that will assist educators in implementation of RTI, including various lists of implementation guidelines, position papers, and brief explanations.

National Center on Response to Intervention

www.rti4success.org

The National Center on RTI provides an assortment of briefs, fact sheets, presentations, media, and training modules relevant to RTI that are divided into eighteen separate categories. Many of the current resources were created by other organizations, associations, state departments, or districts, and center-authored resources will be added on a regular basis. Visitors can sign up to receive an online monthly newsletter, the *RTI Responder.*

National Center on Student Progress Monitoring

www.studentprogress.org

This website was established by the U.S. Office of Special Education Programs under funding for the National Center on Student Progress Monitoring. It is structured as a technical assistance center, working in conjunction with Vanderbilt University in Nashville, Tennessee. The site provides a wide array of resources including online discussions, newsletters, and web-based training on monitoring student performance.

National Wraparound Initiative

www.rtc.pdx.edu/nwi

This website is the home of the National Wraparound Initiative. That initiative provides information on the wraparound process, a widely implemented approach to community-based treatments for students with emotional and/or behavioral disorders.

OSEP Technical Assistance Center on Positive Behavioral Interventions and Supports

www.pbis.org

The OSEP Technical Assistance Center on Positive Behavioral Interventions and Supports was established to address the behavioral and discipline systems needed for successful learning and social development of students. Positive Behavior Support (PBS) aims to prevent inappropriate behavior through teaching and reinforcing appropriate behavior and social skills. The process is consistent with the core principles of RTI as it provides a comprehensive system of interventions based on the needs of all students. The site provides a significant number of planning and evaluation tools, research-based information on PBS, resource links, video links, and PowerPoint presentations. Visitors can also sign up to receive newsletters and new articles as they are added to the site.

RTI Action Network

www.rtinetwork.org

The RTI Action Network was created by the National Center for Learning Disabilities and is dedicated to the effective implementation of response to intervention in school districts nationwide. The site contains a variety of free resources for districts and other stakeholder groups, including webcasts, national online forums, implementation guidelines, and research summaries. Visitors can also sign up to participate in various webcasts or online workshops.

School-wide Information System

www.swis.org

The School-wide Information System (SWIS) is a web-based information system developed to facilitate behavioral intervention planning. This system presents options for inputting behavioral data on the number of office referrals to allow school administrators to compile data in a variety of ways. Individual data may be used to support student behavior for particular students, but administrators may also compile data on specific time periods during the day, specific locations within the school, and so on, to analyze and solve behavioral problems throughout the school. According to the website, the system is currently used by more than 3,700 schools in various countries worldwide.

University of Oregon

http://reading.uoregon.edu

This site provides information on interventions used in RTI, including the essential components of reading instruction, assessment within a comprehensive schoolwide reading model, evaluating and selecting core, supplemental, and intervention reading programs, and links to other helpful reading resources.

Vaughn Gross Center for Reading and Language Arts

www.texasreading.org/utcrla/materials

The Vaughn Gross Center for Reading and Language Arts is dedicated to improving the educational outcomes of traditionally underrepresented student populations, such as English language learners and students with learning difficulties. The Vaughn Center has more than sixty products related to effective research-based reading instruction for prekindergarten, primary, secondary, and special education students. The professional development guides, videos, CD-ROMs, and booklets address a range of reading topics, including phonological awareness, phonics, fluency, vocabulary, and comprehension. Many products and publications can be downloaded and can be explored digitally through an online database such as Searchlight.

References

Abernathy, S. (2008). *Responsiveness to instruction: An overview.* A presentation on RTI results from the North Carolina Department of Public Instruction. Accessed at www.ncpublicschools.org/docs/ec/development/learning/responsiveness/rtimaterials/problem-solving/rtioverview-training-present.ppt on September 9, 2008.

Ardoin, S. P., Witt, J. C., Connell, J. E., & Koenig, J. L. (2005). Application of a three-tiered response to intervention model for instructional planning, decision making, and the identification of children in need of services. *Journal of Psychoeducational Assessment, 23,* 362–380.

Arter, P. S. (2007). The positive alternative learning supports program: Collaborating to improve student success. *Teaching Exceptional Children, 40*(2), 38–47.

AutoSkill. (2004a). *Academy of MATH.* Ontario, Canada: Author.

AutoSkill. (2004b). *Academy of READING.* Ontario, Canada: Author.

AutoSkill. (2008). *RTI toolkit.* Ontario, Canada: Author.

Barberisi, M. J., Katusic, S. K., Colligan, R. C., Weaver, A. L., & Jacobsen, S. J. (2005). Math learning disorder: Incidence in a population-based birth cohort, 1976–1982. Rochester, Minn. *Ambulatory Pediatrics, 5,* 281–289.

Baskette, M. R., Ulmer, L., & Bender, W. N. (2006, Fall). The emperor has no clothes! Unanswered questions and concerns on the response to intervention procedure. *Journal of the American Academy of Special Education Professionals,* 4–24.

Bender, W. N. (2003). *Relational discipline: Strategies for in-your-face kids.* Boston: Allyn & Bacon.

Bender, W. N. (2007). *Relational discipline: Strategies for in-your-face kids* (2nd ed.). Charlotte, NC: Information Age.

Bender, W. N. (2008). *Differentiating instruction for students with learning disabilities: Best practices for general and special educators* (2nd ed.). Thousand Oaks, CA: Corwin Press.

Bender, W. N. (2009). *Differentiating math instruction: Strategies that work for a K–8 classroom* (2nd ed.). Thousand Oaks, CA: Corwin Press.

Bender, W. N., & Shores, C. (2007). *Response to intervention: A practical guide for every teacher.* Thousand Oaks, CA: Corwin Press.

Berkeley, S., Bender, W. N., Peaster, L. G., & Saunders, L. (2009). Implementation of response to intervention: A snapshot of progress. *Journal of Learning Disabilities, 42,* 85–95.

Bishop, D. V. M., & Adams, C. (1990). A prospective study of the relationship between specific language impairment, phonological disorders and reading retardation. *Journal of Child Psychology and Psychiatry, 31,* 1027–1050.

Boyer, L. (2008, June 20). *The West Virginia model for RTI: An update.* Paper presented at the Annual Sopris West Educational Conference, Morgantown, West Virginia.

Bradley, R., Danielson, L., & Doolittle, J. (2007). Responsiveness to intervention: 1997–2007. *Teaching Exceptional Children, 39*(5), 8–12.

Bryant, D. P., Bryant, B. R., Gersten, R. M., Scammacca, N. N., Funk, C., Winter, A., et al. (2008). The effects of tier 3 intervention on the mathematics performance of first-grade students who are at risk for mathematics difficulties. *Learning Disability Quarterly, 31*(2), 47–64.

Buffum, A., Mattos, M., & Weber, C. (2009). *Pyramid response to intervention: RTI, professional learning communities, and how to respond when kids don't learn.* Bloomington, IN: Solution Tree Press.

Bulgren, J., Deshler, D. D., & Lenz, B. K. (2007). Engaging adolescents with LD in higher order thinking about history concepts using integrated content enhancement routines. *Journal of Learning Disabilities, 40,* 121–133.

Chard, D. J., Baker, S. K., Clarke, B., Jungjohann, K., Davis, K., & Smolkowski, K. (2008). Preventing early mathematics difficulties: The feasibility of a rigorous kindergarten mathematics curriculum. *Learning Disability Quarterly, 31*(1), 11–20.

Clark, F. L., Deshler, D. D., Schumaker, J. B., Alley, G. R., & Warner, M. M. (1984). Visual imagery and self-questioning: Strategies to improve comprehension of written material. *Journal of Learning Disabilities, 17,* 145–149.

Conroy, M. A., Sutherland, K. S., Snyder, A. L., & Marsh, S. (2008). Classwide interventions: Effective instruction makes a difference. *Teaching Exceptional Children, 40*(6), 24–31.

Cruz, L., & Cullinan, D. (2001). Awarding points, using levels to help children improve behavior. *Teaching Exceptional Children, 33*(3), 16–23.

Cummings, K. D., Atkins, T., Allison, R., & Cole, C. (2008). Response to intervention: Investigating the new role of special educators. *Teaching Exceptional Children, 40*(4), 24–31.

Deno, S. L. (2003). Development of curriculum based measurement. *Journal of Special Education, 37*(3), 184–192.

Denton, C. A., Fletcher, J. M., Anthony, J. L., & Francis, D. J. (2006). An evaluation of intensive intervention for students with persistent reading difficulties. *Journal of Learning Disabilities, 39,* 447–466.

Deshler, D. D. (2006). An interview with Don Deshler: Perspectives on teaching students with learning disabilities (interview conducted by Steve Chamberlain). *Intervention in School and Clinic, 41,* 302–306.

Deshler, D. D., Schumaker, J. B., Lenz, B. K., Bulgren, J. A., Hock, M. F., & Knight, J. (2001). Ensuring content-area learning by secondary students with learning disabilities. *Learning Disabilities Research & Practice, 16,* 96–108.

East, B. (2006). *Myths about response to intervention implementation.* Accessed at www.rtinetwork.org/Learn/What/ar/MythsAboutRTI on November 21, 2008.

Eber, L., Breen, K., Rose, J., Unizycki, R. M., & London, T. H. (2008). Wraparound as a tertiary level intervention for students with emotional/behavioral needs. *Teaching Exceptional Children, 40*(6), 16–23.

Etscheidt, S. K. (2006). Progress monitoring: Legal issues and recommendations for IEP teams. *Teaching Exceptional Children, 38*(3), 56–60.

Fairbanks, S., Simonsen, B., & Sugai, G. (2008). Classwide secondary and tertiary tier practices and systems. *Teaching Exceptional Children, 40*(6), 44–53.

Fairbanks, S., Sugai, G., Guardino, D., & Lathrop, M. (2007). Response to intervention: Examining classroom behavior support in second grade. *Exceptional Children, 73*(3), 288–310.

Fuchs, D., & Deshler, D. D. (2007). What we need to know about responsiveness to intervention (and shouldn't be afraid to ask). *Learning Disabilities Research & Practice, 22,* 129–136.

Fuchs, D., & Fuchs, L. S. (2005). Responsiveness to intervention: A blueprint for practitioners, policy makers, and parents. *Teaching Exceptional Children, 41*(1), 93–98.

Fuchs, D., & Fuchs, L. S. (2006). Introduction to response to intervention: What, why, and how valid is it? *Reading Research Quarterly, 40*(1), 93–98.

Fuchs, L. S., Compton, D. L., Fuchs, D., Paulsen, K., Bryant, J., & Hamlett, C. L. (2005). Responsiveness to intervention: Preventing and identifying mathematics disability. *Teaching Exceptional Children, 37*(4), 60–63.

Fuchs, L. S., & Fuchs, D. (2007). A model for implementing responsiveness to intervention. *Teaching Exceptional Children, 39*(5), 14–20.

Fuchs, L. S., Fuchs, D., Compton, D. L., Bryant, J. D., Hamlett, C. L., Seethaler, P. M. (2007). Mathematics screening and progress monitoring at first grade: Implications for responsiveness to intervention. *Exceptional Children, 73*(3), 311–330.

Fuchs, L. S., Fuchs, D., Hamlett, C. L., Hope, S. K., Hollenbeck, K. N., & Capizzi, A. (2006). Extending responsiveness-to-intervention to math problem solving at third grade. *Teaching Exceptional Children, 38*(4), 59–63.

Fuchs, L. S., Fuchs, D., & Hollenbeck, K. N. (2007). Extending responsiveness to intervention to mathematics at first and third grades. *Learning Disabilities Research & Practice, 22,* 13–24.

Gerber, A., & Klein, E. R. (2004). A speech-language approach to early reading success. *Teaching Exceptional Children, 36*(6), 8–15.

Gersten, R., & Dimino, J. A. (2006). RTI (response to intervention): Rethinking special education for students with reading difficulties (yet again). *Reading Research Quarterly, 41,* 99–108.

Gillon, G. (2005). Facilitating phoneme awareness development in 3- and 4-year-old children with speech impairment. *Language, Speech, and Hearing Services in Schools, 36,* 308–324.

Ginsburg, H. P., & Baroody, A. J. (1990). *Test of early math ability* (3rd. ed.). *(TEMA-3).* Los Angeles: Western Psychological Services.

Good, R. H., & Kaminski, R. (2002). *DIBELS: Dynamic indicators of basic early literacy skills* (6th ed.). Longmont, CO: Sopris West.

Greene, J. F. (1998). *Language! A comprehensive literacy curriculum* (4th ed.). Longmont, CO: Sopris West.

Gregory, G. H., & Kuzmich, L. (2005). *Differentiated literacy strategies for student growth and achievement in grades 7–12.* Thousand Oaks, CA: Corwin Press.

Haager, D., Calhoon, M. B., & Linan-Thompson, S. (2007). English language learners and response to intervention: Introduction to special issue. *Learning Disability Quarterly, 30*(1), 151–152.

Hall, S. (2006). *I've DIBEL'd, now what? Designing interventions with DIBELS data.* Longmont, CO: Sopris West.

Harn, B. A., Linan-Thompson, S., & Roberts, G. (2008). Intensifying instruction: Does additional instructional time make a difference for the most at-risk first graders? *Journal of Learning Disabilities, 41,* 115–125.

Horner, R., & Sugai, G. (1999). Discipline and behavioral support: Practices, pitfalls, and promises. *Effective School Practices, 17*(4), 65–71.

Horton, S. V., Lovitt, T. C., & Bergerud, D. (1990). The effectiveness of graphic organizers for three classifications of secondary students in content area classes. *Journal of Learning Disabilities, 23,* 12–22.

Howell, R., Patton, S., & Deiotte, M. (2008). *Understanding response to intervention: A practical guide to systemic implementation.* Bloomington, IN: Solution Tree Press.

Hughes, C., & Dexter, D. D. (2008). *Field studies of RTI programs.* Accessed at www.rtinetwork.org/Learn/Research/ar/FieldStudies on November 20, 2008.

Ihnot, C., Mastoff, J., Gavin, J., & Hendrickson, L. (2001). *Read naturally.* St. Paul, MN: Read Naturally.

Jenkins, J. R., Graff, J. J., & Miglioretti, D. L. (2009). Estimating reading growth using intermittent CBM progress monitoring. *Exceptional Children, 75*(2), 151–163.

Jordan, N. C., Kaplan, D., Locuniak, M. N., & Ramineni, C. (2007). Prediction first-grade math achievement from developmental number sense trajectories. *Learning Disabilities Research & Practice, 22,* 36–56.

Kame'enui, E. J. (2007). A new paradigm: Responsiveness to intervention. *Teaching Exceptional Children, 39*(5), 6–7.

Kamps, D., Abbott, M., Greenwood, C., Arreaga-Mayer, C., Wills, H., Longstaff, J., et al. (2007). Use of evidence-based, small group reading instruction for English language learners in elementary grades: Secondary-tier intervention. *Learning Disability Quarterly, 30*(3), 153–168.

Kavale, K. A., & Spaulding, L. C. (2008). Is response to intervention good policy for specific learning disability? *Learning Disabilities Research & Practice, 23*, 169–179.

Kemp, K. A., & Eaton, M. A. (2007). *RTI: The classroom connection for literacy.* Port Chester, NY: Dude Publishing.

King, K., & Gurian, M. (2006). Teaching to the minds of boys. *Educational Leadership, 64*(1), 56–61.

Langdon, T. (2004). DIBELS: A teacher friendly basic literacy accountability tool for the primary classroom. *Teaching Exceptional Children, 37*(2), 54–58.

Lenz, B. K. (2006). Creating school-wide conditions for high quality learning strategy classroom instruction. *Intervention in School and Clinic, 41*, 261–266.

Linan-Thompson, S., Cirino, P. T., & Vaughn, S. (2007). Determining English language learners' response to intervention: Questions and some answers. *Learning Disability Quarterly, 30*(3), 185–196.

Linan-Thompson, S., Vaughn, S., Prater, K., & Cirino, P. T. (2006). The response to intervention of English language learners at risk for reading problems. *Journal of Learning Disabilities, 39*(5), 390–398.

Lindsley, O. R. (1971). Precision teaching in perspective: An interview with Ogden R. Lindsley (A. Cuncan, interviewer). *Teaching Exceptional Children, 3*, 114–116.

Lindsley, O. R. (1990). Precision teaching: By teachers for children. *Teaching Exceptional Children, 22*(3), 10–15.

Lindsley, O. R. (1992). Precision teaching: Discoveries and effects. *Journal of Applied Behaviour Analysis, 25*, 51–57.

Locuniak, M. N., & Jordan, N. C. (2008). Using kindergarten number sense to predict calculation fluency in second grade. *Journal of Learning Disabilities, 41*, 451–459.

Lohrmann, S., Talerico, J., & Dunlap, G. (2004). Anchor the boat: A classwide intervention to reduce problem behavior. *Journal of Positive Behavioral Interventions, 6*, 113–120.

Lovett, M. W., De Palma, M., Frijters, J., Steinbach, K., Temple, M., Benson, N., et al. (2008). Interventions for reading difficulties: A comparison of response to intervention by ELL and EFL struggling readers. *Journal of Learning Disabilities, 41*, 333–352.

Lovitt, T., & Horton, S. V. (1994). Strategies for adapting science textbooks for youth with learning disabilities. *Remedial and Special Education, 15*, 105–116.

Mabbott, D. J., & Bisanz, J. (2008). Computational skills, working memory, and conceptual knowledge in older children with mathematics learning disabilities. *Journal of Learning Disabilities, 41*(1), 15–28.

Montague, M. (2008). Self-regulation strategies to improve mathematical problem solving for students with learning disabilities. *Learning Disability Quarterly, 31*(1), 37–44.

Murphy, M. M., Mazzocco, M. M., Hanick, L. B., & Early, M. C. (2007). Cognitive characteristics of children with mathematics learning disability (MLD) vary as a function of the cutoff criterion used to define MLD. *Journal of Learning Disabilities, 40*(5), 458–478.

National Joint Committee on Learning Disabilities. (2005). Responsiveness to intervention and learning disabilities: A report prepared by the National Joint Committee on Learning Disabilities. *Learning Disability Quarterly, 28*(4), 249–260.

Nunley, K. F. (2006). *Differentiating the high school curriculum.* Thousand Oaks, CA: Corwin Press.

O'Connor, R. E., Fulmer, D., Harty, K. R., & Bell, K. (2005). Layers of reading intervention in kindergarten through third grade: Changes in teaching and child outcomes. *Journal of Learning Disabilities, 38,* 440–455.

Puranik, C. S., Petscher, Y., Otaiba, S. A., Catts, H. W., & Lonigan, C. J. (2008). Development of oral reading fluency in children with speech or language impairments: A growth curve analysis. *Journal of Learning Disabilities, 41*(6), 545–560.

Rinaldi, C., & Samson, J. (2008). English language learners and response to intervention. *Teaching Exceptional Children, 40*(5), 6–15.

Roth, F. P., Troia, G. A., Worthington, C. K., & Dow, K. A. (2002). Promoting awareness of sounds in speech: An initial report of an early intervention program for children with speech and language impairments. *Applied Psycholinguistics, 23,* 535–565.

Roth, F. P., Troia, G. A., Worthington, C. K., & Handy, D. (2006). Promoting awareness of sounds in speech (PASS): The effects of intervention and stimulus characteristics on the blending performance of preschool children with communication impairments. *Learning Disability Quarterly, 29*(2), 67–88.

Silberglitt, B., & Hintze, J. M. (2007). How much growth can we expect? A conditional analysis of R-CBM growth rates by level of performance. *Exceptional Children, 74*(1), 71–84.

Simmons, D. C., Coyne, M. D., Kwok, O., McDonagh, S., Harn, B. A., & Kame'enui, E. J. (2008). Indexing response to intervention: A longitudinal study of reading risk from kindergarten through third grade. *Journal of Learning Disabilities, 41*(2), 158–173.

Simonsen, B., Sugai, G., & Negron, M. (2008). Schoolwide positive behavior supports: Primary systems and practices. *Teaching Exceptional Children, 40*(6), 32–43.

Slavin, R. E., Chamberlain, A., & Daniels, C. (2007). Preventing reading failure. *Educational Leadership, 65*(2), 22–27.

Sousa, D. A. (2005). *How the brain learns to read.* Thousand Oaks, CA: Corwin Press.

Sousa, D. A. (2009). *How the brain influences behavior: Management strategies for every classroom.* Thousand Oaks, CA: Corwin Press.

Spectrum K12/CASE. (2008, March). *RTI adoption survey.* Washington, DC: Author.

Sprick, M., Howard, L., Fidanque, A., & Jones, S. V. (2002). *Read well.* Longmont, Co: Sopris West.

Sugai, G., Guardino, D., & Lathrop, M. (2007). Response to intervention: Examining classroom behavior support in second grade. *Exceptional Children, 73*(3), 288–310.

Sugai, G., Simonsen, B., & Horner, R. H. (2008). Schoolwide positive behavior supports: A continuum of positive behavior supports for all students. *Teaching Exceptional Children, 40*(6), 5.

Tomlinson, C. A. (1999). *The differentiated classroom: Responding to the needs of all learners.* Alexandria, VA: Association for Supervision and Curriculum Development.

Tomlinson, C. A., & McTighe, J. (2006). *Integrating differentiated instruction and understanding by design.* Alexandria, VA: Association for Supervision and Curriculum Development.

Torgesen, J. K. (2007, June). *Using an RTI model to guide early reading instruction: Effects on identification rates for students with learning disabilities.* Accessed at www.fcrr.org/science/pdf/torgesen/Response_intervention_Florida.pdf on December 12, 2008.

Vaughn, S., & Roberts, G. (2007). Secondary interventions in reading: Providing additional instruction for students at risk. *Teaching Exceptional Children, 39*(5), 40–49.

Vaughn, S., Wanzek, J., Murray, C. S., Scammacca, N., Linan-Thompson, S., & Woodruff, A. L. (2009). Response to early reading intervention: Examining higher and lower responders. *Exceptional Children, 75*(2), 165–183.

Vellutino, F. R., Scanlon, D. M., Small, S., & Fanuele, D. P. (2006). Response to intervention as a vehicle for distinguishing between children with and without reading disabilities: Evidence for the role of kindergarten and first-grade interventions. *Journal of Learning Disabilities, 39*(2), 157–169.

White, O. R. (1986). Precision teaching-precision learning. *Exceptional Children, 52,* 522–534.

Index

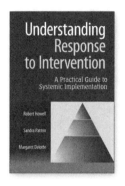

Pyramid Response to Intervention
Austin Buffum, Mike Mattos, and Chris Weber
Foreword by Richard DuFour
Accessible language and compelling stories illustrate how RTI is most effective when built on the Professional Learning Communities at Work™ model. Written by award-winning educators, this book details three tiers of interventions—from basic to intensive—and includes implementation ideas. **BKF251**

Understanding Response to Intervention
Robert Howell, Sandra Patton, and Margaret Deiotte
Whether you want a basic understanding of RTI or desire thorough knowledge for district-level implementation, you need this book. Understand the nuts and bolts of RTI. Follow clear examples of effective practices that include systems and checklists to assess your RTI progress. **BKF253**

Whatever It Takes
Richard DuFour, Rebecca DuFour, Robert Eaker, and Gayle Karhanek
Elementary, middle, and high school case studies illustrate how professional learning communities respond to students who aren't learning despite their teachers' best efforts. Practical wisdom infuses inspiring stories of educators who have implemented school-wide systems of intervention. **BKF174**

Power Tools for Adolescent Literacy
Jan Rozzelle and Carol Scearce
Power Tools for Adolescent Literacy integrates key strategies from Dr. Robert Marzano's meta-analysis and research from top literacy experts in a comprehensive collection of best practices and powerful literacy tools for middle and high school teachers. **BKF261**

Solution Tree | Press
a division of
Solution Tree

Visit solution-tree.com or call 800.733.6786 to order.

DATE DUE